Acknowledgments Love and humble thanks to my wife Keri, son Jonah, and daughter Zinnia for their support and patience throughout the writing of this book.

Special thanks to all of the talented musicians who provided material for use in this edition of the book:

Harrison "Polo" Hedriana and The Colonel's Men for their song "Midnight Wonder"

Grant Levin for his composition "A Blues for Trane"

Rocky Winslow and Randy McKean for playing on "Georgie the Spider"

Steve Martin for the use of the "2nd Impressions" footage

Caesar Filori and Wideband Network for providing "Anatomy of a Human Bomb"

Contents at a Glance

Table of Contents

Getting Started

We are lucky to live during one of the most exciting periods in the history of the music production industry. Just a few years ago, you would need a studio filled with synthesizers, hardware effects processors, mixing consoles, and expensive multitrack tape machines to accomplish what you can now produce in a small project-based environment with a computer, an audio interface, and the right software. It's a good time to be a musician.

Apple Pro Training Series: Logic Pro X Advanced Audio Production: Composing and Producing Professional Audio is intended to help experienced composers, arrangers, and producers enhance their current Logic skills while working with real projects based on real-world scenarios.

You'll learn how to accelerate editing tasks and increase the overall efficiency of your production workflow. You'll refine your mixing techniques, manipulate tempo and pitch, create notated parts and scores, mix for surround sound, and develop music and audio tracks for video and film. You'll unlock the limitless potential of the groundbreaking software instruments in Logic by creating your own sounds from scratch.

Whether you're tweaking a song structure, applying effects processing, or editing audio and MIDI tracks, this book explains insider techniques to make your time with Logic Pro X more productive and creative.

The Methodology

This book is written for users who already have a working knowledge of Logic Pro. (Beginning or less-experienced Logic users should read *Apple Pro Training Series: Logic Pro X 10.1: Professional Music Production* by David Nahmani (Peachpit Press). Composers, audio engineers, and music producers currently working with Logic Pro will have the most to gain from this book.

The book is divided into six sections:

▶ Lesson 1 lays a foundation by helping you customize your Logic workflow. You'll create an environment designed to increase efficiency well after you've completed the exercises in the book.

▶ Lesson 2 reveals the deep Logic feature set for manipulating time and pitch, including Flex Time and the new Flex Pitch feature.

▶ In Lessons 3 through 6, you'll create your own sounds using the most advanced software instruments in Logic: ES2, EXS24 mkII, Sculpture, and Ultrabeat. Gaining an understanding of these powerful synthesizers and samplers will add a wealth of musical resources to your future sessions.

▶ In Lessons 7 through 9, you'll shape your tracks into an arrangement. Using the MIDI and audio editing tools, you will refine the sound and structure of your composition, correcting production problems and making the most of your best takes.

▶ A composition is only as good as it sounds, which makes mixing and mastering your arrangement an essential part of the creative process. Lessons 10 through 12 guide you in taking your composition to the final level. You'll use the Logic Pro Mixer, automation, control surface support, and effects processing to bring your creative output to highest degree of production quality.

▶ For many projects, Logic Pro will be an all-inclusive working environment that carries composers and producers from musical idea to final recording, from manuscript paper to the big screen. Lesson 13 provides a foundation for developing your surround sound mixing skills by using Logic's extensive surround support. In Lesson 14 you'll creatively process MIDI data both with MIDI plug-ins and by creating objects in the Environment. Lesson 15 shows you how to use Logic Pro's extensive notation capabilities to create musical parts and scores. Finally, in Lesson 16 you'll explore Logic Pro's power as a film and video scoring tool.

System Requirements

Before beginning to use *Apple Pro Training Series: Logic Pro X Advanced Audio Production: Composing and Producing Professional Audio*, you should have a working knowledge of your computer and its operating system. Make sure that you know how to use the mouse, navigate standard menus and commands, and also open, save, and close files. If you need to review these techniques, see the printed or online documentation included with your system.

For the basic system requirements for Logic Pro X, go to www.apple.com/logic-pro/specs.

Preparing Your Logic Workstation

The exercises in this book require that you install Logic Pro X along with its default media content. If you have not yet installed Logic, you may purchase it from the App Store. When your purchase is completed, Logic Pro X is automatically installed on your hard drive.

All the instructions and descriptions in this book assume that you installed Logic Pro X on a Mac without any legacy Logic media, and that you downloaded all the additional media except for the Legacy and Compatibility content.

When you first open Logic Pro X, the app will automatically download and install about 2 GB of essential content. An alert then offers to download additional media content.

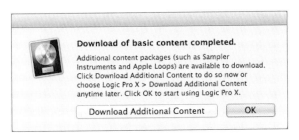

Click Download Additional Content to install all the Logic Pro X media content. In the Additional Content window, click the Select All Uninstalled button at the lower left, and double-click the "Legacy and Compatibility" checkbox to deselect it. Depending on the speed of your Internet connection, the following download may take several hours.

> **NOTE** ▸ If you have already installed Logic Pro X but did not install the additional content, choose Logic Pro X > Download Additional Content, and click Select All Uninstalled (make sure the "Legacy and Compatibility" content is not selected). Finally, click Install.

After you've installed all additional media, your Additional Content window will resemble the following figure:

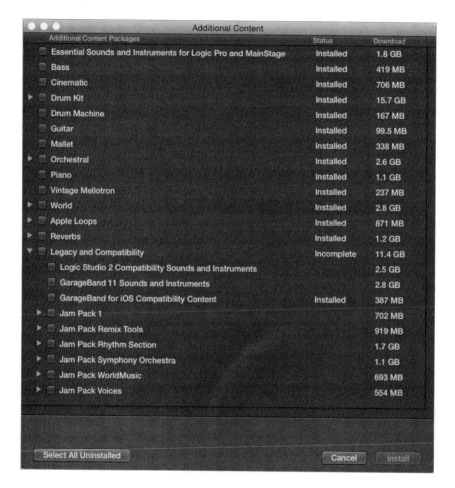

NOTE ▶ If you have previously installed the "Legacy and Compatibility" content, or if earlier versions of Logic are installed on your Mac, you may not always see the same results as those shown in this book, especially when viewing the library, the Loop Browser, or the plug-in settings menus.

Downloading and Using the Logic Lesson Files

The downloadable content for *Apple Pro Training Series: Logic Pro X Advanced Audio Production: Composing and Producing Professional Audio* includes the project and media files you will use for each lesson. After you save the files to your hard disk, each lesson instructs you in their use.

To download these files, you must have your access code, which is available on a card placed in the back of the printed editions or on the "Where Are the Lesson Files?" page in electronic editions. When you have your code, do the following:

1   Using a browser, go to www.peachpit.com/redeem, and enter your access code.

2   Click Redeem Code, and sign in or create a Peachpit.com account.

3   In the Lesson & Update Files tab, locate the downloadable files on your Account page.

4   Click the lesson file link and download the file to your Mac desktop.

> **NOTE** ▶ If you purchase or redeem a code for the electronic version of this book directly from Peachpit, the lesson file link will automatically appear on the Lesson & Update Files tab without the need to redeem an additional code.

5   After downloading the file to your Mac desktop, you'll need to extract the .zip file to your Mac desktop to access a folder titled Advanced Logic X_Files.

The Advanced Logic X_Files folder contains two subfolders—Lessons and Media— that contain the project files for this course. Make sure you keep these two folders together in the Advanced Logic X_Files folder on your hard disk. When you do so, your Mac will maintain the original links between the lessons and media files. Each lesson explains which files to open for that lesson's exercises.

Using Default Preferences and Selecting the Advanced Tools

All the instructions and descriptions in this book assume that you have enabled the Advanced Tools in Preferences. If you haven't, follow these steps:

1   Choose Logic Pro X > Preferences > Advanced Tools.

2   Select Show Advanced Tools.

3   Click the Enable All button.

Using the U.S. Key Command Preset

This book assumes that you are using the default initialized key command preset for a U.S. keyboard. If you are not, you may find that some of the key commands in your Logic installation do not function as described in this book.

If at any point you find that the key commands don't respond as expected, make sure that the U.S. key command preset is enabled on your Mac by choosing Logic Pro X > Key Commands > Presets > U.S.

Screen Resolution

Depending on your display resolution, some of the project files may look different on your screen when compared to the figures in the book. When you open a project, if you can't see the whole window, move it until you can see the three window controls at the left of the title bar, and Option-click the Zoom button (the third button from the left) to fit the window to the screen.

When using lower display resolutions, you also may have to zoom or scroll more often than described in the book to perform some of the exercise steps. In some cases, you may have to temporarily resize or close an area of the Tracks window to complete an action in another area.

About the Apple Pro Training Series

Apple Pro Training Series: Logic Pro X Advanced Audio Production: Composing and Producing Professional Audio is part of the official training series for Apple Pro applications developed by experts in the field. The lessons are designed to let you learn at your own pace. You'll find that this book explores many advanced features and offers tips and techniques for using the latest version of Logic.

Although each lesson provides step-by-step instructions for creating a specific project, there's room for exploration and experimentation. Try to follow the book from start to finish, or at least complete the lessons in each part of the book in order. Each lesson concludes with a review section summarizing what you've covered.

For a complete list of Apple Pro Training Series books, see the ad at the back of this book, or visit www.peachpit.com/apts.

Apple Pro Training and Certification Program

The Apple Pro Training and Certification Program is designed to keep you at the forefront of Apple digital media technology while giving you a competitive edge in today's ever-changing job market. Whether you're an editor, sound designer, special effects artist, or teacher, these training tools are meant to help you expand your skills.

For more information, go to training.apple.com.

Resources

Apple Pro Training Series: Logic Pro X Advanced Audio Production: Composing and Producing Professional Audio is not intended as a comprehensive reference manual, nor does it replace the documentation that comes with the application. For more information about Apple Logic Pro X, refer to these sources:

▶ Logic Pro Help, accessed through the Logic Pro X Help menu, contains a description of most features. Other documents available in the Help menu can also be valuable resources.

▶ The Apple websites www.apple.com/logic-pro/ and www.apple.com/support/logicpro/

Setup and Production

1

Time   This lesson takes approximately 90 minutes to complete.

Goals   Create and save your own custom template

Customize existing screensets for session needs

Learn the advantages and disadvantages of locking screensets

Assign key commands to speed up a workflow

Access needed tools quickly and efficiently

Back up and transport your settings

Speeding Up Your Workflow

Spending a little upfront preparation time saves considerable production time when you are knee deep in a project. The quicker you can get your creative ideas into Logic, the more time you can spend producing music and audio!

This lesson covers techniques to make your Logic sessions more efficient by using advanced techniques to speed up your workflow. Throughout, you will learn how to quickly access common functions and tools and how to customize Logic to suit your individual needs.

NOTE ▸ When working through the exercises in this book, it is important to have Logic configured to show all of its advanced tools and functions. Go to Preferences > Advanced Tools and click the Enable All button to turn on all advanced features.

Creating Your Own Template

Although an extensive collection of templates install with Logic Pro, eventually you will want to create custom templates to suit your personal workflow. You can do this by modifying one of the existing templates or making an entirely new one. In the following exercises, you will create a custom template from scratch and then configure the interface for maximum workflow efficiency.

1   Choose File > New From Template to open the Template dialog.

In this area you can open a recent project, create a new project using an existing template, or create a new project from scratch.

2   Select New Project.

You can create a new project based on one of the many supplied templates or create a new project without any preconfigured tracks, routings, or display settings. In this lesson, you will be populating a new project with everything you will need to form a template to be used throughout this book.

3   In the Templates pane, click Empty Project.

4   Click Choose to create a new project

Creating New Tracks

The New Tracks dialog allows you to quickly create and configure all types of tracks.

1   In the New Tracks dialog, click the Details disclosure triangle, if necessary, to display all the options in the window.

2   At the top of the window, click Audio.

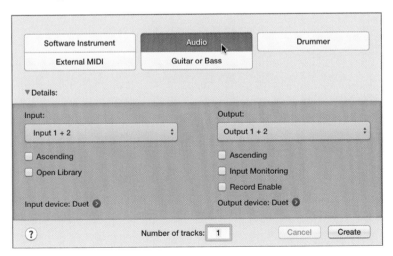

NOTE ▸ Depending on your audio interface, you may see different options listed under the Input and Output menus (also listed under Input and Output device).

3   In the "Number of tracks" field, type 8.

4   In the Input and Output menus, choose the pair of stereo inputs and outputs on your audio interface that you use most often.

5   Click Create.

NOTE ▸ In the New Tracks dialog, you can assign inputs and outputs individually or in ascending order (multiple tracks), as well as set them to open with input monitoring turned on and record enabled. By doing so, you're ready to lay down new tracks immediately.

Eight new stereo audio tracks are created and appear in the main window's track list.

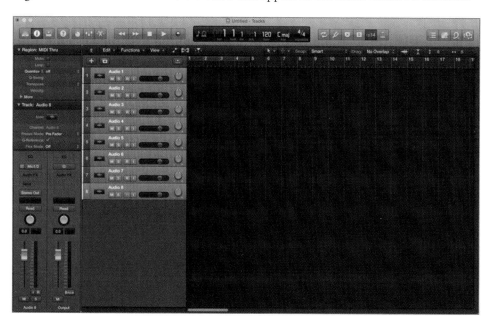

NOTE ▶ On smaller displays (such as 13 inches), some of the buttons might appear in the Control bar due to lack of space. You can still access these buttons by clicking the double arrows in the Control bar. The additional buttons will be available in a menu.

You can create additional tracks at any time by opening the New Tracks dialog.

6   In the menu bar, choose Track > New Tracks.

TIP ▶ You can also open the New Tracks dialog by clicking the Add Tracks (+) button at the top of the track list.

The New Tracks dialog opens.

7   In the Number field, enter *8*.

8   Select the Software Instrument option. Deselect the Open Library checkbox, if necessary.

9   Click Create.

Eight new software instrument tracks appear in the main window's track list.

Customizing the Interface

Logic has a reputation for being a highly customizable software application and with good reason. Not only can you conform the viewing area to a specific workflow, but you can also customize access to the functions you use the most to keep them at your fingertips.

The control bar, which you can also customize, provides immediate access to a variety of project functions and information.

1   Click View > Customize Control Bar and Display.

The Customize Control Bar dialog appears. Let's set it up.

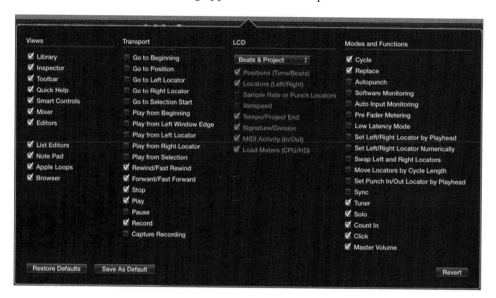

To customize the control bar, you can select each function you want to add.

2   In the Transport column, select Go to Position.

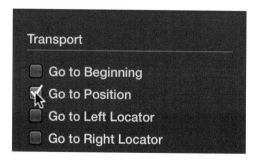

3   Click anywhere outside the Customize Control Bar dialog to close it.

The Go to Position button is added to the control bar's Transport section.

You can also customize the toolbar, which provides access to common editing functions utilized in the main window.

4   In the control bar, click the toolbar button to display the toolbar.

5   Choose View > Customize Toolbar.

The Customize Toolbar dialog appears.

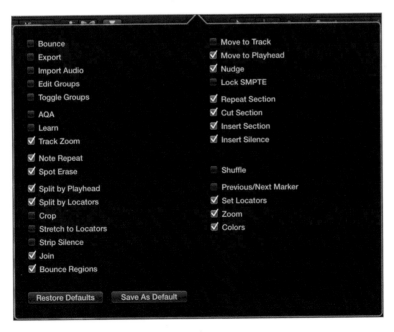

In the Customize Toolbar dialog, you can add and remove functions from the toolbar by selecting and deselecting them.

6   Deselect Colors.

The Colors icon disappears from the toolbar.

7   Select Move to Track.

8   Click anywhere outside the Toolbar dialog to close it.

NOTE ▶ Functions added to the control bar and toolbar appear only in the current project file and will not be present in all project files. Customizations can be saved to a template, however, enabling you to create new projects with your preferred setup already in place.

Creating Screensets

Logic Pro enables direct access to all editing and mixing functions from the main window. The single window interface significantly speeds up workflow, but it can also become a little crowded when many items are displayed at once.

If you've been using Logic for some time, you've most likely used screensets to save multiple area and window combinations. In this exercise, you'll create a few basic screensets customized for editing and mixing workflows and integrate them into a template for future use.

By default, new projects contain only a single screenset, as indicated by the number 1 in the menu bar. Let's start off by optimizing this screenset for editing tasks.

NOTE ▶ Depending on your display size and resolution, you will have more or less visible screen area. Therefore, your view might differ from the screenshots presented throughout this book.

1   At the far right of the Tracks area, drag the vertical zoom control to the left until you can see all 16 tracks.

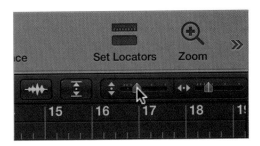

Although this screenset primarily will be used for editing, the ability to access channel strips in the inspector is essential for performing quick fixes. But as it is now, the Track parameter area obscures the top of the channel strip.

2   In the Track parameter area, click the disclosure arrow to collapse the area.

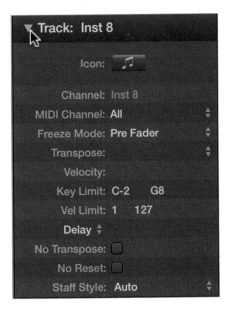

The entire channel strip is now visible. This screenset features areas commonly used when editing, including the Tracks area, control bar, toolbar, Region Parameter box, and inspector, all accessible in one window.

Although you do have some access to the Mixer in the inspector, a separate screenset dedicated to the Mixer can be convenient. Let's customize a new mixing screenset that still contains a small Tracks area that displays an overview of the project tracks.

3   Press 2.

A new screenset is created, represented by a *2* in the Logic menu bar. By default, Logic populates the new screenset with a small main window. First, you'll resize that window to match your screen.

4   At the upper left of the main window, Option-click the full-screen button.

TIP▶ Beginning with OS X Yosemite (OS 10.10 and later), the maximize button was superseded by the full-screen button. However, you can still access the maximize functionality by Option-clicking the button, which resizes the window and fills the screen (but without making the app full screen).

5   Click the Mixer button to open the Mixer.

You now have a screenset consisting of the Mixer area and a small Tracks area.

Maximizing Workspace

For larger productions, you'll want as much screen space as possible to view your music data. You should set up screenset 2 for maximum viewable space in both the Tracks area and the Mixer, while making sure that you're still able to access important project information.

Currently, the Tracks area can display only about six tracks, which requires you to scroll down to see additional tracks. If this small Tracks area is to serve as an overview of the project's tracks, you must adjust the view to display as much of the arrangement and as many of the tracks as possible, both horizontally and vertically.

1   Drag the vertical zoom control to the left until you can see all 16 tracks.

> NOTE ▶ When you created a new screenset, the toolbar was not opened by default. Since you are customizing this screenset for mixing, access to the toolbar's editing and viewing functions is not essential. Even when the toolbar is hidden, the editing and viewing commands are still accessible in the Tracks area's local Edit menu.

Although the inspector's channel strips and parameter boxes are vital when you're working in the Tracks area, they are not needed when you're mixing.

2   In the control bar, click the Inspector button.

The inspector is now hidden, which displays more channels in the Mixer and more measures in the Tracks area.

In Logic (as in any application), windows and areas generally must have key focus for you to make changes in them. That is, you must make interface areas active before you can interact with them. Key focus is indicated by a highlighted top bar and thin blue border. For your customized mixing screenset, it makes sense to have the Mixer area receive key focus.

3   Press the Tab key to make sure key focus is assigned to the Mixer area.

The Mixer's top bar is highlighted in blue to indicate that it has key focus.

2   In the Key Commands window, from the Options menu, choose Expand All.

The list expands to show all possible key commands. Scroll down to get an idea of the breadth of the assignable functions in Logic—a vast number of choices to be sure!

TIP ▶ Assign key commands only to those actions you perform often. By doing so, your most-used actions will always be at your fingertips but you won't be overwhelmed by an overabundance of customized key commands.

3   From the Options menu, choose Collapse All.

Instead of listing every available command, the Commands column now displays only those categories that represent the main application areas. You can view key commands more methodically in this manner.

Assigning Keys to Commands

Let's assign a useful key command that doesn't already have a default assignment. You'll do this by first searching for the command.

1   Click once in the search field, and type *lock*.

NOTE ▶ You do not need to press Return to initiate the search.

2   Click the Lock/Unlock Current Screenset command, located near the top of the currently visible part of the list.

3   Click the Learn by Key Label button.

NOTE ▶ A key label is the actual imprint on an individual key. Logic has been local-ized to support many languages and differing international keyboard layouts. By assigning a function to a key label, you are assured that the function will be assigned to that key, regardless of its position on any given keyboard.

4 Press Shift-L. An alert message appears.

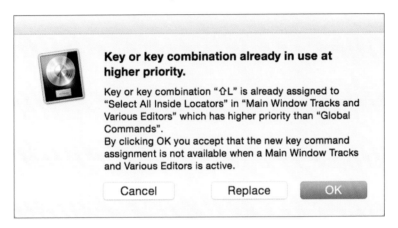

This message is a Logic fail-safe to avoid assigning multiple commands to the same key. It also provides an option for quickly reassigning the command to a new key.

The Key column in the Key Commands window shows the key assignments in use. However, as you remember from scanning the list, not all functions are easily remem-bered, which is why this alert message is beneficial.

5 Click Cancel.

6 With the Learn by Key Label button still active, press Option-L.

The key combination you entered appears in the Key column next to the Lock/Unlock Current Screenset command.

NOTE ▶ This combination of key (L) plus modifier key (Option) is also displayed in the area above the Learn by Key Label button.

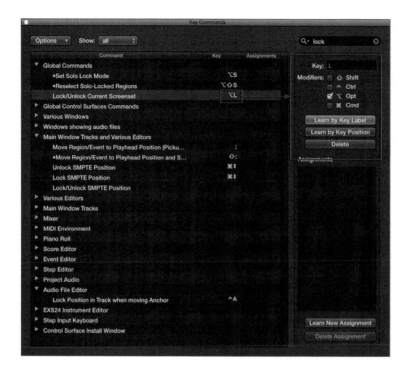

TIP ► The most useful key commands are easy to remember. Therefore, choose assignments that provide a clue to their functions. The first letter of a function, or a graphic representation of it, is a good place to start. (For example, the comma and period keys also have the less-than and greater-than symbols, which visually represent the forward and rewind functions, respectively.) Also try to think about commands as parts of families of similar functionality, then assign related commands to keys with different modifiers. (For example, since comma is the command for Rewind, Control-comma is a logical choice for Rewind by Transient.)

Using Key Command-Only Functions

Some functions are accessible only via key commands and are not available in menus. Don't overlook these functions, however, as they can be quite useful.

In the Key Commands window's search field, you can search for the playback functions in Logic.

1   Click the X button to clear the search field.

2   Click once in the search field, and enter *play*.

The left pane of the Key Commands window now lists every command that has the word *play* in it, regardless of the category. You'll notice that some commands are preceded by a bullet (•).

This bullet indicates that the function is accessible only via key command, and is not available as a menu choice.

3   Scroll down (if necessary), and click "Set Locators and Play."

4   Assign "Set Locators and Play" to Option-Spacebar.

This useful key command packs multiple functions into a single keystroke. Used in the Tracks area or in any editor, it creates a cycle area (setting the locators first) around a selected region or event and then initiates playback. Use this command when you want to quickly audition the section around a given region or event.

5   Close the Key Commands window.

NOTE ▶ Key commands can be triggered via MIDI commands from an external controller, allowing you to control Logic functions remotely. In Lesson 12, you'll try this technique by assigning Logic transport controls to buttons on your MIDI keyboard.

Accessing the Tool Menu

The Tool menus provide access to many ways to manipulate data throughout Logic. In all cases, the Tool menus are located at the top of the screen, usually a distance away from where you will want to use the tool. Even though it's just a short distance, if you find yourself switching tools often while editing (as most of us do), this movement can become tedious and ergonomically annoying. In the following exercises, you will use shortcuts to gain quick access to a Tool menu, enabling you to work more efficiently.

Saving the Alternate Tool to Your Screenset

Tool assignments can be different for each area or window that has a Tool menu. You can save these assignments with the screenset, so let's add a Command-click assignment to the screenset you created earlier in this lesson.

1   Press 1 to open screenset 1.

2   In the Tracks area, from the left (default) Tool menu, choose the Pointer tool if necessary.

3   From the right (alternate) Tool menu, choose the Pencil tool.

4   Unlock screenset 1 by pressing the key command you assigned to Lock/Unlock
Current Screenset (Option-L).

5   Lock screenset 1 by pressing Option-L again.

The Command-click tool designation is saved to the screenset.

TIP ▶ Take some time to think about which tools you use most often in each of the
editors, and then based on those work habits, assign alternate tools in your screensets
using the technique you just learned.

Quickly Accessing the Tool Menu

1   Move your pointer to the middle of the Tracks area.

2   Press T.

A floating Tool menu appears at the pointer position.

3   Click the Eraser tool.

The Tool menu disappears, and the Pointer tool is now an Eraser tool.

This technique can save many a trip across the screen to select a new tool, because it
opens the Tool menu when and where you need it.

4   Press T again.

Instead of choosing the desired tool using the mouse, let's try an even quicker key
command.

5   Press 5.

The Tool menu disappears, and the Eraser tool changes to the Scissors tool.

NOTE ▶ When the floating Tool menu is open, the number keys you usually use for
screensets are overridden until you make a selection.

6   Press T twice to return to the Pointer tool.

Many users assign key commands to their most-used tools. This technique lets you access common tools that are shared by separate editors (the Pointer tool, for instance). Try searching for the tool names in the Key Commands window to see your options.

Working with Hard-Wired Tool Menu Commands

Just as holding down the Command key lets you momentarily toggle to an alternate tool, you can also access common functions by using tools in conjunction with other modifier keys. These "hard-wired" commands aren't listed in menus, so here are the most useful ones:

Key Command	With Tool	Result
Control	Any tool	Open a shortcut menu with associated functions when clicking
Control-Option	Any tool	Change the tool to the Zoom tool
Option	Pointer tool	Create a copy when dragging a region or event
Option-Shift	Pointer tool	Create alias (MIDI) or clone (audio) when dragging a region
Shift	Pointer tool	Change multiple selected region or event endpoints to same absolute time when dragging
Option	Pointer tool	Stretch time stretches or compress region when dragging region endpoint
Option-Shift	Pointer tool	Stretch time stretches or compress multiple regions when dragging endpoint, sets length to same absolute time
Shift	Pointer tool	Select nodes in automation track
Control-Shift	Pointer tool	Create a crossfade between two adjacent regions
Control-Shift	Pointer tool	Adjust curves in automation track
Control-Shift	Pointer tool	Adjust the crossfade curve
Option	Fade tool	Delete crossfade

Key Command	With Tool	Result
Option	Solo tool	Solo and play region from beginning
Option	Marquee tool	Create marquee selection at region borders
Option-Shift	Marquee tool	Add selected region to marquee selection

NOTE ▸ These commands are used throughout the lessons in this book. It's a good idea to place a bookmark at this page for future reference.

Using Tool Click Zones

You can dramatically speed up region editing in the main window by using Tool click zones. For example, you can automatically select a Fade or Marquee tool by positioning the mouse pointer over a specific "hot spot."

Click zones are enabled in Logic preferences.

1   Choose Logic Pro > Preferences > General to open the Preferences window.

Several preference categories (General, Audio, and so on) are available. Once you select a category, you can access various preferences by clicking a tab.

2   Click the Editing tab.

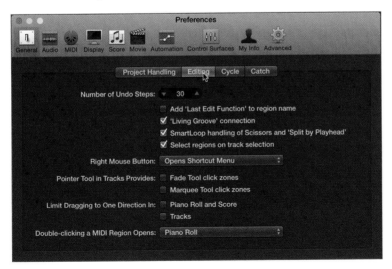

The Editing preferences include the assignment of the Pointer tool click zones in the Tracks area.

Pointer Tool in Tracks Provides: ▢ Fade Tool click zones
▢ Marquee Tool click zones

"Fade Tool click zones," when selected, automatically changes the Pointer tool to a Fade tool when it is positioned over the upper-left or upper-right corners of an audio region.

NOTE ▶ This function is not available for MIDI regions, as they do not allow fades to be created with the Fade tool.

"Marquee Tool click zones," when selected, automatically changes the Pointer tool to a Marquee tool when positioned over the lower half of any region (audio or MIDI).

NOTE ▶ You can utilize the tool click zone settings in combination, and they do not interfere with the Pointer tool's dynamic region loop or length editing capabilities.

Controlling the Tool Menu with a Two-Button Mouse

When using a two-button mouse with Logic, you gain another way to access the Tool menu. To do so, you must first assign the function of the right mouse button to one of four modes of operation.

1   Click the Right Mouse Button pop-up menu to view the options.

The first option, "Is Assignable to a Tool," enables you to assign a tool of your choice to the right mouse button. When this option is chosen, a third Tool menu appears next to the default and alternate Tool menus, representing the right-click tool. Essentially, this assignment works similarly to the Command-click, or alternate, tool you learned about earlier. However, it functions independently of the Command-click tool, in effect providing three tool choices at your disposal at any given time.

The second option, Opens Tool Menu, works similarly to pressing the T key (see "Quickly Accessing the Tool Menu," earlier in this lesson), by displaying a Tool menu at your current mouse position.

The third option, Opens Shortcut Menu, works similarly to pressing the Control key (see "Working with Hard-Wired Tool Menu Commands," earlier in this lesson), displaying a shortcut menu with associated functions at the current mouse position.

The fourth option, "Opens Tool and Shortcut Menu," combines the second and third options, providing access to both menus at your current mouse position.

2   Choose Opens Shortcut Menu, if necessary.

3   Close the Preferences window.

Saving a Project Template

You have spent quite a bit of time customizing this project. Now you can save it as a template for future use.

1   Choose File > Save as Template.

The dialog automatically points to a save location in the Project Templates folder that was created when you first installed Logic Pro.

2   Enter the filename *Advanced Logic*.

3   Click Save.

The template is now saved to your hard disk and will appear in the My Templates area the next time you create a new project.

Opening and Creating Projects Automatically

Having a varied selection of templates at your fingertips can be useful in any given situation. However, most of the time you'll want to start your sessions with the same basic setup. You can configure Logic Pro to automatically open a given template or empty project by setting a startup action preference.

1   Choose Logic Pro > Preferences > General.

2   Click the Project Handling tab.

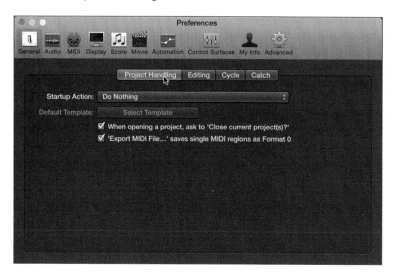

3   Click the Startup Action pop-up menu to view the menu items.

These commands dictate the Logic startup action, ranging from Do Nothing (no project file is loaded) to Create New Project Using Default Template. Once you have created a general-purpose, or default, template (as you did in this lesson), have Logic conveniently base a new project file on it at startup. Doing so will help you get to work as soon as Logic opens.

4   Choose Startup Action > Create New Project Using Default Template.

Now all that's needed is to specify which template Logic will use as the default.

5   Click the Select Template button.

The Template dialog opens.

6   In the column on the left, click My Templates.

7   In the Template pane, click Advanced Logic.

The next time you open Logic, it will automatically create a new project based on the template you created in this lesson.

8   Close the Preferences window.

Backing Up and Transporting Your Setup

After you've spent time customizing your Logic setup, back up your key commands and project templates for future use.

If you work in multiple physical locations, you can take your configurations with you for working on another Logic setup in a different facility. USB flash drives are great for carting around your personal Logic settings. Copy the following files from your main system to the flash drive:

Setting	File Location
Key commands	~/Music/Audio Music Apps/Key Commands
Project templates	~/Music/Audio Music Apps/Project Templates

To benefit from the portability of your Logic settings, you must load these settings files into the host system. You must copy the contents of both your Key Commands and Project Templates folders to the listed locations in the new system to make them available.

NOTE ► The Key Commands folder will be empty unless you export your current setup. You can do so in the Key Commands window by choosing Options > Export Key Commands. You can also import any .logikcs (key commands) file by choosing Options > Import Key Commands.

TIP ► Logic users who work with a laptop that occasionally plugs into an external monitor and keyboard may find that certain keys work better for systems with and without numerical keypads. As a result, you'll need separate key command sets for each keyboard layout. Therefore having both key command files in the ~/Music/Audio Music Apps/Key Commands folder is convenient, and toggle between them by choosing Logic Pro X > Key Commands > Presets.

Importing Screensets

Sometimes when you're working on Logic song files from other people, you may want to import your own screensets so that you can more comfortably navigate through their songs. You can do so by importing settings from one project file to another, which requires only that you have an available copy of one of your project files.

1   Choose File > Project Settings > Import Project Settings.

The Import Project Settings file selector dialog opens.

2   In the dialog, go to Music > Advanced Logic X_Files > Lessons and select 02_The Only Light Thats On_Start.logic.

3   Click Import.

The Import Settings dialog opens.

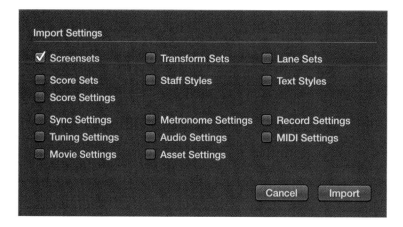

4   Deselect all other selections besides Screensets.

5   Click Import.

6   Press the numbers 1 through 4 to view the imported screensets.

Logic copies the screensets to the current project.

Lesson Review

1. What are project templates?
2. Describe some of the ways you can customize a project file?
3. What is the advantage of using an unlocked screenset?
4. Identify two strategies for creating key commands that help you remember them.
5. Are all key commands accessible via menus?
6. In what ways can you quickly access the Tool menus?
7. In what ways can you back up and share your settings?

Answers

1. Project templates are premade project files containing configurations specific to certain session tasks, such as composing and mixing.
2. Customize project files by adding buttons to the toolbar and Transport bar and by maximizing various areas of the workspace.
3. An unlocked screenset can be advantageous during the editing stage because it allows a dynamic view of the current data.
4. Assign a key command only if you find yourself performing a menu command often. Assign keys that provide a clue to the function of a command, such as a key with a graphic representation or the first letter of the function.
5. No. Some useful functions are accessible only via key command, as indicated by a bullet preceding the name in the Key Commands window.
6. You can access the Tool menus quickly by using alternate tools, using the T key to display the Tool menu at the pointer location, and using a two-button mouse.
7. You can back up custom key commands, plug-in settings, and channel strip settings to traditional storage media, and you can import them into new project files.

2

Time
This lesson takes approximately 90 minutes to complete.

Goals
Manipulate the phrasing and feel of audio tracks using the Flex tool and flex markers

Quantize audio regions with Flex Time to change the feel or tighten the timing

Conform the timing of one region to that of another by creating custom groove templates

Use Flex Pitch to create a convincing doubled part

Use Flex Pitch for creative sound design

Match a project's time grid to a freely played recording for further editing and development

Working with Time and Pitch

Music production has finally reached the age when time and pitch are fluid. Not too long ago, it would have been impossible to alter the overall speed of an audio recording without changing the pitch, along with the phrasing and feel. Recent developments in audio production technology have attempted to address this, incorporating features that allow you to effectively manipulate time and pitch.

Certain approaches aren't always suitable for a specific piece of material and may produce unexpected results (desirable and undesirable). To achieve the best outcome, you need to manipulate the available parameters and help Logic make the most appropriate choices.

In this lesson, you will utilize the Logic Pro Flex Time and Flex Pitch features in both a corrective and creative capacity, fixing problems as well as expanding on the arrangement. In addition, you will explore how to "beat map," or align the Logic Pro time grid to a rubato performance.

Stretching and Compressing Time

Sometimes a small adjustment is all you need to conform slightly slower or faster regions of the project's tempo. Although there are many sophisticated ways of accomplishing this (as you will learn later in the lesson), you can quickly perform basic time stretching and compression in the Tracks area by Option-dragging the endpoints of a region.

1   Choose File > Open, and open Music > Advanced Logic X_Files > Lessons > **02_Georgie the Spider_Start.logic**.

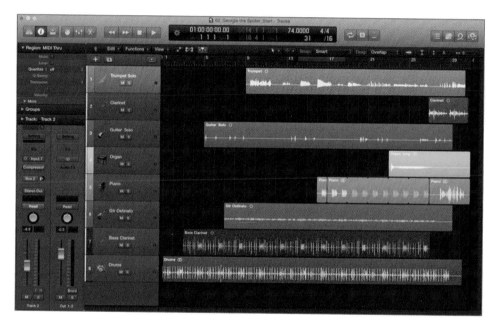

2   Play the project to familiarize yourself with the arrangement.

Most of the necessary pieces are here, but some timing and pitch problems exist in the individual parts. Each will be addressed throughout this lesson.

3   Click the Browsers button, opening the Project tab.

4   Drag **Organ.aif** to the Organ track at the beginning of measure 11.

The Organ region is imported to measure 11.

5   Play the project to listen to the newly imported region. Notice that the Organ region sounds out of sync and doesn't quite extend all the way to the next bar.

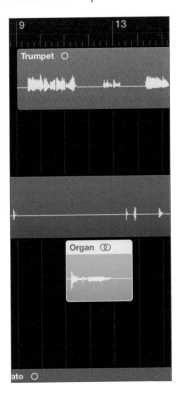

6   Close the Browsers area.

You can manipulate the timing of an audio region by graphically dragging its border to line up with a given bar or beat.

NOTE ▶ This technique can be especially handy for creating a half-time or double-time feel in a given region.

7   Option-drag the lower-right corner of the Organ region, extending it to 14 1 1 1.

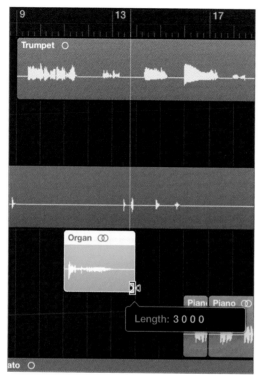

The region is slightly time stretched, conforming to an exact three-bar length. You can now loop the region so it will play in perfect time with the other material.

8   In the Region Parameter box, select Loop parameter.

The Organ region is looped until it reaches the Organ_long region (at measure 23).

TIP ▸ The "Time Stretch Region Length to Nearest Bar" and "Time Stretch Region Length to Locators" commands found in the Edit menu work in a similar fashion. The former conforms the selected region's length to the nearest bar; the latter time stretches or compresses the audio region to the region defined by using the left and right locators. This works for both MIDI and audio regions.

Using Flex Time

Flex Time allows you to manipulate the timing of audio in previously impossible ways, positioning and changing the length of individual notes or phrases as easily as if they were MIDI events. Using Flex Time's many features, you can change the rhythm, phrasing, and feel of individual audio regions or entire tracks.

In the basic Logic Pro book (David Nahmani, *Apple Pro Training Series: Logic Pro X: Professional Music Production*, Peachpit Press), you used Flex Time to tighten the timing of a musical phrase. In the following exercises, you'll revisit some of these techniques to gain a deeper understanding of Flex Time's potential.

1   In the Trumpet track, use the Zoom tool to drag around the phrase from approximately 20 4 1 1 to 23 2 1 1.

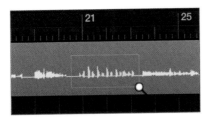

2   Create a cycle region from 20 4 1 1 to 23 2 1 1 (the trumpet phrase).

3   Play the project, and stop playback after you've familiarized yourself with the trumpet phrase.

4   In the main window, click the Flex View button.

5   In the Trumpet track header, click the Enable Flex button.

6   Choose Monophonic for the flex mode, if necessary.

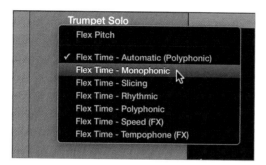

When Flex view is enabled in the Tracks area, transient markers appear as dimmer lines, and the flex markers look brighter and more prominent. This area shows signs of previous Flex Time manipulations, and provides a good starting point for further refinement and understanding of effective flex editing.

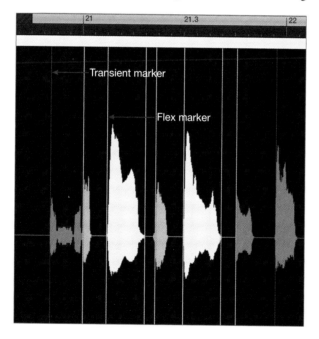

Creating Flex Markers in Flex View

When you perform time compression or expansion, Flex Time uses flex markers as points of reference. When you drag flex markers, time shifting occurs on either side of the edit point, affecting material situated in the surrounding flex markers (if any). In this way, you can think of flex markers as pins, holding down material until you manually adjust or move through them.

In Flex view, the mouse pointer becomes a multifunction tool, allowing you to insert single or multiple flex markers at specific locations, depending on where the pointer is situated.

In this exercise, you will use these tools to manually create flex markers, thereby rhythmically adjusting the phrase.

1   Click the Trumpet track's Solo button to solo the track.

2   Place the mouse pointer at the top of the region area, directly over the transient marker located at 21 4 4 1.

The pointer changes to display a single marker.

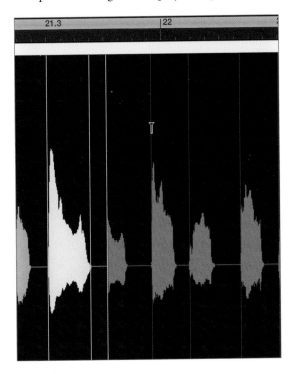

3   Click the transient marker to create a single flex marker at the selected transient marker.

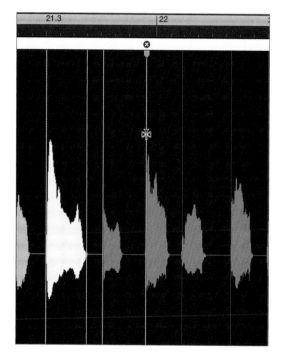

4   Drag the newly created flex marker to the right, and align it to 22 1 1 1.

The audio event is moved to the right, lining up with the downbeat of bar 22. All audio events occurring after the flex marker are moved equally, putting the entire ending of the phrase out of time. In addition, the audio event prior to the flex marker was time stretched (and the shading becomes lighter).

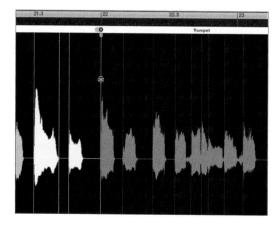

To shift only one desired audio event, you must surround it with more flex markers to pin down the adjacent material.

5   Double-click the flex marker you just created to delete it. The audio returns to its original, pre-adjustment state.

6   Position the mouse pointer at the bottom of the region area, directly over the transient marker at 21 4 4 1.

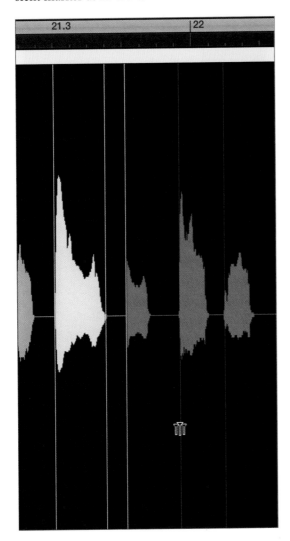

The pointer changes to display three markers. Now you may create three flex markers: one at the selected transient marker location, as well as two surrounding transient markers.

7   Click the transient marker. Two new transient markers are created.

NOTE ▶ Some flex markers are already present in the file.

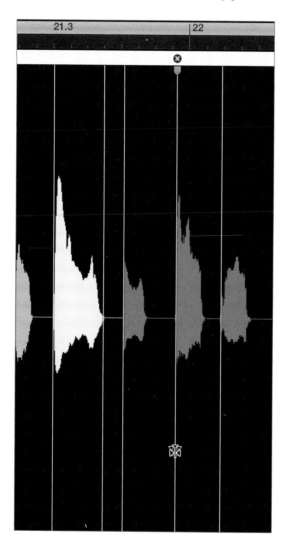

8   Drag the newly created flex marker to the right, aligning it to 22 1 1 1.

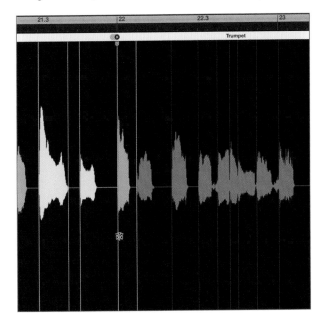

This time, the audio event moves without shifting the material to the right; however, the material to the left is still time stretched (and appears lighter in color). To move the audio event without stretching the previous event, you will need to create an additional flex marker after the tail of the previous audio event, "pinning" it into place.

9   Choose Edit > Undo Drag Flex Marker (or press Command-Z). The audio returns to its previous, preshifted state.

10 Position the mouse pointer in the upper half of the region area, directly after the waveform occurring at 21 4 1 1.

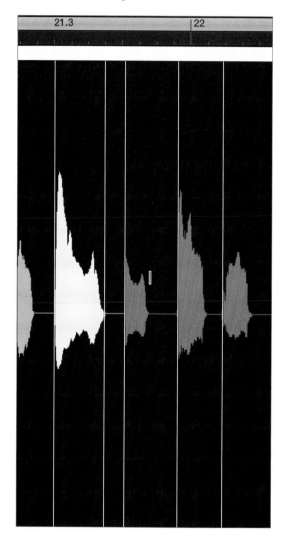

The pointer changes to display a single line. This tool allows you to create a flex marker at a location without a transient marker.

TIP You can also click in the lower half of the region to create three flex markers: one at the selected location (with no existing transient marker), as well as two surrounding transient markers.

11 Click the current location (after the tail of the audio event). A flex marker is created between the two existing flex (and transient) markers.

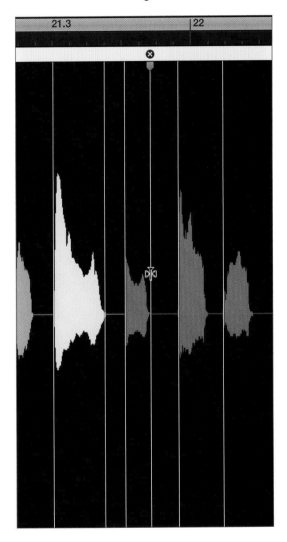

TIP You can change the position of a flex marker without performing any time compression or expansion by Option-dragging the marker.

12 Drag the flex marker you have been working with (at 21 4 4 1) to the right, and align it
to 22 1 1 1. The audio event shifts to the right without affecting the surrounding material.

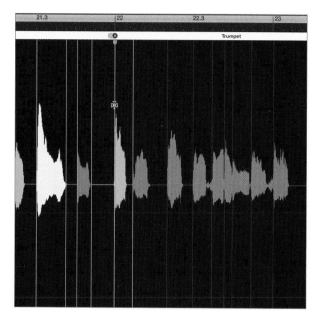

13 Control-Option-click the background to zoom out to the previous level.

> **TIP** ▸ Once you get used to the behavior of creating flex markers, you don't need
> to drag the created marker. Instead, you can quickly create and adjust a flex marker
> in a single action by holding down the mouse button and dragging to achieve the
> same results.

Shifting and Stretching Audio Using Marquee Selections

You can also use the Marquee tool to adjust an entire phrase without manually creating
flex markers. Essentially, you can shift a selection forward and backward in time while
automatically time compressing or expanding the surrounding material to make it fit.

In this exercise, you will use the Marquee tool to quickly select and shift a phrase by half a
beat without making a single region cut.

1 Click the Trumpet track's Solo button to unsolo the track.

2   In the Trumpet track, use the Zoom tool to drag around the phrase that starts at
    approximately 12 1 1 1 and ends at approximately 14 1 1 1.

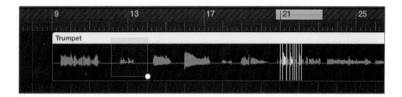

3   Create a cycle region from 12 1 1 1 to 14 1 1 1.

4   Play the project to familiarize yourself with the trumpet phrase.

    The phrase is early, so you're going to shift it later by an eighth note.

5   Using the Marquee tool, drag a marquee selection around the entire phrase.

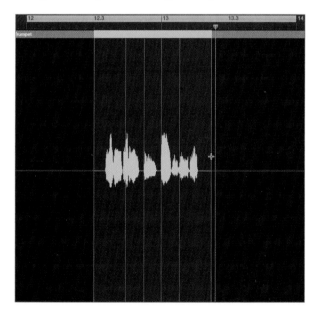

6   Switch to the Pointer tool.

7   Position the mouse pointer at the upper part of the selection area.

The pointer turns into a hand icon, which you can use to shift the entire selection backward or forward in time.

8   Drag the marquee selection to the right by an eighth note (see the following figure for a reference).

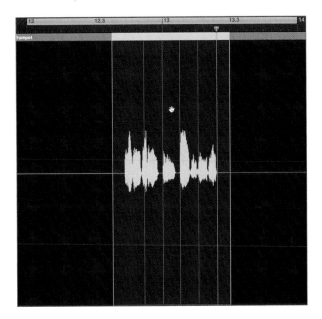

Two flex markers are created at the selection borders (as well as at the surrounding transient markers), and the selected audio material is shifted to the right.

NOTE ▶ The audio on either side of the selection is time stretched or compressed, as evidenced by the color change of the waveforms to the left and right of the selection. In the current example, the time compression and expansion is slight.

9   Play the project, listening to the results.

10   Turn off Cycle mode.

11   Control-Option-click the background to zoom out to the previous level.

12 Click anywhere in the background of the Tracks area to release the Marquee selection.

> **TIP** ▶ You time stretch or time compress an entire marquee selection by dragging the lower half of the region.

Quantizing Audio Using Flex Time

As you discovered in the previous exercises, Flex Time allows you to edit audio events as freely as you would edit MIDI events, adjusting length and shifting the timing manually using the mouse. This functionality also extends to a technique such as quantization, which is used to tighten the timing of an entire region.

When applying quantization with Flex Time, you use both flex markers and transient markers to adjust the timing in relation to the time grid. You do not first need to create flex markers to perform simple, region-based adjustments like quantization.

In this exercise, you will use Flex Time in conjunction with quantization to change the feel of the Drums track.

1 Select the Drums track.

2 Click the Drum track's Solo button to solo the track.

3 In the Drums track, use the Zoom tool to drag around the area starting at approximately 1 1 1 1 and ending at approximately 3 1 1 1.

4   Create a cycle region from 1 1 1 1 to 3 1 1 1.

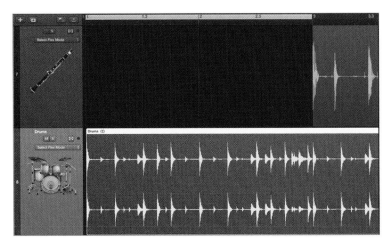

5   Play the project to familiarize yourself with the drum groove.

Although Flex view is still active, you still need to enable flex mode for each track to be edited.

6   Click the Flex button for the Drums track.

Logic takes a moment to analyze the track, and then it displays the detected transient markers.

> **TIP** Although flex modes are set for an entire track, you can enable or disable flex mode for individual regions by selecting or deselecting the Flex option in the inspector's Region Parameters.

This time, Logic selected a less-than-optimal flex mode for the material (Monophonic). Instead, let's utilize Slicing mode, which is unique among the flex modes in that it does not apply time compression or expansion. Instead, it places slices at transient markers, playing each at its original speed, which makes it an excellent choice for editing non-pitched instruments such as drums and percussion.

You choose the mode for the track from the Flex Mode menu, located in the track header.

7   From the Flex Mode menu, choose Flex Time - Slicing.

8   In the Region Parameter box, from the Quantize pop-up menu, choose 1/16 Note.

9   Play the project to listen to the change in feel. The Drums track now plays with a straight sixteenth-note feel.

> **TIP** ▶ Each flex mode offers associated parameters you can use to fine-tune the way Flex Time is applied to selected material. These parameters are accessed in the inspector's Track Parameter box. To find out more about these parameters, see the "Flex Time algorithms and parameters" section of the Logic Pro User Manual.

10 In the Region Parameter box, from the Quantize pop-up menu, choose 16 Swing F.

11 Play the project to listen to the change in feel.

The Drums track now plays with a swing feel, slightly delaying every other sixteenth note.

12 Click the Drums track's Solo button to unsolo the track.

13 Turn off Cycle mode.

14 Control-Option-click the background to zoom out to the previous level.

> **TIP** ▸ You can align flex markers to the transients of other tracks by first creating the flex marker and then dragging it up or down to adjacent tracks. A yellow guide-line appears that snaps to the transients in the adjacent region and aligns the flex markers to match. This technique is especially useful for aligning doubled parts, or multitracked drums, or for getting the bass to lock in with the kick drum.

The Gtr Ostinato audio file could also benefit from a bit of tightening by quantization.

15 Select the Gtr Ostinato track.

16 Click the Gtr Ostinato track's Solo button to solo the track.

17 Play the project to familiarize yourself with the part.

18 In the Gtr Ostinato track's header, enable flex mode.

19 From the Gtr Ostinato track's Flex Mode menu, choose Rhythmic.

NOTE ▶ The Polyphonic and Rhythmic modes are similar in that they both work well on material that contains multiple notes played simultaneously, such as guitar chords. Polyphonic mode is recommended for timbrally complex material, including material with reverb or delay tails. Rhythmic mode is best used for drier, rhythmically active material such as rhythm guitar, keyboard/piano, and other harmonic parts.

20 In the Region Parameter box, from the Quantize pop-up menu, choose 1/16 Note.

21 Play the project to hear the results of the quantization.

Activating Flex Time tightens up the timing considerably.

22 Click the Gtr Ostinato track's Solo button to unsolo the track.

23 Play the project, listening to the quantized track within the context of the composition. Stop playback.

Editing Transient Markers in the Audio Track Editor

Although Flex Time usually does a good job of creating transient markers at appropriate locations, you occasionally will need to manually adjust marker locations to better serve the audio material. These manual adjustments can be of major importance because processes such as quantization rely on the location and number of transient markers to align the material to the time grid.

You perform deletion, creation, and adjustment of transient markers in the Audio File Editor.

1 Select the Bass Clarinet track.

2 Click the Bass Clarinet track's Solo button to solo the track.

3 In the control bar, click the Metronome button to turn on the metronome click.

4 Play the project to familiarize yourself with the part in comparison to the metronome click.

The part purposely rushes beats 2 and 4 by approximately one sixteenth note. However, the part is rhythmically uneven and needs to be tightened up.

5   In the Bass Clarinet track header, click the Flex button to enable it. Logic analyzes the track.

6   In the Bass Clarinet track header, choose Monophonic for the Flex mode, if necessary.

7   Using the Scissors tool, separate the Bass Clarinet region at measure 5, creating a two-bar region starting on measure 3.

8   Double-click the two-bar Bass Clarinet.1 region to open the Audio File Editor. (Click the File tab, if necessary.)

9   In the Audio File Editor, adjust the Zoom controls to view the entire region's contents.

10   Click the Transient Editing Mode button.

The transient markers detected by Flex Time are displayed in the Audio File Editor.

11   Click the Prelisten button to audition the audio file in the Audio Track Editor. Note where the transient markers fall in relation to the material. Click the Prelisten button again to stop playback.

The Flex Time analysis created unneeded transient markers for quieter (smaller) transients such as key clicks and breaths. These unnecessary transient markers will cause unwanted artifacts when applying quantization. Fortunately, you can use the Delete (–) and Add (+) buttons to decrease and increase the amount of detected transients, respectively.

12 Click the Delete (–) button seven times to decrease the number of transient markers.

Most of the transient markers assigned to quieter waveforms disappear.

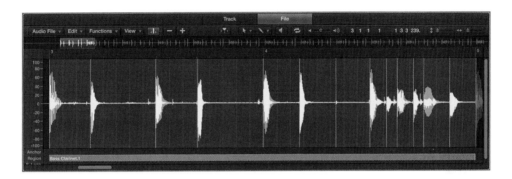

Now that the unneeded transient markers are eliminated, you can apply quantization to the remaining, more important transient markers, thereby creating a more accurate result.

Creating and Using Groove Templates with Flex Time

Groove templates are essentially customized quantization maps taken directly from the timing of the selected region. They are useful to apply the rhythmic feel of one region to another.

In this project, the Bass Clarinet part has a unique feel, purposefully rushing beats 2 and 4. The part needs a little tightening, however, and because of its unique rhythm, it cannot be aligned to the time grid using one of the available quantize settings. You could tighten up the timing manually by inserting and dragging flex markers, but repeating this process for an entire track becomes tiresome.

In this exercise, you will create a groove template from a portion of the track on which you performed flex editing and then apply it to the remaining portion, thereby tightening up the timing for the entire Bass Clarinet part.

In addition to performing flex edits in the Tracks area, you can also use the Audio Track Editor to zoom in and edit selections of audio.

1 Click the Audio Track Editor button.

2 Zoom in horizontally until you can see the entire two-bar region you have been working on.

3   Set a cycle region from 3 1 1 1 to 5 1 1 1.

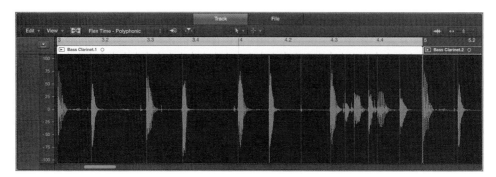

4   Using the method you applied earlier in the Tracks area, create and drag a flex marker, lining up the transients occurring near 4 1 4 1 to the time grid (see the following figure for reference), placing it exactly a sixteenth note before the beat.

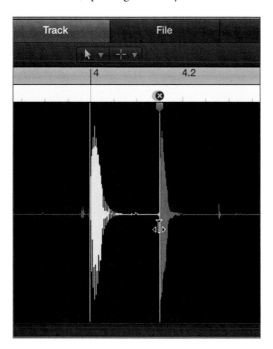

5   Play the project and listen to the time-adjusted part in reference to the metronome.

The timing for the selected region is much tighter now. The goal is to have this rhythmic timing be consistent for the entire track. Rather than move through the entire part,
eliminating unneeded transient markers in the Audio Track Editor, and then manually
creating flex markers—you can simply create a groove template out of the "fixed" region.
Then you can apply the same feel to the rest of the track. Groove templates are created in
the Region Parameter box's Quantize menu.

6   Close the Audio Track Editor.

7   Turn off the metronome.

8   Turn off Cycle mode.

9   In the Region Parameter box, from the Quantize pop-up menu, choose Make Groove
Template.

10   Select the Bass Clarinet.2 region (the remaining part of the track).

11   In the Region Parameter box, from the Quantize pop-up menu, choose Bass Clarinet.1.

The Bass Clarinet.2 region takes on the rhythmic characteristics of the Bass Clarinet.1 region, which tightens the timing.

12   Click the Bass Clarinet track's Solo button to unsolo the track.

13   Play the project, listening to the timing of the track within the context of the composition.

> **TIP** ▶ Try experimenting with both Tempophone and Speed flex modes for special effects. Tempophone mode breaks the signal into a stream of tiny grains, whose size can be set in the Track Parameter box. Here, you can also control how these grains overlap by adjusting the crossfade parameter. Speed mode works similar to changing the playback speed of a tape recorder, adjusting both speed and pitch.

Using Flex Pitch

New to Logic Pro X is Flex Pitch, which offers the same deep control over the pitch of an audio track as Flex Time provides over the timing. This amazingly powerful tool permits you to manipulate not only the pitch of individual notes in audio regions but other aspects as well.

In *Logic Pro X: Professional Music Production*, Flex Pitch was used to correct the tuning of a recorded part, salvaging an otherwise perfect performance. In this set of advanced exercises, you'll expand on that knowledge, applying Flex Pitch's features to create a convincing doubled part.

Using Flex Time and Pitch to Double a Part

Flex Pitch isn't limited to correcting pitch. It also can be a creative tool when arranging material. In this exercise, you will use Flex Pitch to create a pitch-shifted copy of the ending clarinet melody that harmonizes with the original.

1   Select the Clarinet track.

2   Click the Clarinet track's Solo button to solo the track.

3   Play the project from measure 26 to audition the Clarinet region, and stop playback when you are familiar with the material.

4   Click the "New Track with Duplicate Settings" button to create a copy of the Clarinet track.

NOTE ▶ Don't be confused because Logic initially names the duplicate track, "Trumpet". You'll be addressing this in the following steps.

5   Option-Shift-drag the Clarinet region down, and copy it to the newly created duplicate track at the same position.

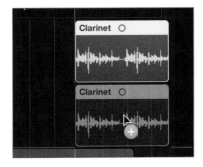

You will use this new region for the harmony part.

6   Using the Text tool, change the name of the new region to *Clarinet harmonized*.

7   Double-click the track header for the newly created track, and rename it *Clarinet 2*.

8   Click the Clarinet track's Solo button to unsolo the track.

9   Solo the newly created track (Clarinet 2).

10 With the newly copied region selected, open the Audio Track Editor.

    To streamline the editing workflow, the Audio Track Editor has its own Flex button, as well as a menu in which to choose the mode.

11 At the top of the Audio Track Editor, click the Flex button to enable it.

A dialog appears asking if you want to turn on Flex for the new track.

12 Click "Turn on Flex."

13 From the Flex Mode menu, choose Flex Pitch, if necessary.

The Audio Track Editor displays the audio waveform with beams floating above the respective notes.

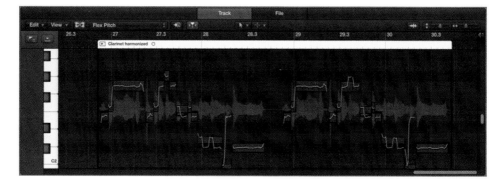

To create the harmony part, you need to change all notes at once, so that every pitch will be raised or lowered by the same interval.

14 In the Audio Track Editor, choose Edit > Select > All (or press Command-A) to select all note beams.

15 Drag the phrase's first note beam up from E2 to G2.

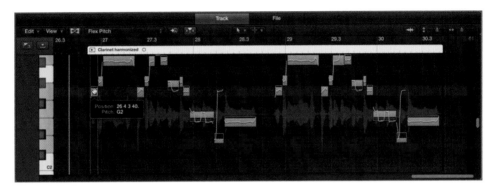

16 In the Audio Track Editor, double-click the ruler to play the Clarinet harmonized region, listening to the results of the pitch change.

The part has been transposed a minor third higher.

Using Formant Correction with Flex Pitch

Pitch transposition usually involves shifting the entire frequency spectrum up or down by a constant value. In effect, everything within the sound source is shifted, including natural resonances (called *formants*). This process works well for some material, but it can also create unnatural results when the material (such as instruments or voices) contains a harmonic structure that is integral to the sound.

A good example occurs when pitch shifting a cello note. When all the material is shifted upward (including formants), the pitch changes, and the "body," or timbre, of the instrument changes as well. The result is a higher pitch that sounds as if it were emanating from a smaller instrument (such as a viola or violin, in this case), rather than from the original instrument.

What's more, some instruments (such as the clarinet) often display distinct timbral changes when moving up and down in register, resulting in mellower or brighter sounds. Whether used to create a more realistic sound, or as a special effect, Flex Pitch has the capability of shifting the formant individually for each note, regardless of whether or not you change the pitch.

Let's try this out by changing the formants of the Clarinet harmonized region in the Audio Track Editor. The transposition you performed earlier works well but sounds a little dull. The goal is to keep the transposition of a minor third while independently altering the inherent resonances of the sound.

1   With all the notes still selected in the Audio Track Editor, drag up the Formant Shift hotspot (lower-right) on any of the beams to a value of 150.

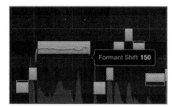

2   Double-click the ruler in the Audio Track Editor to play the Clarinet harmonized region, listening to the results of the pitch change.

The part has a distinctly brighter timbre.

3   For the track you've been working with, Option-click the Solo button to disable solo mode for all tracks.

4   Play the project to hear the new region within the context of the composition.

The Clarinet part is now harmonized.

Adjusting Timing with Flex Pitch

Although the doubled clarinet's pitch and timbre relationship sounds good, the combined pair sounds a bit unnatural as their rhythm is too tightly in sync. You can solve this by slightly changing the timing of the doubled part, without leaving Flex Pitch mode.

1   Click the background of the Audio Track Editor, or press Option-Shift-D, to deselect the notes.

2   Hover the pointer tool over the left edge of any note beam.

The cursor changes to indicate that you can resize the note.

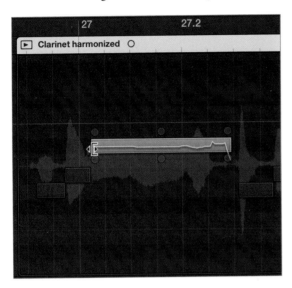

3   Drag the selected note *slightly* to the left or right, resizing its length a few ticks.

These small changes in the timing will better emulate a human performance for the doubled part.

4   Repeat this process on a few notes of your choice within the phrase, adjusting either the beginning or the end of the note to slightly change its length.

5   Close the Audio Track Editor.

6   Play the project, listening to the result.

> **TIP** You can also use this technique to closely approximate the sound of Automatic Double Tracking (ADT).

Sound Design with Flex Time

In addition to correcting timing problems, Flex Time can be used creatively as a sound design tool. In particular, its Tempophone mode offers unique sound mangling capabilities when its parameters are set correctly. Named after a historical tape-based effect, Tempophone mode can create results similar to granular synthesis, wherein the waveform is divided into tiny "grains" of sound that are then manipulated and recombined to produce surprising results. Let's try this out on the final Piano region and create a strange new ending for the song.

1 Click the Piano track header to select it.

2 Solo the track.

3 On the Piano track header, enable Flex view and select Tempophone for the Flex mode.

4 Control-click the last Piano region located at bar 27, and choose "Slice at Transient Markers."

The region is now separated into individual regions that equal the size of each note.

5   Use the Zoom tool to drag around the last few bars of the song (from about bar 28 onward).

6   Option-click the lower-right corner of the last Piano region, dragging out the end of the region for an additional three bars or so.

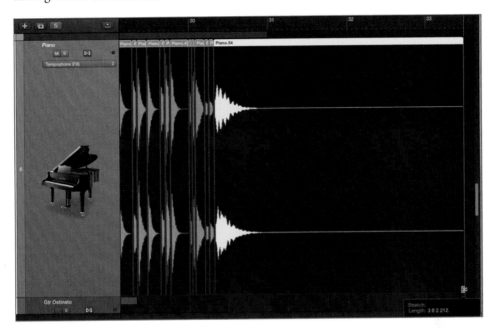

NOTE ▶ The project's end point adapts to the additional length of the region.

7   Play the project from bar 30 to hear the result.

The last piano note now sounds very bizarre with interesting artifacts introduced through the use of Tempophone. Let's finish things up by tweaking the Tempophone parameters, processing the original sounds even more.

8   Click the disclosure triangle for the Track Parameter Box to view its contents.

The Flex Time parameters for the track are located in the lower portion of this area. Any adjustments made here will change the Flex properties for the entire track. For the final "icing on the cake," let's reduce the size of the grains along with the amount of crossfade time between them.

9   Double-click the Grain Size parameter, and enter a value of *1.3* (ms). Press Enter.

10 Double-click the Crossfade parameter, and enter a value of *25* (%). Press Enter.

11 Play the project from bar 30, listening to the result.

The sound is now quite other-worldly, a perfect way to end a quirky song.

12 Click the Solo button on the Piano track to unsolo the track.

13 Using the Zoom tool, Option-click anywhere to return to the previous zoom level.

14 Play the entire project, listening to all you've done throughout these exercises.

15 Choose File > Save As.

16 Name the project *02_Georgie the Spider_Finished* and save it to Music > Advanced Logic X_Files > Lessons > Completed.

17 Close the project.

Working with Rubato Passages

In Logic, you will generally be working with music based on a constant tempo and/or recorded to a metronome click. In this common situation, the Logic tempo and time-signature settings create a time grid in which you can plot events. As a result, the musical data can be displayed accurately in relation to bars and beats.

However, sometimes you will record without a guiding metronome click to gain the freedom to freely vary the tempo and play with rhythmic flexibility (to "play with rubato," in music parlance). In this situation, the trick is to maintain a performer's interpretation with its deviations in tempo, while displaying the musical data in correct and clear time (bars and beats). You can use beat mapping to align the Logic time grid with these tempo variations.

Once the time grid matches the performance, you can use the compositional and arranging features (quantization, time-based effects, notation, Apple Loops, and so on) to work with data as if it were recorded to a metronome click.

For this exercise, you will use the Logic Beat Mapping track to create tempo changes for each event that deviates from a constant tempo.

Using the Beat Mapping Track

The Beat Mapping track, one of the global tracks in Logic, works hand in hand with related tracks such as Signature and Tempo. It works like an adaptive ruler that lets you graphically tie events to particular bars and beats (all derived from the Signature track). When events are defined according to their bar positions in the Beat Mapping track, tempo changes are created in the Tempo track to align the grid.

Both MIDI and audio tracks can form a basis on which to generate a beat map. Let's start by opening a project file that contains both MIDI and audio versions of a rubato piano performance.

1   Open Music > Advanced Logic X_Files > Lessons > 02_The Only Light Thats On_ Start.logic.

The project contains a single MIDI track output through the EXS24 mkII instrument (a piano sample), along with a muted audio track of the same performance.

2   Play the project to familiarize yourself with the material.

3   In the control bar, click the Metronome button to turn on the click.

4   Play the project again, this time listening to the tempo deviations of the piece against the click.

Things start off without too much tempo deviation, but the click is really out of sync by measure 4.

5   At the upper-left corner of the Arrange area, click the Global Tracks button.

The global tracks appear, displaying only the tracks used for this exercise: Signature, Tempo, and Beat Mapping.

> **TIP** You can display any or all of the global tracks by choosing Tracks > Global Tracks and selecting whatever you wish to view. This setting is saved with the screenset and can be hidden or exposed at any time using a key command or menu selection.

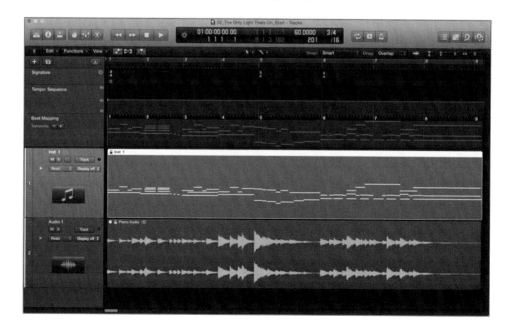

As you can see in the Signature track, the piece starts in 3/4 meter but also contains bars of 5/4 and 4/4. The time signatures are reflected in the Beat Mapping track with bars and beats displayed graphically using lines representing the time grid (not unlike the Bar ruler).

If this grid is to be used as a reference, the division value in Logic Pro (a freely definable part of a beat) must reflect the smallest rhythmic value played within the performance. The music you are using has a triplet feel, so it is necessary to select a division of 12 instead of 16 (the default).

6   In the control bar, click the Division field in the LCD display and choose /12.

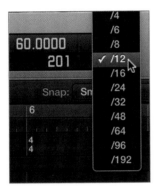

The ruler and grid now display triplet divisions instead of sixteenth notes.

Beat Mapping a MIDI Region

To start aligning the grid to the music, you need to select the material you want to work with.

> **NOTE** ▸ The Beat Mapping track works with regions, and not tracks (which contain multiple regions).

1   If not already selected, select the MIDI region on the Inst 1 track.

Light-blue lines appear in the Beat Mapping track to indicate each MIDI event in the selected region. You will tie together these lines and the bar/beat lines above to realign the grid.

2   Zoom in horizontally until about two bars are visible in the Arrange area. This enables you to see greater detail when working in the Beat Mapping track.

3   In the upper portion of the Beat Mapping track, drag down the line representing measure 1, beat 2 (1 2 1 1) and connect it to the event (at 1 1 3 305) in the lower portion of the track.

As you are connecting the line, a help tag (Position) displays the event's position before alignment.

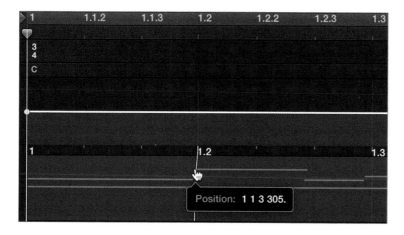

When you release the mouse button, the points are aligned, and a new tempo event is created (61.0071) in the Tempo track.

NOTE ▸ Logic uses very fine tempo increments (as small as one ten-thousandth of a beat!) to realize accurate alignment.

4   Using the same technique, connect the line representing measure 1, beat 2, division 3 (1 2 3 1) to the line located below and slightly to the left (1 2 2 294).

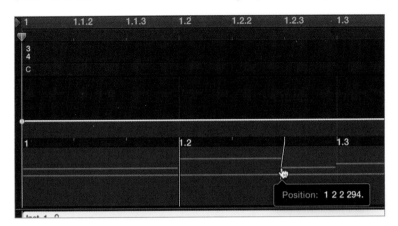

Another tempo event is created in the Tempo track.

5   Connect the line representing measure 1, beat 3 (1 3 1 1) to the line located below and slightly to the right (1 3 1 34).

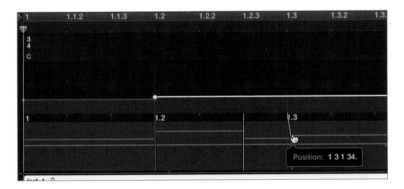

Another tempo event is created in the Tempo track.

6   Connect the line representing measure 1, beat 3, division 3 (1 3 3 1) to the light-blue line located below and slightly to the left (1 3 2 293).

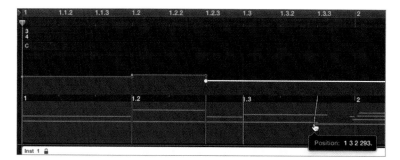

For every note event you connect, a new tempo is indicated to create an accurate depiction of the region's timing. The more events you beat-map, the closer the Logic Pro time grid will conform to the music.

For the rest of this exercise, you will finish beat mapping the entire piano part, creating an accurate time map of the piece.

Here are two areas to watch out for:

Position	Situation	Recommendation
2 1 1 1	The slur and slightly staggered chord entries create multiple possibilities to draw connections.	Try experimenting with what works best to represent the downbeat.
3 1 2 1	Deviates from triplet feel to eighth notes for one beat.	Change the division to /8 (eighth notes) to work with the grid above the two eighth notes.

7   Continue connecting related lines in the Beat Mapping track, moving from left to right for the entire region.

TIP ▶ If you make a mistake, you can erase any beat allocation by double-clicking it or by using the Eraser tool.

8   When you are finished, check your work by listening to the EXS24 mkII piano part along with the metronome click.

For comparison, a beat-mapped Tempo track has been created for you as a reference. You can access this in the Tempo Sets menu in the Tempo track.

NOTE ▶ The Tempo Sets menu allows you to save and recall up to nine tempo "maps" created in the Tempo track.

9   From the Tempo pop-up menu, choose Tempo Sets > Beat map MIDI.

The Tempo track now displays the premade tempo events created by beat mapping.

10 Play the project with the click to compare the premade Tempo track with your results, toggling between tempo sets using the first two Tempo Sets menu choices.

Checking Your Results in the Piano Roll Editor

You can check how well you performed beat mapping by viewing the events in the Piano Roll Editor. Here you can graphically see the individual events lined up on the time grid and compare the results achieved with beat mapping to the original, non-beat-mapped track.

1   With the MIDI region selected, click the Editors button to display the MIDI events in detail.

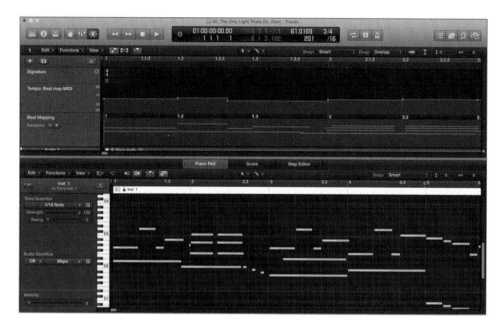

2   In the Tempo pop-up menu, switch among the options 1 (your beat map), 2 (Beat map MIDI), and 3 (No beat map), comparing how the note events align to the grid.

You can see major discrepancies between the beat-mapped (1 and 2) and non-beat-mapped (3) versions, especially from measure 4 forward.

Beat Mapping an Audio Region

Using an audio region as the source for beat mapping involves a technique similar to using a MIDI region. Instead of relying on MIDI note events, however, the Beat Mapping track uses audio transients as alignment points. To do this, Logic needs to analyze the source to detect the transients (similar to the function in Flex Time).

Let's mute the MIDI track and unmute the audio track before you start working with the audio track version.

1   Click the Editors button to hide the Piano Roll Editor.

2   Use the Mute tool to mute the Inst 1 region.

3   Use the Mute tool to unmute the Piano Audio region.

4   From the Tempo pop-up menu, choose Tempo Sets > No beat map.

5   Click in the track header of the Beat Mapping track (but do not click the buttons or menus) to select everything in the track, and press Delete.

    All beat events are erased, allowing you to continue with a fresh slate.

    NOTE ▶ Neither the work you performed with beat mapping or the premade Tempo track is deleted when you do this because they were saved to the first two Tempo Sets slots.

6   In the Audio 1 track, select the Piano Audio region. The audio waveform is displayed in the Beat Mapping track.

7   In the Beat Mapping track, from the Beat Mapping pop-up menu, choose Analyse Transients.

The detected transients appear in the Beat Mapping track as vertical blue lines.

8   Zoom out horizontally so that you can see the entire track.

Take a close look at the results displayed in the Beat Mapping track. As you experienced earlier with Flex Time, some unnecessary transients are detected. You can increase or decrease the detected transients in the Beat Mapping track by clicking the Add (+) or Delete (–) buttons in the track header.

9   In the Beat Mapping track header, click the Delete (–) button a few times to reduce the number of transients detected.

The number of transients is reduced, thereby providing a better picture of the relevant timing events in the audio file.

Now that you have accurate timing events in the Beat Mapping track, you are ready to begin the process of aligning the time grid.

10   Connect related lines in the Beat Mapping track as you did in the previous exercise, moving from left to right for the entire region.

11   When you're finished, play the track with the metronome click to check your results.

Lesson Review

1.   What does Flex Time use as a point of reference when time compressing or expanding?

2.   When performing region-based time adjustments such as quantizing on audio content, what does Flex Time reference to adjust the timing in relation to the time grid?

3.   Where can you edit Flex Time transient markers?

4.   Flex Pitch allows the independent adjustment of what note parameters?

5.   Which global track lets you graphically align the Logic Pro time grid to a rubato part?

6.   True or false? Both audio and MIDI regions can be beat-mapped.

Answers

1. Flex markers are used as points of reference for time manipulation, and they may be created independently of (or on top of) transient markers.

2. When making region-based time adjustments such as quantizing, Flex Time uses both flex markers and transient markers as timing references aligning to the Logic time grid.

3. You can edit Flex Time transient markers only in the Audio Track Editor.

4. Flex Pitch allows you to adjust a note's pitch, pitch drift, formants, gain, and vibrato independently in the Audio Track Editor.

5. The Beat Mapping track allows the accurate rescaling of the time grid to a rubato part.

6. True. Both audio and MIDI regions can be used as the basis for beat mapping.

Creating Your Own Sounds
with Software Instruments

3

Lesson Files	Advanced Logic X_Files > Lessons > 03_ES2_Start.logicx
Media	None
Time	This lesson takes approximately 60 minutes to complete.
Goals	Trace the signal flow through the ES2
	Select, combine, and blend multiple waveforms from all three oscillators to generate interesting sounds
	Shape the generated sound with the filters
	Modulate parameters with low-frequency oscillators and envelopes
	Add additional processing through output parameters

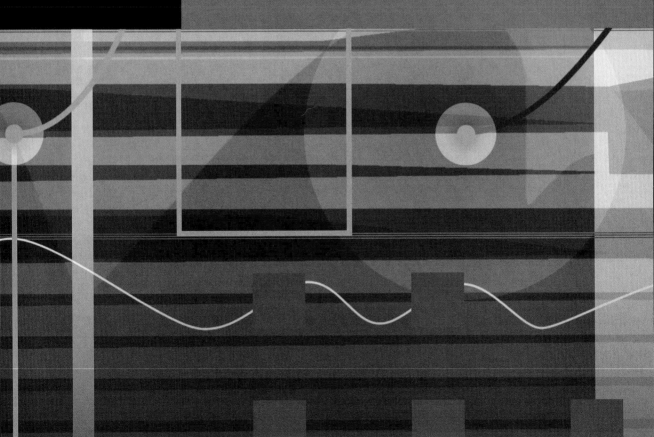

Lesson **3**

Synthesis with the ES2 Synthesizer

The ES2 Synthesizer is a hybrid synthesizer, inspired by the designs of well-loved analog and digital synthesizers of both past and present. From large-sounding leads to evolving pads, classic analog waveforms to digital waveforms and FM, the ES2 offers a wide array of tools for synthesizer enthusiasts.

With so much available here, starting off creating your own sounds can be overwhelming. In this lesson, you will walk through the various sections of the ES2, learning how to create new sounds from scratch. Even if you are not that interested in creating new sounds, you can also apply these skills to modifying stock presets to better fit your needs.

> **NOTE** ▶ Middle C may be designated as either C4 or C3, depending on the manufacturer of your MIDI keyboard. To accurately follow the directions in this lesson (and others throughout the book), you will need to set the "Display Middle C as" preference to C3 (Yamaha). You'll find this command in the Preferences > Display > General tab.

> **TIP** ▶ To learn more about the basic properties of synthesizers and how they generate and modify sound, check out Appendix B, "Synthesizer Basics" in the Logic Pro X Instruments manual. It serves as an excellent introduction for beginners to the synthesis aspects explored in this lesson.

Understanding the User Interface

Most of the Logic software instruments share interface features that represent how sound is generated and shaped. With synthesizers, tracing the signal flow through controls that affect a particular aspect of the sound is especially important.

1   Choose File > Open.

2   Navigate to Music > Advanced Logic X_Files > Lessons and open 03_ES2_Start.logicx.

The project opens, displaying the ES2 Synthesizer interface.

Let's look at the ES2 interface and trace the signal flow through the instrument.

Sound generation section   Filter section   Output/processing section

Modulation section

On the upper-left side, you can see the three oscillators that are responsible for the ES2's sound generation. Surrounding each oscillator are controls for tuning and mixing.

Moving to the right, you find the filter section, where the frequency spectrum of the raw sound is shaped.

At the far right is the output section for the ES2, with controls for volume and effects (distortion, chorus, flanger, and phaser).

In the lower half of the interface is the modulation section, comprising the modulation router, and below that, the modulation sources. Here you can manipulate any of the ES2 controls via any other parameter and real-time input.

In general, signal flow moves from left to right for almost all the Logic software instruments, with few exceptions.

TIP ▶ To hear how and what each section contributes to the overall sound, begin with a stripped-down preset using a single oscillator and no modulation routings. Doing so allows you to construct a sound from the ground up, engaging specific portions of the synthesizer one at a time, as needed.

Exploring the Oscillator Waveforms

The ES2 sound generation section consists of three oscillators capable of producing everything from classic analog waveforms to digital waves. The oscillators' raw signals are sent to the other sections of the synthesizer for further sound shaping.

Let's start by exploring all the waveforms for each oscillator and examining the unique potential of each.

1   Play your MIDI keyboard, listening to the sounds.

You currently hear Oscillator 1 generating a sawtooth wave, as shown in green surrounding the knob.

TIP ► When you select a software instrument in the track list for the first time, you may hear a slight delay (around 100 milliseconds) at first. This is because Logic does not engage live mode until it receives its first MIDI message. The delay doesn't affect the playback of sequenced material, but it can interfere with live performance and tracking. If you require perfect timing for the first played note, you need to send silent MIDI events in advance of that note (for example, sustain pedal, pitch bend, or modulation wheel).

2   Drag Oscillator 1's wave knob up and down, listening to the various waveforms available (sine, triangle, square, pulse, and so on).

In addition to dragging the knob with the mouse, you can quickly and precisely select a waveform by clicking it in the ring around the wave knob.

3   Click the sine selection, located at the bottom of the ring around Oscillator 1's wave knob.

In addition to the choices depicted on the ring, all three oscillators offer 100 sampled digital waveforms, called Digiwaves. These are accessed in a scrollable parameter located at the bottom (which defaults to sine).

4   Play a key on your MIDI keyboard while slowly dragging upward on the sine selection (Digiwaves). Listen to the result, and settle on a waveform you like.

5   Click the on/off button for Oscillator 2 to turn it on.

If you played your MIDI keyboard at this point, you wouldn't hear Oscillator 2 at all because the Oscillator Mix control is set to output only Oscillator 1. You can set the proportional mix level of each oscillator using the Triangle to the right. Each point of the Triangle represents one of the three oscillators.

6   In the Triangle, drag the square icon to the far left (Oscillator 2).

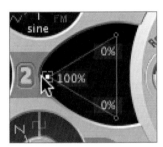

Just as does Oscillator 1, Oscillator 2 offers a variety of analog waveforms in addition to the 100 Digiwaves. Although you'll find some waveform overlap (sawtooth, triangle, square), Oscillator 2 offers unique functionality, including a variable-width pulse wave. As you move the wave knob from the 12 o'clock to the 5 o'clock position, the square wave's pulse-width proportions change to create different timbres.

7   Play a key on your MIDI keyboard while slowly dragging Oscillator 2's wave knob from the 12 o'clock to the 5 o'clock position. Listen to the result.

8   Click the on/off button for Oscillator 3 to turn it on.

Oscillator 3 has similar waveforms to Oscillator 2 but with a slight variation: a noise generator you can use for nonpitched percussive sounds or to blend in with other waveforms.

9 In the ring around Oscillator 3's wave knob, click Noise.

10 In the Triangle, drag the square icon to the bottom (Oscillator 3).

11 Play a key on your MIDI keyboard while dragging the square icon in the Triangle toward the center, and blend the output of the three oscillators to suit yourself.

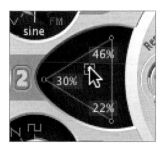

Just like Oscillator 2, Oscillator 3 has a pulse wave with variable pulse width.

12 On the ring around Oscillator 3's wave knob, click the square wave located at the 12 o'clock position.

13 Play a key on your MIDI keyboard, and listen to the result.

14 Move the square in the oscillator mix Triangle until the outputs of Oscillator 1 and 2 are roughly equal in volume.

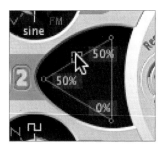

Each oscillator has dedicated tuning controls located immediately to its left. These frequency knobs allow you to set the pitch offset of the oscillators in a three-octave range. They enable harmonization, octave doubling, and the introduction of slight tuning variances to fatten up your sounds.

15 While holding down a key on your MIDI keyboard, drag Oscillator 2's frequency knob counter-clockwise down to –12 (semitones), listening to the results.

Oscillator 2 sounds an octave below Oscillator 1.

Just as you can click the settings in the ring around the wave knob, on the outside of the frequency knob, you can click the octave settings (12, 24, 36) to quickly change the setting.

16 On Oscillator 2's frequency knob, click the 0 setting to negate the tuning offset.

The tuning change you just imparted to Oscillator 2 was in semitones. You can also adjust tuning by cent intervals (100 cents/semitone) for subtle detuning of one oscillator against the other. You can do so by dragging the cents setting (indicated with the letter *c*) in the frequency value field.

17 Play a key on your MIDI keyboard while dragging the cents setting in Oscillator 2's frequency field downward to –3.

The slight, 3-cent detuning between Oscillator 1 and 2 creates a bigger, lusher sound, similar to a chorusing effect.

18 In the frequency field, Option-click the cents setting to return it to 0.

Using Oscillator Modulation to Create Interesting Sounds

You may have noticed that we didn't explore specific waveform settings on each oscillator. These settings do not specifically produce sounds on their own, but depend upon the settings of the other oscillators to produce a sound.

Using Frequency Modulation

Frequency Modulation, or FM, synthesis has been around since the late '60s and provides a unique way to create harmonic timbres using two audio-range oscillators. Using even simple sine waves, you can modulate, or modify, the frequency of one oscillator (called the *carrier*) by another (called the *modulator*) to produce complex results. You can think of FM simply as fast vibrato, wherein the rate of pitch change is in the audible range (20 Hz to 20 kHz).

With the ES2, Oscillator 1 acts as the carrier with a frequency you can modulate by the frequency of Oscillator 2. To best hear the effect of the modulation source upon the carrier, you need to hear only Oscillator 1's output in the mix.

1 Drag the Triangle to set the mix output to Oscillator 1 only (all the way to the upper right).

2 At the top of the ring around Oscillator 1's wave knob, click the sine wave.

When you select this waveform, FM is also selected, which indicates that Oscillator 1 is set to FM mode.

3 Hold down a key on your MIDI keyboard while dragging Oscillator 1's wave knob upward, thereby increasing the intensity of FM from Oscillator 2.

The sound becomes increasingly complex with the addition of new harmonics called *sidebands*.

NOTE ▸ Hearing only the carrier's output (and not the modulator) in FM synthesizers is normal, but you can certainly hear both outputs with the ES2 by positioning the square in the mix Triangle between Oscillator 1 and 2.

With FM synthesis, the tuning relationship between the carrier and modulator oscillators directly affects the sidebands that are produced. You accomplish this on the ES2 by changing the tuning of Oscillator 2 using the frequency knob.

4 Hold down a key on your MIDI keyboard while dragging Oscillator 2's frequency knob upward.

The sound becomes more inharmonic and metallic.

5 Option-click the frequency knob for Oscillator 2 to return it to 0.

TIP ▸ You can generate even more complex sounds using complex source waveforms for the modulator (Oscillator 2). Try using Digiwaves for interesting modulation sources.

Using Ring Modulation

Whereas frequency modulation uses one oscillator to modulate the frequency of another, ring modulation modulates the amplitude of the carrier. You can simply think of this as fast tremolo (instead of vibrato).

An interesting effect of ring modulation is that you hear only the sidebands it creates, which are made up of the sum and differences between the frequency of the carrier and modulator oscillator. This creates inharmonic frequencies, which results in a metallic sound. Although ring modulation doesn't always produce useful sounds for pitched melodic instruments, it is an excellent sound design tool for creating otherworldly timbres and textures.

With the ES2, Oscillator 2 both outputs the sound and supplies a simple square wave signal that is modulated with the output of Oscillator 1.

1   Use the Triangle to set the mix output to Oscillator 2 only. (Drag the square all the way to the left.)

2   At the bottom of the ring around Oscillator 1's wave knob (at about the 7 o'clock position), click the triangle wave shape. This will be the modulation source.

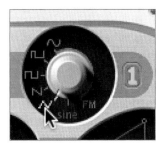

3   At the bottom of the ring around Oscillator 2's wave knob (at about the 7 o'clock position), click Ring. This will be the carrier source.

Just as with frequency modulation, the tuning relationship between the carrier and modulator oscillators directly affects the sidebands that are produced. You adjust this relationship on the ES2 by changing the tuning of *either* Oscillator 1 or 2 using the frequency knob.

4   Hold down a key on your MIDI keyboard while dragging Oscillator 1's frequency knob upward, listening to the result.

As you can hear, a complex metallic sound is produced that changes in relation to the tuning of Oscillator 1.

5   Option-click the frequency knob for Oscillator 1 to return it to 0.

Using Oscillator Synchronization

With oscillator synchronization, the start time (phase) of one oscillator is slaved to another. If the synced oscillators are set to the same frequency, you simply get a doubled waveform. However, if the oscillators are set to different frequencies, the slaved oscillator is forced to reset before it finishes a complete cycle, which results in oscillators that are not harmonized (separate pitches) but instead produce an interesting timbre change.

With the ES2, oscillator synchronization can be set for both Oscillator 2 and Oscillator 3, slaving to the frequency of Oscillator 1. On both oscillators, you can synchronize either a generated sawtooth or square wave to the chosen waveform of Oscillator 1.

1   In the ring around Oscillator 2's wave knob (at about the 8 o'clock position), click the sawtooth sync setting.

2   Hold down a key on your MIDI keyboard while dragging Oscillator 2's frequency knob upward, listening to the result.

The sound changes in timbre as you adjust the frequency of the slaved oscillator (Oscillator 2) in relation to the triangle wave generated by Oscillator 1.

3   In the mix Triangle, position the square somewhere close to the middle to create an equal mix of all oscillators.

Sculpting Your Sound Using the Filters

A synthesizer's filter section allows you to carve out only those frequencies generated by the oscillators you want to hear. Of utmost importance to the quality of sound is the character and flexibility of the filter or filters.

The ES2 provides two independent filters you can set in series or in parallel for flexible routing and sculpting of the sound generated by the oscillators. With the stripped-down preset you are using, the two filters are set in series by default with the signal feeding from one filter to the other.

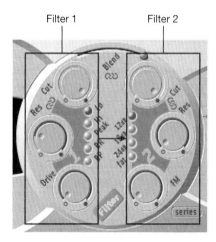

To gain an understanding of how each filter can influence the generated sound, you need to listen to them one at a time. When in series, the Blend slider at the top of the filter section acts as a cross-fader between Filter 1 and Filter 2. As you can see, the Blend control is currently set all the way to the right (above Filter 2), so only Filter 2 will affect the sound from the oscillators.

Characteristic of subtractive synthesis, Filter 2 is a dedicated low-pass filter with variable cutoff, slope, and resonance. Let's listen to its effect on the sound.

1   Hold down a key on your MIDI keyboard while dragging Filter 2's Cutoff knob downward to the midpoint, listening to the result.

As you decrease the cutoff frequency, high frequencies are reduced, allowing only low frequencies to pass (hence the name, "low-pass filter"). You set the way frequencies past the cutoff frequency are attenuated by selecting a slope setting (12 db, 18 db, or 24 db).

2   Press a key on your MIDI keyboard while selecting each of the slope settings (12 db, 18 db, and 24 db), listening to their differences.

NOTE ▶ Slope is measured in decibels per octave. A higher number generates a steeper slope, which attenuates more frequencies higher than the cutoff frequency.

You can boost the gain at the cutoff frequency using the Resonance knob, which will emphasize the filter's cutoff point and even self-oscillate when boosted at high levels.

3   Hold down a key on your MIDI keyboard while dragging Filter 2's Resonance knob upward to about the 2 o'clock position, listening to the result.

You can really hear the effect that resonance offers by sweeping the filter cutoff when resonance is boosted.

4   While holding down a key on your MIDI keyboard, drag Filter 2's Cutoff knob down and up, listening to the result.

5   Set the filter's cutoff frequency back to about the 2 o'clock position.

You might have heard a drop in low frequencies when you boosted the resonance of the filter. This behavior mimics the original circuits in vintage synthesizers. If you'd like, you can add the low frequencies back in while using high resonance by selecting the Fat setting.

NOTE ▶ The Fat setting has little or no effect on low-resonance settings.

6   Click the Fat setting, and then play a key on your MIDI keyboard to hear the result.

The low frequencies are restored, giving more weight to the sound.

You can modulate Filter 2's cutoff frequency in a manner similar to the FM setting discussed earlier in the "Using Frequency Modulation" section. In this case, the cutoff frequency is the carrier, and the modulator source is Oscillator 1. The amount of frequency modulation is set by Filter 2's FM knob.

7   While holding down a key on your MIDI keyboard, drag Filter 2's FM knob upward, listening to the result.

This produces a different sound than the oscillator frequency modulation explored earlier, but it offers a unique way to create interesting timbres.

8   Option-click Filter 2's FM knob to return it to 0.

Now that you've explored what Filter 2 has to offer, let's direct our attention to Filter 1.

9   Drag the Blend control to the far left, over Filter 1.

Filter 1 is a multimode filter, providing not only low-pass (Lo) but also high-pass (Hi), peak, band reject (BR), and band pass (BP) modes. Adjusting its cutoff frequency can have a different effect depending on the mode selected.

10   Drag Filter 1's Cutoff knob to about the 2 o'clock position.

11   To the right side of Filter 1, try clicking the filter mode buttons one at a time while holding down a key on your MIDI keyboard to hear how they affect the sound.

Lo pass lets through only those frequencies *below* and around the cutoff frequency (as you heard with Filter 2); Hi pass lets through only those frequencies *above* and around the cutoff frequency. Band pass (BP) lets through only a narrow band around the cutoff frequency, while band reject (BR) does the opposite, cutting out those frequencies around the cutoff frequency. Peak mode simply boosts frequencies around the cutoff frequency, acting similar to parametric equalizers.

NOTE ▶ Filter 1's high-pass and low-pass filter modes have a fixed slope of 12 db.

12 Select high-pass mode for Filter 1 by clicking its mode button.

Below Filter 1 is a Drive knob, which distorts the signal before it is fed into the filter section (both Filter 1 and 2). Boosting this knob adds pleasant harmonic distortion that can add grit or fatten up a sound considerably.

13 While holding down a key on your MIDI keyboard, drag the Drive knob upward, listening to the result.

So far you've been listening to only a single filter at a time. You can blend the output of Filter 1 and 2 by sliding towards the middle of the Blend control.

14 While holding down a key on your MIDI keyboard, drag the Blend control about midway between the two filters, listening to the result.

As you can hear from the dip in volume, the high-pass and low-pass filter settings for Filter 1 and 2, respectively, almost cancel each other out. This occurs because the two filters are in series. Therefore, the low frequencies are first cut out by Filter 1's high pass, and then some of the remaining low frequencies are cut out by Filter 2's low pass. You can hear the effect of both filters equally by putting them in parallel, in effect splitting the sound generated by the oscillators to feed both filters at once, thereby combining the result.

15   At the lower right of the filter section, click the Series/Parallel button.

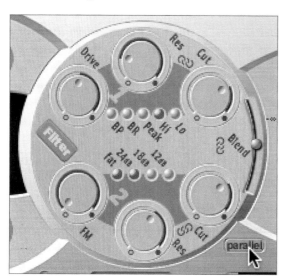

The filters change orientation to illustrate parallel processing.

16   Play a key on your MIDI keyboard to hear the result of the filters working in parallel.

Now you can blend the output of the split signal passing through the separate filters using the Blend control.

17   While holding down a key on your MIDI keyboard, drag the Blend control to about 0.54 (three-quarters of the way toward Filter 2), and listen to the result.

Using Modulation

Now that you've shaped the raw sound using the oscillators and filters, you can have some fun changing the sound dynamically using the modulation section. Your sound so far, while interesting in timbre, is quite static, and it doesn't respond to performance input (velocity and so on.). By applying modulation, you can, in effect, change the ES2 settings dynamically to create evolving sounds that respond to touch and gesture.

The heart of the modulation section is the modulation router. Like a virtual patch bay, it routes all modulation from source to target. The modulation router contains ten slots that you can assign individual routings to affect the sound.

To better explain how this works, let's start by taking a look at one of the pre-existing routings that is standard on almost all synthesizers.

1   Look at the second slot in the modulation router.

Each slot in the modulation router has assignable Target, Source, Intensity, and Via parameters. The Target parameter represents values that will be changed dynamically. In this example, the target is the tuning of all three oscillators (Pitch123). The Source parameter represents what will generate the change: in this case, one of the two low-frequency oscillators (LFO1) offered by the ES2.

NOTE ▶ An LFO is just like one of the oscillators you looked at earlier, except that the frequencies it affects are low (typically well below the frequency of human hearing). As such, the LFOs are perfect for invoking gradual change over a parameter.

The arrows immediately to the right of the slot represent the intensity of the effect (how much the LFO will change the pitch).

The Via parameter assigns a source to control the modulation intensity. In this routing, the mod wheel (Controller 1) is assigned.

In effect, the pitch of all three oscillators is gradually changed back and forth by the LFO, with the mod wheel giving the user control over the pitch-change depth. This all translates to vibrato.

2   Hold down a MIDI key while turning the mod wheel up and down on your MIDI keyboard.

The intensity of the vibrato effect changes as you adjust the mod wheel.

In this instance, intensity is given a range, represented by the split arrows showing minimum and maximum values. You can change the range by dragging the top or bottom arrow, or you can even move the whole range up and down by dragging between the arrows. When dragging, pay attention to the help tags to better position the intensity slider.

3 Drag the top arrow (the orange one) of the intensity range upward to 1.00.

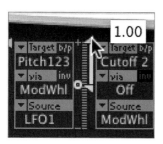

4 Hold down a MIDI key while turning up the mod wheel on your MIDI keyboard all the way.

The pitch change is more significant (and extreme) at the top of the range.

You can quickly return to an intensity of 0 by clicking the little zero symbol immediately to the left of the intensity slider.

5 Click the zero symbol.

6 Drag the top arrow (the orange one) of the intensity range upward to around 0.25.

Using the Low-Frequency Oscillators

You can modify the speed and shape of the routed vibrato by working with the source (LFO1) settings, which are displayed below the modulation router.

1 While holding down a key on your MIDI keyboard, drag LFO 1's Rate slider downward, listening to the result.

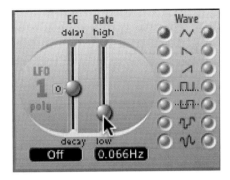

The rate of vibrato slows.

2 Set LFO 1's rate back to about three-quarters of the way up (5.500 Hz).

Just like the oscillators in the sound generation section, the ES2 LFOs can have different waveforms that dictate how the Target parameter will change during the LFO cycle. You can select waveforms by clicking the column of buttons adjacent to LFO 1 and LFO 2, respectively.

3 While holding down a key on your MIDI keyboard, select LFO 1's Wave buttons one at a time, listening to the result.

The effect on oscillator pitch changes shape, depending on the waveform selected.

TIP ▶ The bottom two waveforms output random values. The uppermost of the two steps from value to value, and the bottom choice smoothly transitions between the values. These are excellent for applying subtle, unpredictable variations to a parameter.

4   Select the triangle wave for LFO 1.

Unique to LFO 1 is the addition of its own envelope generator, labeled EG, to the left of the Rate slider. It enables you to fade in or out the modulation. You can use this to emulate the natural vibrato a musician might employ on a conventional instrument.

5   Drag LFO 1's EG slider up to around 3600 ms toward the delay side.

6   Hold down a key on your MIDI controller, listening to the result.

The vibrato fades in gradually after the sound starts.

NOTE ▶ Another unique feature of LFO 1 is that it is polyphonic; that is, each voice played (via a key press) has its own wave cycle that is independent of the others. This feature helps to avoid static, phase-locked modulation. In the case of the vibrato example, each note in a chord would have its own unique LFO, no matter when it was played.

7   Turn the mod wheel all the way down on your MIDI keyboard, turning off the vibrato effect.

NOTE ▶ LFO 2, while monophonic, offers the capability of syncing to bars and beats in Logic to create tempo-based effects. Do so by dragging the Rate slider to the bottom half.

Using the Envelope Generators

The ES2 offers three envelope generators per voice. Both Envelopes 1 and 2 do not do anything unless you assign them as modulation sources. Envelope 3, on the other hand, is hard-wired to the volume of the sound. You can use it to define how a sound changes in dynamics when you strike, hold, or release a key.

You will use this envelope to change the organ-like dynamics your sound has now to those of a swelling pad or string sound.

1   Drag Envelope 3's Attack slider (A) upward about halfway (1000 ms).

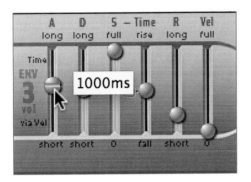

2   Play a key on your MIDI keyboard, listening to the result.

The sound swells, and then dies out quickly when you release the key.

3   Drag Envelope 3's Release slider upward to about 1800 ms.

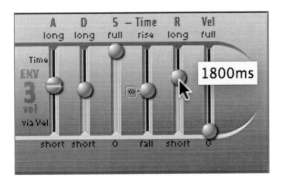

4   Play a key on your MIDI keyboard, while listening to the result.

The sound swells, and then dies out slowly when you release the key.

Using an adjustment similar to the intensity slider you looked at earlier in the modulation router, you can set the attack of each envelope to a range hard-wired to respond to velocity. If you set a range, playing softly will increase attack time (toward the top of the range), and playing hard will decrease attack time (toward the bottom of the range).

5   Drag the bottom of Envelope 3's Attack slider downward to around 280 ms to create
a range.

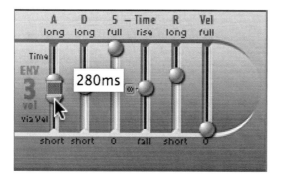

6   Play a key on your MIDI keyboard multiple times using varying velocity, listening to
the result.

As mentioned earlier, you can assign all three envelope generators as modulation
sources. The first modulation slot is set to modulate the cutoff frequency of Filter 2 by
Envelope 2. Currently, it is bypassed. (The b/p button is orange.) Let's turn it back on
to hear the result.

7   Click the bypass (b/p) button next to the Target parameter in the first slot of the
modulation router.

8   Play a key on your MIDI keyboard, listening to the result.

The cutoff frequency of the low-pass filter (Filter 2) changes over time, as dictated by
Envelope 2.

> **TIP** ▶ Understanding the differences between LFOs and envelope generators can be
> confusing at first. Think of LFO modulation as regular, or cyclic, change between two
> states (like a pendulum). Think of envelope generators as change that happens over
> time and are therefore linear (like a timeline).

Now that you've explored some existing routings, you can create your first modulation routing. This routing will change the blend between the two parallel filters, using Envelope 1 as the modulation source.

9   In the fourth slot in the modulation router, from the Target menu, choose FltBlend.

10 From the Source menu, choose Env1.

11 Drag the intensity slider upward to around 0.77.

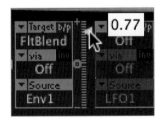

NOTE ▶ You can set intensity to a negative value to create a negative offset to the target instead of a positive one.

Now that you've set up the modulation routing, you can set Envelope 1's parameters as you wish.

12 Drag Envelope 1's Attack slider to around 1200 ms.

13 Drag Envelope 1's Decay slider to around 4900 ms.

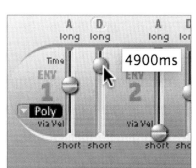

14 Play a key on your MIDI keyboard, listening to the result.

The sound slowly crossfades between Filter 1 and 2, as governed by the settings of Envelope 1.

Using the Vector Envelope Generator

The ES2 vector envelope generator is unique among the other envelopes in its ability to evoke change at specific points along an adjustable timeline that triggers with each key pressed. You can loop these points, offering myriad ways to change the sound over time.

To keep screen real estate demands to a minimum, the vector envelope controls are hidden behind the modulation router.

1 Click the Vector button, located to the right of the modulation router.

The vector envelope controls open.

The vector envelope controls only two targets: oscillator mix (Triangle) and parameters assigned to the X-Y (Planar) pad in the output section. You assign the targets in the Vector Mode menu.

2   From the Vector Mode menu, choose Mix.

Look at the main area of the vector envelope. Three numbered points are positioned along a timeline, each of which can store different states of the target control (in this case, the mix Triangle). Essentially, the vector envelope moves from state to state along the timeline, changing the target parameters.

You set these states by first selecting a point and then setting the square in the Triangle.

3   Click the first point to select it.

4   In the Triangle, drag the square to approximately the middle (all oscillators).

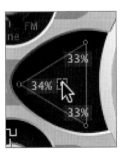

This sets the beginning state of the sound, which is almost identical to its previous sound.

5   Select the second point.

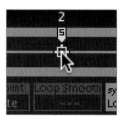

NOTE ▶ By default, the second point is designated as the sustain point (represented by the small *s* symbol above it). It is similar to a standard envelope generator, wherein the sustain point is held for as long as you press the key. You can change the sustain point by clicking the blue strip above the designated point.

6   In the Triangle, drag the square to the lower-right corner (Oscillator 3).

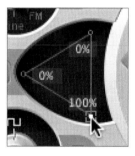

7   Select the third point.

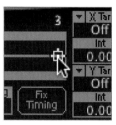

8   In the Triangle, drag the square to the far left (Oscillator 2).

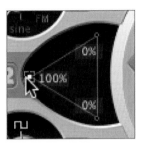

By default, the vector envelope is set to Solo Point, which will let you hear only the state of the selected point in the timeline. To hear the sound move from state to state, you need to turn off this mode.

9   In the lower-left corner of the vector envelope area, click the Solo Point button to deselect it.

10 Hold down a key on your MIDI keyboard, and listen to the result.

When you press a key, you can hear the oscillator mix change from all three oscillators sounding equally to just the sound of Oscillator 3. When you release the key, the mix shifts from Oscillator 3 to Oscillator 2.

You can change the amount of time it takes to move from one point to another by dragging the numerical time display between the points.

11 Drag the time display between points 1 and 2 downward to 380 ms.

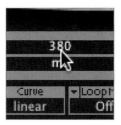

12 Hold down a key on your MIDI keyboard while listening to the result.

The oscillator mix changes between the first two states a bit more quickly.

NOTE ▶ You can add additional points by Shift-clicking the desired location in the vector envelope timeline. To delete a point, Control-click it, and from the shortcut menu, choose Delete Selected Point.

You can add further sonic movement by looping points in the timeline. These loops can move forward, backward, and alternately forward and backward, depending on the settings.

13 At the bottom of the vector envelope area, from the Loop Mode menu, choose Alternate.

A loop area is defined starting at point 1 and ending at point 2.

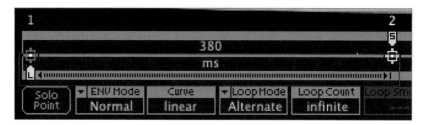

14 Hold down a key on your MIDI keyboard, listening to the result.

The oscillator mix changes, going back and forth from the states defined in points 1 and 2.

NOTE ▶ You can define loop start and end points by clicking below the points on the blue strip below the timeline.

The rate of the loop is usually determined by the timing between the two points. You can, however, adjust the rate proportionally using the Loop Rate control. You can set the rate to free time (as Hz) or as divisions of the beat (Sync), which locks to tempo.

15 Drag the Loop Rate control to the left, setting the rate to a 1/2-note interval.

16 Hold down a key on your MIDI keyboard, listening to the result.

The oscillator mix changes, going back and forth from the states defined in points 1 and 2 at the rate of a 1/2 note. (The default tempo of the project is 120 bpm.)

TIP ▶ You can always revert to the original timeline by clicking the As Set button just below the Loop Rate slider.

The X-Y, or Planar, pad is a freely assignable controller that enables you to control two parameters at once. You can assign these parameters as sources in the modulation router; but if you are planning on using the vector envelope, you can conveniently assign them without leaving Vector mode.

In the following steps, you will assign X in the Planar pad to modulate the pitch of Oscillator 2 (which changes the character of the oscillator synchronization), and you'll assign Y to modulate the pulse width of Oscillator 3.

17 From the X Target menu at the far right, choose Pitch 2.

18 Double-click the Int (intensity) setting under X Target, and enter *1*. Press Return.

19 Using the same method, assign the Y Target to Osc3Wave with an Int of 1.

20 Hold down a key on your MIDI keyboard while dragging the square in the Planar pad, and listen to the result.

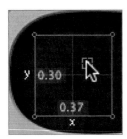

Now that you've heard the modulation effect controlled manually, let's assign it to the vector envelope to change the settings on the Planar pad over time.

21 From the Vector mode menu, choose Mix+XY.

22 Select the vector envelope points one by one as you did earlier, but this time change the Planar pad square location for each point.

23 Hold down a key on your MIDI keyboard, listening to the result.

You can now hear the oscillator mix, pitch of Oscillator 2, and pulse width of Oscillator 3 change dynamically over time.

Exploring the Output/Processing Section

Now you're ready to add the finishing touches in the output/processing section. You can attenuate overall volume level, add an additional sine wave oscillator, or apply processing to further shape the sound.

You may have noticed that the levels on the channel strip are getting pretty "hot," especially at high velocities. To rectify this, you can turn down the Volume knob.

1 Drag the volume knob downward to approximately –8.5 db.

You now have a little more dynamic headroom in which to add some further processing.

In addition to distortion effects, the ES2 offers modulation effects (chorus, flanger, and phaser) to further develop your sound at the output stage. You can select these effects only one at a time by clicking the appropriately labeled buttons (chorus is selected by default) and adjusting the Intensity and Speed knobs.

2   Drag the Intensity knob upward to around 52.

3   Hold down a key on your MIDI keyboard, listening to the result.

The chorus effect increases, thereby creating a spacious, swirling stereo sound.

Now that you've expended quite a bit of effort creating your sound with the ES2, saving it is a good idea.

4   From the preset menu, choose Save As.

5   Name the preset *Advanced Logic*, and then click Save.

> **TIP** ▶ If you are feeling stuck, or need some inspiration, try using the ES2's Randomize function (located just below the filter section). With it you can set a target for randomization in the menu on the right and then use the slider to set the intensity of randomization (1 to 100%). When you click the Randomize button to the left, all specified parameters in the target are randomized by the amount specified. You can also make variations of existing sounds by using low intensity values with limited parameter targets (filters, LFOs, and so on).

Lesson Review

1. Which direction does signal flow in the ES2?

2. What do each of the three oscillators in ES2 offer in addition to analog-style wave-forms and modulation options?

3. When in FM mode, Oscillator 1 acts as the carrier. What does Oscillator 2 act as?

4. When in Ring Modulation mode, Oscillator 2 acts as the carrier. What does Oscillator 1 act as?

5. When using oscillator synchronization, which oscillator is the master?

6. How can the ES2 filters be configured?

7. In the ES2, where is modulation assigned?

8. To which two targets can you assign the ES2 vector envelope?

Answers

1. Signal flow moves from left to right, which helps in understanding the instrument as well as locating controls.

2. Each oscillator offers 100 Digiwaves.

3. Oscillator 2 acts as the modulation source.

4. Oscillator 1 acts as the modulation source.

5. Oscillator 1 is the master when using oscillator synchronization.

6. The filters can be configured in either series or parallel.

7. Modulation is assigned in slots of the modulation router.

8. The ES2 vector envelope can be assigned to Mix (Triangle) and the X-Y (Planar) pad.

4

Lesson Files   Advanced Logic X_Files > Lessons > 04_EXS24_Start.logicx

Media   Advanced Logic X_Files > Media > EXS24

Time   This lesson takes approximately 60 minutes to complete.

Goals   Build new sampler instruments from audio regions

    Assign pitch mapping and tuning to zones

    Create loop points for sustaining sounds

    Use groups to assign common parameters to multiple zones

    Use filters and modulation to change the character of sampled material

    Route output of specific groups for individual processing

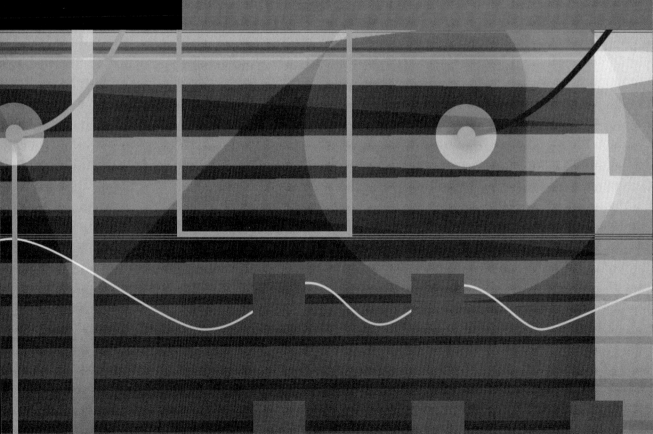

Sampling with the EXS24

A sampler is an extremely versatile tool. Essentially, it allows you to map digital audio files, or *samples*, across pitch ranges for triggering via MIDI. It does this by dynamically changing the playback speed of the samples in real time to match the pitch specified by the MIDI note value.

Individual samples are referenced and mapped in a *sampler instrument*. In this lesson, you will explore the abilities of the EXS24 by creating unique sampler instruments using specific audio regions from the Tracks area.

Creating Sampler Instruments

Traditionally, new sampler instruments are produced by first creating a blank sampler instrument, and then adding and mapping individual samples one by one, building the instrument from the ground up. However, Logic can also use a single command to automatically create a new EXS24 track loaded with a new sampler instrument wrapped around a selected audio region in the Tracks area. With this feature, extending the creative possibilities of audio files is especially easy, placing triggering and processing capabilities right under your fingertips.

1   Choose File > Open.

2   Open Music > Advanced Logic X_Files > Lessons > **04_EXS24_Start.logicx**.

3   Use the Mute tool to unmute the Vox Note region on Track 1.

4   Play the project, listening to the Vox Note audio region. You will use this recording of a singer holding a single pitch for your first sampler instrument.

5   Stop playback.

6   Go to the beginning of the project.

7   In the Tracks area, select the Vox Note region, if necessary.

8   From the Track menu, choose Convert Regions to New Sampler Track.

In the Convert Regions to New Sampler Track dialog, you can set how the selected audio region will be initially mapped in the new sampler instrument. Samples are mapped in zones, which contain settings that control how the sample is played back, including key ranges.

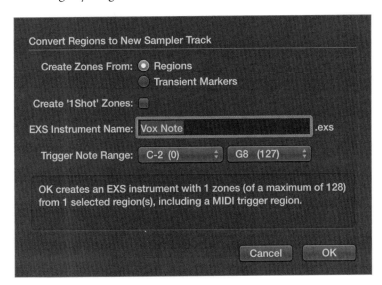

9   Select Create Zones From Regions, if necessary.

A single zone will reference the Vox Note audio region (as outlined at the bottom of the dialog).

You can also set the pitch range of the created zone, as specified by the Trigger Note Range menus (low to high). Because only a single audio region was selected (you can also select multiple regions), it will utilize only the lowest trigger note to map the region.

10   From the first Trigger Note Range pop-up menu, choose C3 (60) to create a new zone at C3, right in the middle of the keyboard.

11 Click OK.

A new EXS24 track (named Vox Note) is created below the original track, along with a new MIDI region. This new region contains a held C3 note that triggers the newly mapped audio file for the same duration as the original audio region. Note that the original region is muted. The new MIDI region, in effect, replaces the original one in the arrangement.

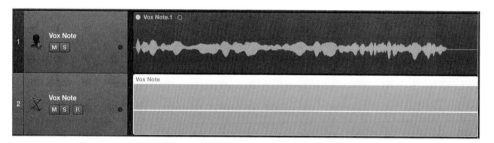

12 Play the project while listening to the new Vox Note MIDI region played through the EXS24. The playback sounds identical to the original.

This new zone will be automatically velocity mapped so that the harder you strike the key, the louder the sample will play.

13 Press C3 on your MIDI keyboard at varying velocities and listen to the results.

The Vox Note audio file plays as long as you hold down the key, while changing volume (amplitude) depending on hard you hit the key.

Using the EXS24 Instrument Editor

Let's take a look inside the newly created sampler instrument with the goal of exploring the creative potential offered by the EXS24. You edit Sampler instruments in the EXS24 Instrument Editor, which is accessible from the EXS24 interface.

1 In the inspector, double-click the EXS24 in the channel strip to open the EXS24 interface.

The EXS24 Parameter window opens with the newly created sampler instrument, Vox Note, displayed. You will be working with the parameters in this window later in the lesson; but for now, you will use it to quickly access the EXS24 Instrument Editor.

2   Click the Edit button.

The EXS24 Instrument Editor opens.

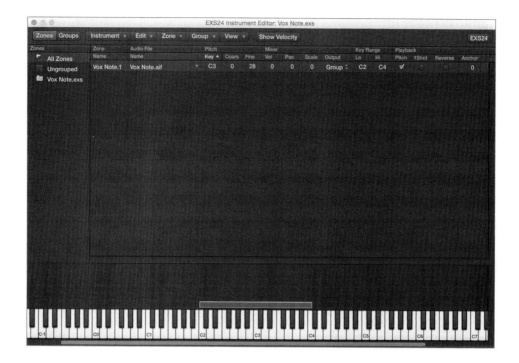

3   To save some screen real estate, close the EXS24 Parameter window (but not the EXS24 Instrument Editor).

The EXS24 Instrument Editor has two views: Zones and Groups. You are currently looking at the Zones view (more on Groups later), as indicated by the selected button at the upper left.

The top portion of the EXS24 Instrument Editor is called the Parameters area, and it displays the settings of each sample referenced by the sampler instrument. The bottom portion of the window displays how each sample is mapped to various pitches, as represented by the keyboard at the bottom of the window. As you can see, a new zone named Vox Note.1 was created, mapped to C3 on the keyboard.

When you create a sampler instrument with the Convert Regions to New Sampler Track command, the zone created is without range—that is, mapped to only a single pitch.

You can, of course, extend the zone's range to map the audio file to multiple pitches, either by changing settings in the Key Range columns of the Parameters area, or by directly dragging the zone in the lower area.

4   In the Key Range parameters, double-click the Hi field and enter *c4*. Press Return.

The zone extends in range to the right, from C3 to C4.

5   In the lower area of the EXS24 Instrument Editor, drag the zone's left border toward the left, extending the range to C2.

6   Play the C2 to C4 keys on your MIDI keyboard, listening to the result.

The pitch (and speed) of the sample shifts up and down, mapped in relation to your MIDI keyboard input.

NOTE ▶ You can also create new sampler instruments by choosing New from the EXS24 Instrument Editor's Instrument menu, or by clicking the Edit button on the EXS24 interface when an instrument isn't currently loaded. Doing so creates a blank sampler instrument in which you can manually add zones by choosing New Zone or Load Multiple Samples from the Zones menu. You can also create new zones by dragging audio files from the Project Audio, Media, or All Files Browser, or even the Finder.

If you have perfect pitch, you might have noticed that the sung note is a little flat compared to standard tuning (A440). It wouldn't be a problem if this were the only instrument used in the project, but if other instruments will be played at the same time, it would sound out of tune. Using the zone's Pitch parameters in the Instrument Editor, you can compensate for tuning discrepancies in Coarse or Fine degrees. (Coarse equals semitones, and Fine equals cents, or 1/100th of a semitone.)

The best way to tune a zone by hand is by inserting a Tuner plug-in on the EXS24 channel, monitoring the results as you adjust parameters.

7 Click the Audio FX slot of the new Vox Note (EXS24) channel, and choose Metering > Tuner > Stereo to open the Tuner.

8 While watching the Tuner readout, hold down the C3 key on your MIDI keyboard and drag the zone's Fine parameter upward to about 28 cents. (The Tuner's readout will bob around the 12 o'clock position.)

The sample plays in tune relative to standard tuning.

9 Close the Tuner window.

Creating Loop Points

Looping is a technique that stems from the days when samplers had tiny memory stores (by today's standards) in which to load samples. Many sounds start off with complex attacks but soon settle into a more or less steady waveform. By repeating this "settled" area, a sample can be sustained indefinitely without using up limited memory space. Even with modern software samplers that have access to gigabytes of memory (like the EXS24), looping is a useful technique to create sustaining sounds out of samples that are otherwise quite short, such as the audio file you are working with in this exercise.

By default, this editor displays only some of the Zone parameters, while hiding others, including the Loop parameters. You can select the parameters you want to display in the View menu.

1   From the local View menu, choose View All.

All Zone parameters are displayed, including the Loop parameters.

NOTE ▸ Depending on the size of your EXS24 Instrument Editor window, you might need to scroll to the right to view the Loop parameters.

To enable looping, you first need to select the Loop On option.

2   In the Loop parameters, select Loop On.

Although you could enter start and end times (by sample number) in the parameters area, doing so would be arbitrary and counterintuitive. Selecting an area on the waveform itself using the Audio File Editor is much easier.

3   In the Audio File parameters for the zone, click the disclosure triangle to the right of the audio file name and choose "Open in Sample Editor."

The Audio File Editor opens, displaying the referenced audio file, **Vox Note.aif**.

NOTE ▶ You most likely will need to expand the Audio File Editor window to complete the following exercise. If you have limited screen real estate, you can minimize the EXS24 Instrument Editor window, temporarily storing it in your Dock.

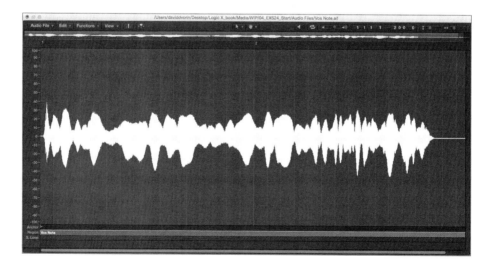

TIP ▶ Double-clicking an audio file in a zone also opens the audio file in the Audio File Editor.

You can set the Audio File Editor's timeline to display time using various units of measurement, depending on which is most useful for the task. For example, when setting loop points, you may find it most helpful to view the timeline in samples (1 sample = 1 ÷ sample rate per second.) That type of timeline setup corresponds to the numerical display in the EXS24 Instrument Editor.

NOTE ▶ Don't confuse samples (as a measurement of time) with audio samples, as mentioned earlier in the chapter. The latter is another way of saying "digital audio files," while the former refers to the tiny components that make up a digital waveform.

4   From the local View menu, choose Samples, if necessary.

The timeline is now displayed in samples.

The trick to setting loop points is to find a sustaining portion in the audio file you can repeat without interruption. To make smooth edits, you must make selections that do not interrupt the waveform above or below the zero axis (thereby creating an audible click). When you enable "Snap Edits to Zero Crossings" in the Audio File Editor, all new selections will be justified to the nearest point the waveform crosses the zero axis.

5   If not set already, choose Snap Edits to Zero Crossings from the local Edit menu.

6   Using the help tags, select an area from approximately 28800 to 91900 samples (refer to the following figure).

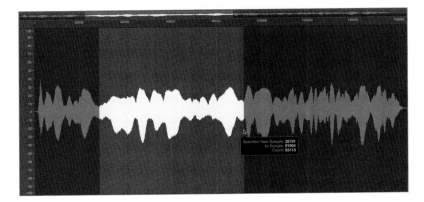

You can audition your selection by selecting the Prelisten and Cycle buttons at the top of the Audio File Editor.

7 Click the Prelisten and Cycle buttons to listen to your selection looping.

8 Click the Prelisten button to stop playback.

> **TIP** Your loop points may sound a bit rough at first, but with further massaging, you can create a smoother result. You do this by zooming in on the start and end loop points and fine-tuning the selection while auditioning the results.

Now that you've identified the area you want to be looped, you need to set the start and end loop points to the zone in the EXS24 Instrument Editor.

9 From the Audio File Editor's local Edit menu, choose Selection > Sample Loop.

The Sample Loop lane in the Audio File Editor displays the selected area in orange.

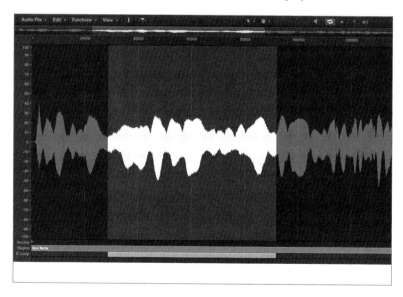

10 Close the Audio File Editor.

The results of your selection appear in the Loop parameters of the EXS24 Instrument Editor.

11 Hold down C3 on your MIDI keyboard, listening to the result.

The sample plays, now looping the selected area for as long as you hold down the key.

To aid you in smoothing out the repeating loop's start and end points, you can apply a short crossfade (much as you would smooth region transitions in the Tracks area).

12 In the Loop parameters, double-click the Xfade field and enter *30*. Press Return.

An option is also available to make the crossfade equal powered, which creates an exponential curve with a 3 db volume boost in the middle to compensate for the volume dip that normally occurs in a linear crossfade.

13 In the Loop parameters, select the E. Pwr option.

14 Hold down a C3 on your MIDI keyboard, listening to the result.

The sample plays, smoothly looping the selected area for as long as you hold down the key.

Using the Parameter Window

After a sampler instrument is loaded, the triggered sounds are further refined and processed by the global playback parameters located on the interface of the EXS24 itself. These parameters, which are nearly identical to the sound processing functionality of a synthesizer, allow you to further shape your sampler instrument sounds.

1   In the EXS24 Instrument Editor window, click the EXS24 button.

The EXS24 Parameter window (interface) opens. It offers a convenient way to access the EXS24 playback parameters without having to go back to the channel strip.

2   Close the EXS24 Instrument Editor.

A Save dialog appears.

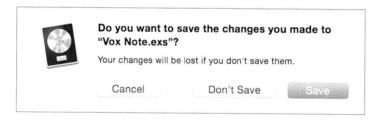

3   Click Save.

Now look at the EXS24's interface. Note that the EXS24 shares many interface characteristics with the ES2 synthesizer covered in Lesson 3. It has filter, output, modulation routing, and modulation source sections in similar places in the interface.

Filter section

Output section

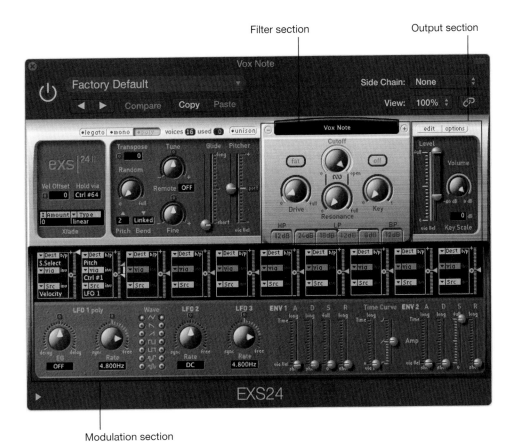

Modulation section

In this exercise, you will use the amplitude envelope to change the Vox Note sampler instrument's character to that of a swelling choir-like pad that decays slowly. In the EXS24, Envelope 2, which is hardwired to amplitude, controls the dynamics of how the sound is shaped over time for each key pressed.

4   In the controls for Envelope 2, drag the bottom half of the Attack slider upward to about 820 ms.

TIP ▶ You can split the Attack controls of both Envelopes 1 and 2 to create a range. This intensity range is modulated via note velocity, wherein high values trigger the sound more quickly (represented by the lower half of the control), and low values trigger the sound more slowly (represented by the upper half of the control).

5   In the controls for Envelope 2, drag the Release slider upward to about 820 ms.

6   Hold down a chord between C2 and C4 on your MIDI keyboard, listening to the result.

You should hear a swelling, sustained choir sound, based on the original audio file, **Vox Note.aif**.

7   From the preset menu in the EXS24 window, choose Save As.

8   Name the preset *Vox Note* and click Save.

9   Close the EXS24 window

Creating Multiple Zones from Region Transients

In the previous exercises, you created a single zone sampler instrument from an audio file in the Tracks area. Using a similar technique, you can create a sampler instrument with multiple zones based on detected transients in the audio file. This is especially useful when dealing with rhythmic material such as drum and percussion loops that have clear transients.

In the following exercises, you will create a new sampler instrument from a basic drum loop and explore ways to extend and transform the sound using the EXS24 playback parameters and routing flexibility.

1   Use the Mute tool to mute the new Vox Note region (Track 2).

2   Select the Basic Drums track (Track 3).

3   Unmute the Basic Drums region on Track 3.

4   Play the project, and listen to the Basic Drums region to become familiar with the material.

5   From the Track menu, choose Convert Regions to New Sampler Track.

The Convert Regions to New Sampler Track dialog appears.

6   Select Create Zones From Transient Markers.

NOTE ▶ When you create zones from transient markers, Logic performs a quick transient detection similar to the one performed when you first activate Flex on a track. The number of detected transients appears in the info area at the bottom of the Convert Regions to New Sampler Track dialog.

7   Click OK.

A new EXS24 track (also named Basic Drums) is created, along with a new MIDI region. This new region contains multiple note events that trigger each of the created zones in order, and for the same duration as the original audio region, thereby replacing the original audio region in the arrangement.

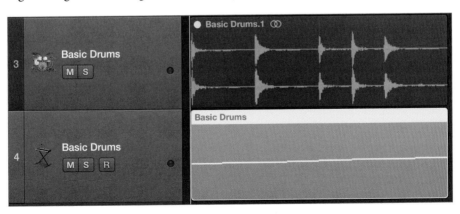

NOTE ▶ This operation is similar to using the Slicing Flex mode, wherein an audio region is chopped up according to its transients.

8   Play the project, listening to the new Basic Drums MIDI region played through the EXS24. The playback sounds identical to the previous version.

9   In the inspector, double-click the EXS24 in the channel strip to open the EXS24 interface.

10   Click the Edit button, located at the upper right.

The EXS24 Instrument Editor opens, displaying the multiple zones created from transients.

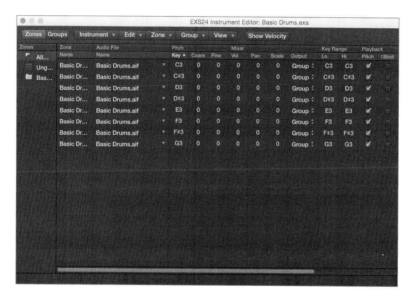

As you can see in the Parameters area, each transient from the original audio file is mapped chromatically to MIDI pitches C3 through G3.

11   Play the C3 through G3 keys on your MIDI keyboard, listening to the results.

When playing the associated MIDI pitches on the keyboard, you hear each individual slice. However, the slice plays only for as long as you hold down the key, and it can sound truncated if you release the key before the slice plays in its entirety. To allow the sample to play its complete length irrespective of the key release, you need to enable 1Shot in the Zone parameters.

12 With the EXS24 Instrument Editor window having key focus, press Command-A to select all of the zones.

13 On any of the selected zones, select the 1Shot checkbox to select it for all.

NOTE ▸ You can create 1 Shot zones automatically when converting audio files to sampler tracks by selecting Create '1 Shot' Zones in the Convert Regions to New Sampler Track dialog.

14 Play the C3 through G3 keys on your MIDI keyboard, and listen to the results.

The slices play in their entirety.

Although this method provides an effective way to trigger the drums as a performance instrument, let's explore additional playback parameters in the EXS24 Instrument Editor to further process the sound.

15 Click in the background of the EXS24 Instrument Editor to deselect all zones.

16 In the Parameters area, Command-click the zones mapped to C#3, D#3, and G3 to select them.

TIP ▸ To use your MIDI controller to select zones, choose Zone > Select Zone of Last Played Key.

17 Select the Reverse checkbox for one of the selected zones to enable it for all selected zones.

18 Play the C#3, D#3, and G3 keys on your MIDI keyboard, listening to the result. The samples play in reverse.

19 Close the EXS24 Instrument Editor window.

20 In the dialog that appears, click Save.

Using Filters and Modulation to Process the Sound

Just as you used the ES2 synthesizer to process the oscillators' signal, you can use the EXS24 filter and modulation options to process a sampler instrument you created. In fact, the EXS24's filter and modulation routers directly mirror the ones in the ES2, with the exception of offering only a single filter, instead of a pair.

The filter in the EXS24 is a multimode filter that includes high-pass, low-pass, and band-pass modes. To take advantage of its sound-shaping properties, you need to turn it on.

1 Click the filter on/off button located at the right side of the filter section.

NOTE ▸ The on/off switch for this filter enables you to quickly audition sounds with and without the filter's influence. Also note that when the filter is active, Logic uses more processor power, so switch off the filter when you don't need it.

Now that the filter is turned on, you can apply filter settings to shape the sound.

2   Do the following with the EXS24's filter settings (as in the following figure):

▶ Click the 6 db low-pass (LP) filter mode/slope button to gradually attenuate frequencies above the cutoff frequency.

▶ Drag the Cutoff knob to about 68%.

▶ Drag the Resonance knob to about 45% to accentuate the cutoff frequency by applying a gain boost.

▶ Click the Fat button to retain the low frequencies that are naturally diminished by high-resonance settings.

▶ Drag the Drive knob to about 20% to distort the filter and add harmonics.

Now that you've adjusted your filter settings, it's time to hear the result.

3   Play the C3 through G3 keys on your MIDI keyboard, listening to the results of the filter settings.

You can further expand the filter's sound-shaping properties by applying modulation to the cutoff frequency. The goal is to create a surging filter sweep that is timed to the tempo of the song. You can do so by using the EXS24's modulation router, which is nearly identical to the ES2's modulation router except that it calls a parameter that is changed dynamically the "destination" instead of the "target."

4   In the third (empty) slot in the modulation router, choose filter cutoff (Flt Cutoff) as the destination (Dest), and LFO1 as the source (Src).

5   Drag the Intensity slider to about +7.7%.

6   Select the top sawtooth setting for LFO1's waveform.

7   Drag LFO1's Rate knob to the left to 1/8.

You now have a filter sweep for every eighth note, regardless of the project tempo.

NOTE ▸ The EXS24's LFO1 is polyphonic with its own envelope generator, just like the ES2.

Now you'll test your modulation routing. Because it's tempo dependent, let's listen to it playing in the Tracks area.

8   In the Transport bar, click the Cycle button.

9   Play the project, listening to the result.

You should hear a sweeping, pulsing, swelling drumbeat that is significantly transformed from the original.

10   Stop playback.

While the loop was playing, you might have noticed that the EXS24 was distorting,
and the channel volume pushed well into the red. This is because of the extra gain
introduced by boosting the Drive and Resonance controls. You can recover a little
headroom by lowering the EXS24 Volume control, located to the far right of the
interface.

11   Drag the Volume knob downward to a value of –7 db.

Using Groups

In the EXS24 Instrument Editor, you can organize zones into groups to apply common
parameters to multiple zones simultaneously. Groups contain many of the same parameters you use in zones, but they also offer some unique parameters. For example, you can
offset both the filter settings and the envelopes, which allows you to create different cutoff
and resonance values for different zones.

In the sampler instrument you created, the low-pass filter cut out the high frequencies of
all samples. By using groups, you can, in effect, apply a different cutoff frequency for just
the snare hits.

1   In the EXS24 interface, click the Edit button to open the EXS24 Instrument Editor.

2 From the local menu, choose Group > New Group.

A new group, named Group #3, appears in the Zones column.

NOTE ▶ In addition to the newly created group, the Zones column displays All Zones, Ungrouped, and Basic Drums groups. The All Zones group contains all zones, regardless of their assignments. The Ungrouped group contains only zones that have no assignment whatsoever. The Basic Drums group, created by default when you imported the samples into the EXS24 Instrument Editor, contains all the slices created using the Convert Regions to New Sampler Track setting.

3 In the Zones column, double-click the new group name (Group #3), and enter *Filter*. Press Return.

To display the newly created group's parameters, you need to switch to Groups view.

4 Click the Groups view button.

The group parameters appear.

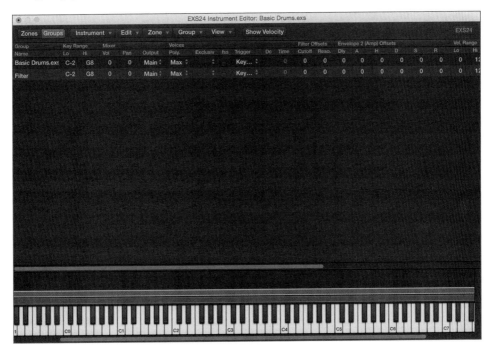

NOTE ▶ By default, the editor displays only some of the group parameters, while hiding others. As you did with zones in an earlier exercise, while in Groups view you can select the parameters that will appear in the View menu.

5   In the Filter Offsets parameters, double-click the Cutoff field and enter –5 to lower the filter cutoff frequency for any zone assigned to this group. Press Return.

Now that you created and modified the group, you'll assign the zones to it using the Zones view.

6   Click the Zones view button.

You might be asking yourself, "Where did the zones go?" Not to worry; you are currently viewing the Filter group, which does not yet have any zones assigned to it.

7   Click the All Zones group to display all zones.

You can easily assign zones to groups by dragging them onto the groups in the Zones column.

8   Command-click the zones mapped to D3 and F#3 to select them.

9   Drag the selected zones to the Filter group.

10 In the Zones column, select the Filter Group.

The two zones you added appear.

11 Play the project, listening to the result.

The snare samples mapped to D3 and F#3 have a slightly different filter cutoff frequency, thereby changing their sounds.

Routing Individual Sounds for Processing

As if the options offered by the EXS24's modulation and filter sections weren't enough, Logic allows you to further process the EXS24 sound by placing plug-ins into the signal chain. When you do so, the entire EXS24 signal is processed. Although processing the entire signal normally isn't a problem, in some instances you may want to apply separate processing to individual zones in a sampler instrument. To do so, you need to isolate the zone or group on its own mixer channel for individual processing.

Fortunately, the EXS24 allows you to route individual sounds through separate virtual "outputs" to accomplish just that. These routings are selected by the Output menu in the Mixer parameters in either the Zone or Group parameters.

1   Click the Groups view button.

2   Click the Output field for the Filter group (currently set to Main), and choose 3-4.

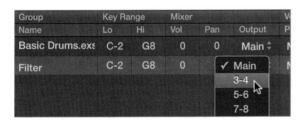

> **NOTE** ▶ The selections with dashes separating numbers represent stereo routings, and the selections with single numbers (without dashes) represent mono routings.

3   From the local Instrument menu, choose Save.

To use this special function, you need to instantiate the EXS24 as a multi-output instrument. So far you've been working with the EXS24 as a stereo instrument and have done quite a bit of work modifying the zones and groups. Luckily, Logic allows you to keep all your current settings when changing from stereo to multi-output instantiations.

> **NOTE** ▶ Logic transfers all settings and content contained in a software instrument when you switch modes (mono, stereo, multi-output, and 5.1).

4   Close the EXS24 Instrument Editor window.

5   Click the Mixer button to open the Mixer.

6   On the Basic Drums channel strip (Track 4), click and hold down the mouse button over the Instrument slot to open the Instrument Plug-in menu. Choose EXS24 (Sampler) > Multi Output.

The EXS24 interface opens after reloading the associated samples and current settings.

7   If necessary, move the EXS24 window so that you can see the EXS24 Basic Drums channel strip (Track 4).

8   Just under the Solo button, click the small + (plus sign) button on the EXS24 Basic Drums channel strip (Track 4).

A new Aux 1 channel strip is created immediately to the right of the EXS24 Basic Drums channel strip (Track 4). It will be the receiving channel for your Filter group. By default, Logic creates an aux channel with the default stereo input of 3-4 for the associated multi-output instrument (in this case, the EXS24).

9   Play the project, stopping playback after you've had a chance to hear the output of the Aux 1 channel.

The zones assigned to the Filter group play through the Aux 1 channel, while the remaining zones play through the EXS24 Basic Drums channel (Track 4).

TIP ▶ This technique works well for drum sampler instruments that need separate compression, EQ, and ambience treatments for individual drums (kick, snare, and so on).

Now that the snare slices are isolated on their own mixer channel, you can insert plug-ins or apply send effects for further processing without affecting the other slices in the sampler instrument. In the following steps, you will send the snare slices through a simple Echo plug-in to create rhythmic echoes.

10   Click the Aux 1 channel's top insert slot, and choose Delay > Echo >Stereo.

The Echo plug-in is instantiated, and its interface window opens.

11 Click the Time menu, and choose 1/8 T to set the repeat time to eighth-note triplets.

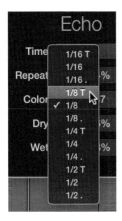

12 Drag the Wet slider down to 23% to lower the repeats' volume level so they do not overpower the original signal.

13 Play the project, listening to the effect of all the EXS24 programming you've done in the previous exercises.

The result is a surging, shuffling, processed drum loop, quite abstracted from the original audio file.

14 From the Echo plug-in's preset menu, choose Save As.

15 Name the preset *Snare Repeats* and then click Save.

To gain perspective on just how much you changed the original loop, let's finish by listening to it.

16 Close both the Echo and EXS24 windows.

17 Close the Mixer.

18 Using the Mute tool, select the Basic Drums.1 region on Track 3, thereby unmuting the original region.

19 In the Transport bar, click the Solo button to enable it.

20 Play the project.

21 While the project is playing, select the original Basic Drums audio track (Track 3) and EXS24 Basic Drums software instrument track (Track 4) alternatively to solo them.

22 Stop playback.

23 In the Transport bar, click the Solo button to disable it.

Lesson Review

1. Where are individual samples referenced and mapped?
2. Where do you find the settings that determine how a sample is played, including key ranges?
3. Which tuning parameter in the EXS24 Instrument Editor is used to tune by cents: Coarse or Fine?
4. Are loop points set in zones or groups?
5. Which EXS24 Instrument Editor parameter is used to smooth out transitions between the end points and start points of a loop?
6. How are groups used in the EXS24 Instrument Editor?
7. Are filter and envelope offsets set in zones or groups?
8. What do multi-output instruments do?

Answers

1. Samples are mapped in sampler instruments.
2. Zones contain the settings for sample playback and key range.
3. The Fine parameter is used to tune by cents.
4. Loop points are set in zones because they refer to specific samples.
5. The Xfade parameter allows you to assign a crossfade between the end and start points of a loop, making it smoother.
6. Groups are used to assign common parameters to multiple zones.
7. Filter and envelope offsets are set in groups.
8. Multi-output instruments (such as Ultrabeat and EXS24) can route individual sounds to separate channel strips for isolation or further processing.

5

Lesson Files   Advanced Logic X_Files > Lessons > 05_Sculpture_Start.logicx

Media   None

Time   This lesson takes approximately 45 minutes to complete.

Goals   Explore different material characteristics on which to base your sound

Apply different objects to select how the material is played

Process the sound using the Waveshaper and Body EQ

Morph between variances of the sound using the Morph Pad

Record your movements in the Morph Pad to use as a modulation envelope

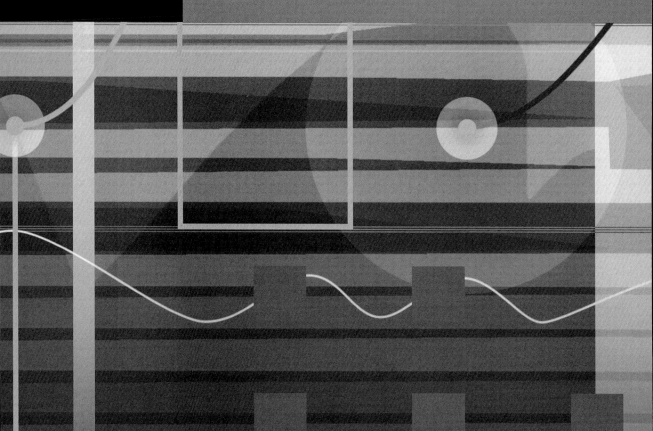

Lesson 5

Sound Design with Sculpture

Sculpture represents a unique approach to synthesis. It uses sophisticated algorithms to recreate the way sound is generated in the natural world, by a vibrating string or bar, for example. This technique is called *component* or *physical modeling*, and it closely mirrors the sound generation found in some of Logic's instruments such as Vintage Clav and Vintage Electric Piano.

One way to wrap your head around Sculpture is to imagine a synthesizer that lets you control how all the components of a real "physical" instrument interact, and what materials they are made from. In effect, you are building a physical instrument from scratch.

Because Sculpture is so innovative, many people have difficulty when they first approach it, unsure of how to begin designing sounds and editing settings. In the next exercise, you will walk through the key components of Sculpture and create a sound from scratch.

Understanding the User Interface

Your journey in sound design starts with a brief look at the Sculpture interface to identify where essential controls are located.

1   Choose File > Open.

2   Open Music > Advanced Logic X_Files > Lessons > **05_Sculpture_Start.logicx**.

The project opens, displaying the Sculpture interface.

Although many unique controls are available here, the Sculpture interface also aligns itself closely with the instruments discussed in previous lessons. Sections are dedicated to sound generation, filtering, processing, and modulation.

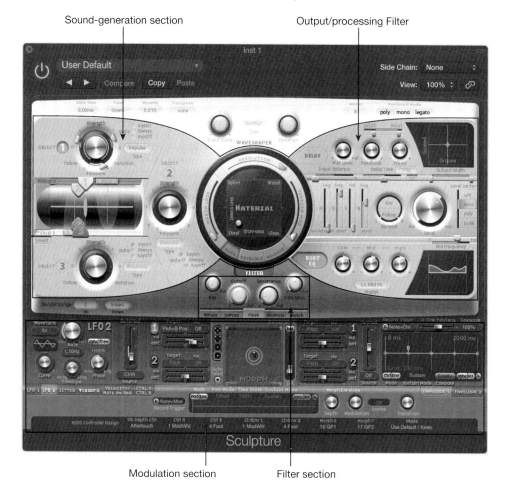

Sound-generation section

Output/processing Filter

Modulation section

Filter section

Signal flow generally follows a path similar to the previously discussed instruments, going from left to right.

Understanding the String

In Sculpture, the central synthesis element is called the string. This is a bit of a misnomer because the basic physical material it represents can be anything that would generate sound as the result of a physical action—striking, picking, blowing, and so on.

1   Play your MIDI controller.

    The string animates, depicting its vibration. When you're programming sounds with Sculpture, this animation provides helpful visual feedback that reflects how your choices are affecting the string.

    TIP ▶ You can turn off the string animation by Control-clicking the string and choosing Disable Screen Animation from the shortcut menu. Doing so can conserve the CPU resources used to generate the animation.

    Using the Material Pad in the center of the interface, you can construct the string by blending the properties of four basic materials: steel, nylon, wood, and glass.

2   Drag the ball in the Material Pad around the square while playing your MIDI controller.

    The sound changes as you move the ball, modifying the Inner Loss (damping) and Stiffness (rigidity) of the string material.

3   Position the ball about halfway between nylon and steel at the far-left edge of the Material Pad.

The outside ring of the Material Pad contains additional parameters that determine the sound-making properties of the selected material.

4   Drag the Media Loss slider. Listen to the sound by playing your MIDI controller, and eventually settle on a value of about 0.25.

Media Loss controls the damping of the string caused by its environment. Imagine a string vibrating in air, water, or pea soup to visualize what this parameter does.

5   Drag the Resolution slider. Listen to the sound by playing your MIDI controller, and eventually settle on a value of about 55.

The material's resolution has to do with the number of harmonics it generates. The higher the value, the richer and more complex the sound as more overtones are produced. Be aware that higher resolution values carry a higher CPU load.

6   Drag the Tension Mod (modulation) slider. Listen to the sound by playing your MIDI controller, and eventually settle on a value of about 0.25.

The Tension Mod control adds pitch displacement of the string to higher note velocities. It is similar to the slight initial pitch change that occurs when you strongly pluck a stringed instrument.

Using Objects in Sculpture

Sculpture has three objects that determine how the string is excited or disturbed (how it is played). Remember that physical instruments need an action applied to a sound-producing material to make a sound: A guitar string must be plucked or picked, a violin string is bowed, a marimba bar needs to be struck with a mallet, and so on.

1   Click the 1 button next to the Object 1 controls (to the left of the interface).

The button turns from blue to gray, indicating that the object is off.

2   Play your MIDI controller.

Why is no sound produced? The lack of sound illustrates the dependent physical interaction between objects and strings. Without an object exciting the string, nothing happens, just as in the real world.

3   Turn on Object 1 again by clicking the 1 button.

4   Click the Type button located to the right of Object 1's Strength knob.

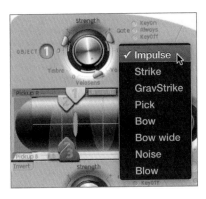

The menu that appears lists various exciter types for exciting the string.

5   Try choosing each exciter type one at a time, testing each sound by playing your MIDI controller and observing the effect on the string animation.

6 Conclude by choosing the Pick exciter type for Object 1.

Object 1 is now set to simulate the action and sound of a guitar pick acting on a string. The parameters are controlled by the object's Strength knob and surrounding sliders: Variation, Timbre, and, for Objects 1 and 2, VeloSens (velocity sensitivity). The parameters are context sensitive, meaning that the exciter type determines what the controls do. For example, the Timbre slider sets hammer mass when the exciter type is Strike, and bow pressure when the type is Bow.

MORE INFO ▸ See the "Sculpture Excite Table (Objects 1 and 2)" section in the Logic Pro X Instruments manual for a chart describing the parameters for each exciter type.

7 Drag the Strength knob and try different values, while playing your MIDI controller and listening to the result.

In the case of Pick, the Strength parameter determines pick force and speed.

8 Option-click the Strength knob to return to the default value.

TIP ▸ You can Option-click most controls in Logic to return them to their default settings.

9 Drag the Variation slider, playing your MIDI controller and listening to the sound. Eventually settle on a value of about 0.61.

The Variation slider determines plectrum stiffness when the exciter type is set to Pick.

10 Click the 2 button next to Object 2 to turn it on.

11 Click the Type button to open the menu, and choose Disturb.

Note that this menu is considerably longer than the Object 1 menu. Object 2 includes all the same exciter types as Object 1 but also contains a variety of others, which are referred to as *disturbers*. The nature of a disturber type is not to start the string material vibrating (as the exciter types do) but to disturb the vibration in some way through a physical interaction. Therefore, disturbers work in conjunction with exciters to produce a complex result.

12 Play your MIDI controller to hear the result of the applied disturber.

With Disturb chosen, you are introducing a physical object at a fixed distance from the string that keeps it from freely vibrating. Think of an object positioned close to the strings of a guitar so that it is nearly touching. When the guitar strings are plucked, the strings hit the object to create a buzzing sound.

13 Adjust the Strength of Object 2 to about 0.43. Play your MIDI controller and listen to the results.

Just as with the exciter types, the Strength, Variation, and Timbre controls modify aspects of the chosen disturber. In the case of Disturb, Strength sets the hardness of the object positioned near the string.

MORE INFO ▶ See the "Sculpture Disturb and Damp Table (Objects 2 and 3)" section in the Logic Pro X Instruments manual for a chart describing the parameters for each disturber type.

14 In the Gate settings for Object 2, select the Always button, and then play your MIDI controller to hear the result.

The Gate settings determine when the object interacts with the string in relation to the MIDI controller keystroke: on depressing the key (and not when the key is let go), on letting go of the key (and not when the key is pressed), or always.

15 Click the 3 button, and then choose Bouncing from the Type menu, if necessary.

Notice that Object 3's Type choices are limited to disturbers (no exciters). Bouncing simulates a loose object lying on the vibrating string. Imagine a piece of paper or small wood block lying directly on a guitar's strings to get an idea of what this produces.

16 Set Strength to about 0.11, playing your MIDI controller to hear the results as you adjust the value.

Strength controls the effect of gravity on the bouncing object.

17 Adjust the Timbre slider to approximately –0.24, listening to the results as you do so.

In the case of a bouncing object, the Timbre parameter controls the stiffness of the object.

Now that you have determined the basic sound generation by choosing object types, you can further work with the sound by determining where each object interacts on the length of the string. This is similar to picking a guitar string at the bridge, at the neck, or in the middle.

You can position objects by moving sliders representing each object in the Pickup display.

18 Drag the Object 1 slider in the Pickup display to the right, positioning it in the middle of the string.

19 In the Pickup display, drag the Object 2 slider to the left, positioning it slightly to the right of the left end (a value of 0.03).

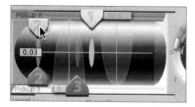

20 In the Pickup display, drag the Object 3 slider to the left, positioning it between the Object 1 and Object 2 sliders.

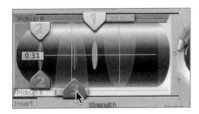

21 Listen to the sound by playing your MIDI controller.

Adjusting the Pickups

To sense vibrations from the string, Sculpture uses pickups that function identically to an electric guitar's electromagnetic pickups. As on an electric guitar, the pickup's location is of importance; different positions along the length of the string create different timbres.

TIP ▶ To hear these subtle differences, play your MIDI controller while you make the following adjustments.

1 Drag the Pickup A slider to the left, roughly between Objects 2 and 3.

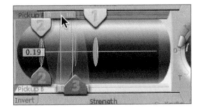

2 Drag the Pickup B slider over Object 1.

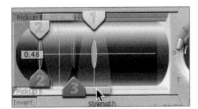

The resulting sound emphasizes the Pick exciter, similar to the way the neck pickup works on an electric guitar.

Processing the Sound

The extensive processing options in Sculpture allow you to further shape the sound using a variety of means (multimode filter, Waveshaper, stereo delay, and Body EQ). Examine some of the choices, while working with the sound you have constructed so far.

1   Turn on the Waveshaper by clicking the Waveshaper button above the Material Pad.

The Waveshaper provides interesting distortion effects, including tube simulation, for harmonically rich results.

2   Drag the Input Scale knob to a value of 0.39.

3   Drag the Variation knob to a value of –0.69.

4   Play your MIDI controller to audition the sound.

You have just applied soft, tube-like saturation to the sound.

The Body EQ section uses a unique approach to equalization, providing some great sound-shaping possibilities. A standard EQ changes individual frequency bands, but Body EQ also offers spectral models that emulate the resonating properties of specific instruments. You can shape these models by adjusting formant-related parameters.

5   If Body EQ is not already turned on, click the Body EQ button to the right of the Material Pad.

By default, Body EQ is set to the Lo Mid Hi model to emulate a standard three-band EQ.

6   Click the Model button to open the Model pop-up-menu.

As you can see, the choices range from various string instruments (guitars, violin, cello, double bass, and so on) to kalimba and types of flutes (alto and bass).

7   Choose Dobro Guitar.

The controls change to reflect the formant parameters of the resonating body (Dobro Guitar), and the graphic display to the right now depicts a detailed spectrum.

8   Play your MIDI controller to hear the Dobro Guitar spectral model applied to your sound.

In effect, you are coupling the sound generator you constructed (through the interaction between string and objects) with the resonating body of a Dobro guitar (a metal-body guitar with an acoustic speaker cone).

9   Try changing the three formant-related controls, which adjust to what degree the harmonics are emphasized (Intensity), how closely they are spaced (Stretch), and how far their frequency moves up or down (Shift).

Using Modulation in Sculpture

The modulation section in Sculpture is extensive, offering everything from low-frequency oscillators (including two jitter generators that produce random variations) to Note On Random modulators and user-created envelopes.

Of special interest is the Morph Pad, which enables you to morph between parameter settings for the entire instrument. You can control the Morph Pad manually by MIDI controllers or by its own time-based envelope.

1   If the Morph Pad is not already turned on, click the Pad button in the morph envelope display.

The Morph Pad has five morph points: one center and four corner points (A, B, C, D). Think of each point as a memory location that stores the parameter settings of everything from string material to object and pickup placement.

Instead of setting each state manually, you'll randomly generate deviants of the original state in each point.

2   Select the 4 Points button located to the left of the Morph Pad.

By selecting this button, you are targeting only the four outermost points (A, B, C, D) for randomization, leaving the original (center point) sound unchanged.

3   Drag the Intensity (Int) slider to the right of the Morph Pad to a value of 25%.

4   Click the Randomize (Rnd) button above the Intensity slider.

To see what just happened, examine how the controls for the various states (points) were affected.

5   Click each point in the Morph Pad (click the letters), one at a time, looking at how the Material and Object controls change.

NOTE ▶ The small red dot appearing in the controls' graphic readout represents the original state (at the center point in the Morph Pad). Each state, then, is a variation of these original settings, depending on how much randomization (Intensity) was applied.

6   Hold down a note on your MIDI controller. On the Morph Pad, move the morph (red) ball to various points, listening to the sound.

The controls (and the sound) change smoothly to reflect the various states.

Sculpture even allows you to record your movements in the Morph Pad to create a unique envelope that animates the sound whenever you press a key.

In order to record your movements, you must first "arm" the morph envelope record function by clicking the Record Enable button to the left of the morph envelope display.

7   Click the Record Enable button.

The Record Enable button flashes while waiting to record.

To guarantee an accurate start time, Sculpture is set by default to trigger recording only when it detects a MIDI note *and* you move the morph ball in the Morph Pad. This ensures that you will be recording only your movements in the Morph Pad, and not the time it takes to prepare your mouse and keyboard.

NOTE ▶ You can also set Sculpture to trigger a Morph Pad recording with just a simple MIDI note-on message or a note plus sustain pedal. You can set these trigger modes in the Record Trigger menu, next to the Record Enable button.

8   Hold down a key on your MIDI controller while moving the morph ball around the Morph Pad. Release the key when you are done.

NOTE ▶ Your morph ball movements record for the length of the sound's decay phase, after you release the key.

When the note completes its decay phase, the recording stops. The envelope information is now displayed in both the Morph Pad itself as well as in the morph envelope display, located directly below.

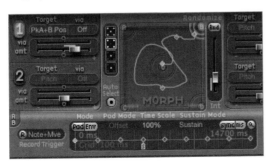

9 Hold down a key on your MIDI controller again, while watching the envelope move along the path and recreate your movements.

Saving and Trying Presets

As you can see, Sculpture is a truly exceptional instrument. You'll now save your new sound as a preset.

1 Click the Settings button to open the menu, and then choose Save As.

2 In the Save As field, enter a name that suits the sound you just made.

3 Click Save.

Let's conclude by taking a brief look at some of the expertly programmed settings in Sculpture, which show off the diverse capabilities of the instrument. With each of these, try playing your MIDI controller while holding chords and single notes to hear the sound evolve over time. Also try playing with the Morph Pad (if active) and modulation wheel of the MIDI controller, as these are frequently deployed to control sound changes.

Some Presets to Try

Preset Location	Description
Blown Instruments > Saturated Air	Highly expressive modeled flute sounds
Modeled Pads > Ambient Light	Evolving harmonic pad
Motion Sequences > Reverse Rhythms	Rhythmic groove using extensive modulation
Warped Sculptures > Marble on a Journey	Randomly bouncing and rolling marble using Morph Pad

Lesson Review

1.   What is the basis for sound generation in Sculpture?

2.   What controls the basic material of the string?

3.   What does an object do?

4.   What do you use to control where each object interacts with the string?

5.   What is used to sense vibrations along the string?

6.   In addition to the sound-generation and modulation tools in Sculpture, what other components are used to further process the sound?

7.   Which modulation control enables you to program smooth transitions between various parameter states?

Answers

1.   Sculpture utilizes a string acted upon by objects as the basis for sound generation.

2.   The Material Pad controls the damping and stiffness of the string.

3.   An object determines how the string is excited or disturbed (how it is played).

4.   You position an object slider anywhere along the length of string by adjusting it in the Pickup display.

5.   Pickups are used to sense vibrations along the string, similar to an electric guitar.

6.   Components such as the Waveshaper, Body EQ, and Delay allow you to further process the instrument in interesting ways.

7.   The Morph Pad enables you to smoothly move from various states of control settings.

6

Lesson Files	Advanced Logic X_Files > Lessons > 06_Ultrabeat_Start.logic
Media	None
Time	This lesson takes approximately 60 minutes to complete.
Goals	Create drum sounds using Ultrabeat's synthesis and sample playback sound generators
	Modulate targets using envelopes and LFOs as sources
	Use the filter and distortion circuit to process drum sounds
	Create and edit drum patterns using Ultrabeat's step sequencer
	Automate parameters with step sequencing

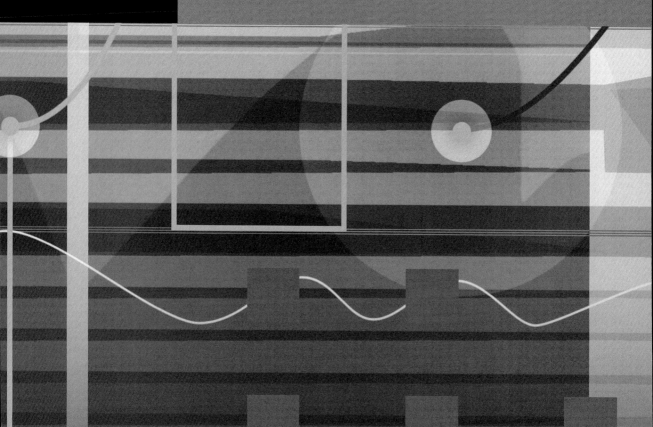

Lesson **6**

Building Drum Sounds with Ultrabeat

Ultrabeat's inspiration stems from the drum machines of the 1980s, as well as more current sample-based hardware groove boxes. Ultrabeat is functionally similar to those devices, offering both sound generation and integrated step sequencing.

What sets Ultrabeat apart, however, are its multiple sound sources, built-in signal processing, sophisticated step sequencing, and highly flexible sound architecture.

In this lesson, you will explore the many synthesis features available in Ultrabeat, as well as the unique traits it offers for triggering and modifying sound.

Selecting Sounds in the Assignment Section

When you look at Ultrabeat for the first time, you can tell that its interface is based on classic synthesizer design with sound-generation, filter, modulation, and output sections. It also reflects a signal flow path that is similar to the other Logic software instruments you looked at in previous lessons.

1   Choose File > Open.

2   Navigate to Music > Advanced Logic X_Files > Lessons and open 06_Ultrabeat_Start.logic.

The project opens, displaying the Ultrabeat interface.

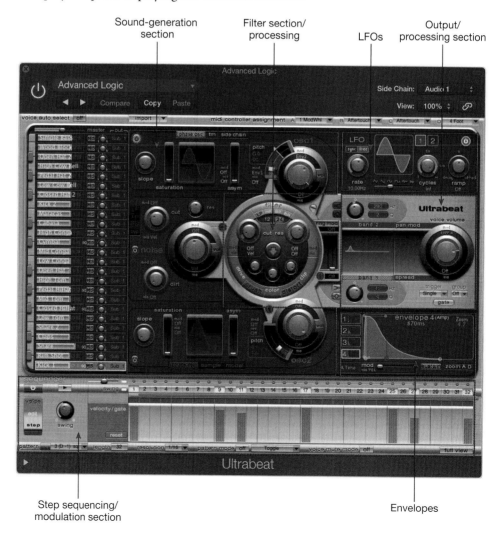

Sound-generation section

Filter section/ processing

LFOs

Output/ processing section

Step sequencing/ modulation section

Envelopes

Although Ultrabeat's interface is unique in its incorporation of a step sequencer area, its sound-generation, filter, and output/processing sections are located in roughly the same places as the software instruments discussed in earlier lessons.

At the left side of the interface is the Assignment section, which contains 25 drum sounds and a mixer. Each drum sound, or voice, has independent parameters you can adjust for volume, soloing, muting, pan position, and audio output.

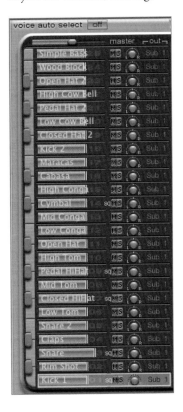

3   Select a few drum voices by clicking their names (kick, snare, and so on).

The main interface section changes with each selected voice. This is because each drum voice has its own independent sound-generation, filter, modulation, processing, and volume settings, which you can view by clicking its name.

NOTE ► In addition to two octaves (C1 to B2) of individually mapped percussion sounds, each kit reserves the C3 slot for a sound that is automatically pitch-mapped over three octaves.

4   At the upper left of the interface, click the "voice auto select" button to turn it on.

5   Play a few notes in the C1 to B2 range.

The interface changes with each note played. When "voice auto select" is turned on, the most recent note triggered is displayed.

> **TIP** ▶ If you do not have a MIDI controller, try clicking the onscreen musical keyboard to the left of the drum name to audition the sound in the Ultrabeat window. You can also use Logic's Musical Typing as you program the sounds in this lesson.

Exploring the Sound Generators

Ultrabeat represents an amalgamation of the synthesis features you looked at in the previous three lessons: analog waveforms (including noise), frequency modulation (FM), ring modulation, sample playback, and physical modeling.

Creating Kick Drum Sounds

Creating your own drum sounds from scratch can be a little daunting for the novice programmer. To speed up voice construction, Ultrabeat offers a few handy presets you can use as starting points.

1   Control-click the kick drum voice (C1), and from the shortcut menu, choose Init > Kick.

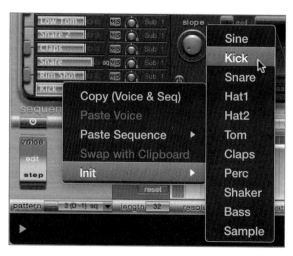

The parameters in the main area change.

2   In the main part of the interface, look at the uppermost oscillator (Osc1).

It is the only oscillator currently active (indicated by the lit power button), so it is responsible for generating the raw sound that makes up the kick drum.

The oscillator is set to Phase Osc, which uses the Slope, Saturation, and Asymmetry (asym) controls to shape a waveform into almost any basic analog synthesizer waveform. The best way to understand how each control shapes the sound is to apply them and listen to the sound each produces.

3   Repeatedly press the C1 key on your MIDI controller as you drag the Slope, Saturation, and Asymmetry controls. Listen to the results.

The sound changes timbre as you shape the waveform.

You can alter the pitch and volume of the signal generated by Oscillator 1 using the controls located immediately to the right of the Phase Osc controls.

Modulation routing in Ultrabeat is not done using a dedicated modulation router (as it is with the ES2 and EXS24) but by choosing from small menus located around the targeted control. These routings are displayed in blue (source) and green (via) around the pitch and volume controls for Oscillator 1.

Ultrabeat has four assignable envelopes you can apply for modulation sources. One of the tricks you can use when creating analog kick drum sounds is to apply an envelope to quickly drive the oscillator pitch downwards, thereby creating an immediately familiar, deep, vintage kick sound. The initialized kick preset puts this routing in place for you by default, as evidenced by the Env3 mod setting in the pitch parameters.

To investigate the shape and timing of envelope 3, you need to select the corresponding button in the lower-right area of the interface.

4   Click button 3 to select envelope 3.

TIP ▶ When you click any of the four envelope buttons, all modulation assignments that use it as a source will highlight on the interface. This also applies to the two LFO buttons at the top right of the Ultrabeat interface. These highlights enable you to easily trace modulation routings in complicated setups.

You can adjust Ultrabeat's envelopes graphically by dragging the attack and decay time handles, and you can further shape the envelopes by using Bezier curves.

5 Drag the decay time handle to the right, leaving it at a setting of around 740 ms.

6 Play C1 on your MIDI controller, and listen to the result.

The pitch change of Oscillator 1 now decays at a slower rate.

Although this is an exaggerated example, it illustrates the ingenuity of using envelopes to quickly modulate pitch and create a unique bass drum sound.

7 Drag the decay time handle to the left, leaving it at its original setting of around 50 ms.

Now that you've dialed in your kick drum sound, let's name it.

8 In the Assignment section, double-click the kick voice (currently Init:Kick), and enter *Kick*. Press Return.

Creating Snare Drum Sounds

Snare drums are traditionally built with noise generators that supply nonpitched, irregular vibrations to define the snare drum character. Ultrabeat has a dedicated noise generator, which is placed between the two oscillators in the sound-generation section.

1 Control-click the snare drum voice (D1), and from the shortcut menu, choose Init > Snare.

The parameters change, turning on the noise generator.

2   Audition the snare by clicking the musical keyboard to the left of the Assignment section or playing your MIDI controller (D1).

> **TIP** ▶ The sound you hear is primarily created by the noise generator, with some bottom-end resonance supplied from Oscillator 1's Phase Osc setting. This layered technique is highly recommended in your own drum sound construction.

The noise generator has its own multi-mode filter (in addition to the main filter section) that offers low-pass (LP), high-pass (HP), and band-pass (BP) modes. By default, high-pass is enabled, which allows you to attenuate unwanted low frequencies produced by the noise generator.

3   Repeatedly press the D1 key on your MIDI controller while you drag the Cutoff knob to a setting of about 0.75, listening to the result.

The snare becomes brighter.

To make the sound more responsive to player input, a common technique is to modulate the cutoff frequency using an envelope with intensity governed by velocity. Let's duplicate this routing for the snare drum.

4   Click the blue Mod menu above the Cutoff knob, and choose Env3.

Look closely and you will see that an indented blue control has appeared on the outer edge of the Cutoff knob. This control adjusts the depth of the assigned modulation source.

5   Click the green Via menu below the Cutoff knob, and choose Vel (velocity).

A green control "handle" appears on the outer edge of the Cutoff knob. It controls the intensity of the modulation, in this case governed by velocity.

6   Drag the green via control to a value of 0.90 (+0.15).

7   Drag the blue Modulation control to a value of 0.66 (−0.09).

NOTE ► The values displayed in parentheses reflect the offset to the current state.

The controls now look like the following:

8   Play the D1 key on your MIDI controller at varying velocities, while listening as the cutoff opens up a bit at higher values and closes at lower ones.

NOTE ► The snare init setting utilizes Ultrabeat's two bands of EQ to further shape the sound after the filter section.

9   In the Assignment section, double-click the snare voice (currently Init:Snare), and then enter *Snare*. Press Return.

Creating Hi-Hat Sounds

As you explored in the ES2 lesson, you can apply frequency modulation (FM) and ring modulation to create metallic timbres with lots of harmonics. You can use these effects in Ultrabeat to create interesting hi-hat sounds.

1   Control-click the closed hi-hat voice (F#1), and from the shortcut menu, choose Init > Hat1 to change the parameters.

This setting contains the routing necessary to create FM with Oscillator 1 as the carrier and Oscillator 2 as the modulator. You set the FM depth using the FM Amount knob located to the left of the waveform display in Oscillator 1.

2 Repeatedly press the F#1 key on your MIDI controller as you drag the FM Amount knob to a value of about 0.86, and listen to the result.

A metallic ringing sound is produced as the harmonics are increased.

3 In the Assignment section, double-click the hi-hat voice (currently Init:Hat1), and enter *Closed Hat*. Press Return.

Oscillator 2 is set to Phase Osc by default in the Init:Hat1 setting, but you can also use the other sound-generation modes—including physical modeling—to modulate the carrier. Doing so will result in an entirely different, but related, timbre you can assign to another drum voice.

4 Control-click the Closed Hat voice (F#1), and from the shortcut menu, choose Copy (Voice & Seq).

5 Control-click the Pedal Hat voice (G#1), and from the shortcut menu, choose Paste Voice.

Your original hi-hat sound is copied to the new voice and made ready for variation.

6 In the Assignment section, double-click the newly copied hi-hat voice (currently Closed Hat) and enter *Pedal Hat*. Press Return.

7   In Oscillator 2, click the Model button to switch the synthesis mode to physical modeling.

Like Sculpture, Ultrabeat's model utilizes a string that is excited by objects. Ultrabeat's component model sound generation is greatly simplified compared to Sculpture, offering only two types of exciters, a material pad, and resolution controls. Even so, you can generate interesting sounds, including sounds created using the component model sound generator as a modulation source.

8   Repeatedly press the G#1 key on your MIDI controller while you click the two exciter buttons, and compare the results. After you've had a chance to listen to both results, select type 2.

▶ Processing Audio Input with Ultrabeat

In addition to offering Phase Osc and FM choices, Oscillator 1 has a side chain setting that enables you to route external audio signals into the signal flow, triggered by incoming MIDI notes or the step sequencer. To set this up, do the following:

1.   From the Side Chain menu at the top right of Ultrabeat's interface, choose the channel that will send the signal.

2.   Mute the channel sending the side chain signal so it doesn't reach the outputs. (If you want to hear the original track in addition to Ultrabeat's processing, you must unmute this signal.)

3.   Play the project.

Whenever MIDI messages are sent to Ultrabeat (MIDI keyboard, recorded regions, triggered patterns, and so on), the side chain signal should be heard, layered with the other sound generators, and processed by the filters and modulation of Ultrabeat.

For more information on side chaining, see "Using Side Chain Effects" in Lesson 11.

Loading Samples

Ultrabeat offers sample playback through Oscillator 2, much like the EXS24 (as discussed in Lesson 4).

1   Control-click the Cymbal voice (C#2), and from the shortcut menu, choose Init > Sample.

The oscillator switches to sample mode, and displays "No Sample Loaded."

If you were to hit the C#2 key now, you wouldn't hear anything because you haven't yet loaded a sample. You can add one by dragging your own audio files from the Finder, or by loading one of Ultrabeat's large library of samples.

2   Click the disclosure triangle next to No Sample Loaded, and from the shortcut menu, choose Load Sample.

A dialog displays the contents of the Ultrabeat Samples folder.

NOTE ▶ Executing the Load Sample command conveniently takes you to the location where Logic Pro installed the default Ultrabeat samples (Library/Application Support/ Logic/Ultrabeat Samples), so you can easily browse samples specially designed for use in Ultrabeat. You can also drag audio files into this folder from the Finder.

3   Open the Crash Cymbals folder, and select Special Crash.ubs.

> **NOTE** ▸ The .ubs extension indicates a proprietary sample format with multiple velocity layers built into the file. Although you can't easily create files in the .ubs format, you can convert velocity-mapped EXS instruments into .ubs files by clicking the Import button at the top of the Ultrabeat window.

4   Click the Open button.

5   Play the C#2 key on your MIDI controller, or click the musical keyboard to the left of the Assignment section, to trigger the crash sample.

Similar to using the EXS24, you can change the pitch of the sample by dragging the Pitch slider next to the oscillator's volume controls.

6   Repeatedly press the C#2 key on your MIDI controller while you drag the Pitch slider to E4 (659.3 Hz).

The sample plays back at a higher pitcher (and is shorter in duration).

Let's finish by creating a fast tremolo (amplitude modulation) using one of Ultrabeat's two LFOs to modulate volume. You can do this by first assigning the routing around the oscillator's Volume knob.

7   Click the blue Mod menu (currently set to Max) above Oscillator 2's Volume knob, and from the menu, choose Lfo1.

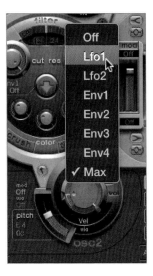

8   Drag the blue modulation control to –14 dB (+36 dB).

9   Play the C#2 key on your MIDI controller and listen to the result (a pulsing cymbal sound).

Ultrabeat's two LFOs are located at the upper right. They contain rate, wave shape, and envelope controls with functions similar to LFO controls you encountered in previous lessons. What makes Ultrabeat's LFOs unique, however, is that they can limit the number of cycles the LFO generates (from one to infinity). This feature enables you to evoke change in limited doses, applying modulation only at the beginning of a sound.

10 Drag the Cycles knob to a setting of 4.

11 Play the C#2 key on your MIDI controller, listening to the result.

The pulsing enacted by the LFO is limited to only four cycles.

> **TIP** ▸ You can easily create your own sample-based kits by dragging audio files to Oscillator 2. A special Ultrabeat preset saves you the hassle of configuring each drum voice's Oscillator 2 setting for samples. You can find this preset under Drum Kits > Drag & Drop Samples.

Processing with the Filter and Bitcrusher

In the middle of the Ultrabeat interface, you'll find a circular area that contains the filter and distortion circuit. To send a signal from the sound generators to the filter and distortion circuit, you must select the Signal Flow buttons located next to the oscillator's Volume knob.

Using the ability to send signal from the oscillator to the filter, let's process the cymbal sound.

Similar to the ES2 and the EXS24, Ultrabeat has a multimode filter you can set for low-pass (LP), high-pass (HP), band-pass (BP), or band reject (BR) with adjustable slope and resonance.

1   Click the Filter button to enable the filter.

2   Click the HP button to select high-pass mode.

3   Drag the Cutoff knob to 0.60.

4   Drag the Resonance knob to 0.75.

5   Play the C#2 key on your MIDI controller, and listen to the result.

The timbre changes slightly with some of the lower frequencies attenuated.

You can use Ultrabeat's distortion circuit to add grit and harmonics to a sound, and also apply a bitcrushing mode for lo-fi sounds.

6   At the bottom of the circle, click the Crush button to enable it.

7   Drag the Drive knob to 5.0 dB.

8   Drag the Color knob to 6x.

9   Play the C#2 key on your MIDI controller while listening to the result.

The cymbal sound's sample rate is reduced, adding grit to the sound.

NOTE ▸ You can determine whether the distortion circuit is inserted before or after the filter by clicking the arrow button located at the center of the circular area.

10   In the Assignment section, double-click the cymbal voice (currently Init:Sample), and enter *Cymbal FX*. Press Return.

Creating Drum Patterns with Step Sequencing

The integrated 32-step sequencer located at the bottom of Ultrabeat's interface greatly aids in the production of drum loops and beat patterns. These patterns, including any user-created patterns, are saved in each of the Ultrabeat settings and can be recalled instantly.

In this exercise, you'll test the kit you've constructed by playing it using a few of Ultrabeat's step sequences. Then, you'll learn how to further customize the sequence to create unique patterns you can save for later use.

By default, Ultrabeat's step sequencer is turned on, as indicated by the highlighted power button at the upper left of the sequencer.

1   Click the Play/Stop button located immediately to the right of the power button.

    The sequencer starts, and Ultrabeat plays a sequenced pattern. Sequences are stored and accessed via the Pattern menu located in the lower left.

2   With the sequencer still playing, from the Pattern menu, choose a few other patterns.

    In addition to choosing a pattern from the menu, you can trigger a pattern in Ultrabeat with an incoming or recorded MIDI note. Doing so allows you to start and stop patterns on the fly (which is especially advantageous for live performance). Each pattern has a number to designate its slot, as well as a MIDI note number displayed next to it in parentheses. This MIDI note number indicates the incoming MIDI note that will trigger the pattern.

    To change Ultrabeat patterns using MIDI notes, you need to enable pattern mode.

3   At the bottom of the interface, click the Pattern Mode button to enable it.

4   With the sequencer still active, play the A-1 through C-1 keys on your MIDI controller, and listen to the results.

    NOTE ▶ The specific trigger notes were chosen because they are located far below the most commonly used range on a MIDI keyboard. You may have to transpose your MIDI controller (using its octave buttons) to activate the pattern triggers. You can double-check your octave range in the Transport's MIDI Activity display at the bottom of the screen.

5   Play G-1 on your MIDI controller, or from the Pattern menu, choose 8 (G-1) sq.

6   Click the Play/Stop button to stop sequencer playback.

NOTE ▶ In the Playback Mode menu immediately to the right of the Pattern Mode button, you can change the pattern trigger behavior when receiving an incoming MIDI note. Choosing One Shot Trig mode will play the pattern only once, whereas choosing Sustain mode will play the pattern as long as the key is depressed. Toggle mode repeats the pattern indefinitely even after you release the key, stopping only when you press same key again. Finally, "Toggle on Step 1" mode acts similarly to Toggle mode, except that it triggers a new pattern only on step 1 of the sequence, enabling you to trigger the next pattern perfectly in time regardless of when you pressed the key.

The pattern located at 8 (G-1) will be used as a base for a new pattern. You can copy and paste any sequence from one location in the Pattern menu to another.

7   Control-click the Pattern menu and choose Copy.

When looking at the Pattern menu previously, you might have noticed that some of the patterns were marked with "sq" following the note pitch. The "sq" indicates that a sequenced pattern was saved to this location. To avoid writing over the default patterns, you will need to paste the copied sequence pattern to one of the available locations that are not marked with "sq". Do so by first selecting the pattern, and then pasting into a location.

8   From the Pattern menu, choose 11 (A#-1).

9   Control-click the Pattern menu, and from the shortcut menu, choose Paste to copy the pattern from one location to another.

Sequencing Sounds

The actual sequencing of a given sound is performed in an area called the *step grid*. Here, you can graphically insert events and edit them to create each element of a pattern.

1   Select the snare drum sound (D1). The snare sound's sequence is displayed in the step grid.

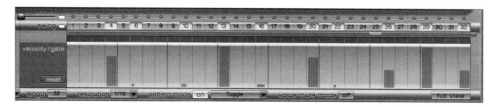

2   To the right of the drum name, click the Solo (S) button to solo the snare drum.

NOTE ▶ The "sq" next to the name indicates that this sound has a step sequence in the current pattern.

3   Play A#-1 on your MIDI controller to start the sequence. The snare sound is triggered whenever an event is displayed in the step grid.

4   Click the 2 button above the step grid.

This array of buttons is called the trigger row.

The next time the pattern cycles, you will hear a soft snare attack on step 2.

5   In the step grid, drag up the event at step 2 until the event stretches to the top.

The next time the pattern reaches this step, the event will be played louder.

6   Click the Solo button for the snare drum to hear the entire pattern (with all drum sounds).

> **NOTE ▶** The step width indicates the length (gate time) of the notes in the trigger row. In this case, the sound being triggered has an extremely short release, so this parameter does not audibly affect the sound.

Applying Swing to a Pattern

The Swing knob, located to the left of the step grid, lets you adjust the rhythmic feel of the pattern by increasing the distance between notes. Notes on odd-numbered steps remain unchanged, while even-numbered notes are shifted slightly. This control affects all drum sounds that have swing enabled in the pattern. (Different swing amounts cannot be assigned to sounds individually.)

1   While the sequencer is playing, drag the Swing knob up and down to adjust the value. Listen to the results.

2   To the left of the trigger row, click the Swing button to turn off swing for the snare part.

The snare drum sequence's "feel" changes in relation to the rest of the drum sounds in the pattern.

3   Click the Swing button to turn on swing again for the snare drum.

4   Drag the Swing knob to return the swing value to about 58%.

5   Play the A#-1 key on your MIDI controller to stop playback of the pattern.

Using Full View

When creating or editing step sequences for multiple sounds, use the full-view function, which displays all sounds at once in the Ultrabeat window. Full view also helps to show the relationship between the various sounds used in the pattern.

1 In the lower-right corner of the Ultrabeat interface, click the Full View button.

The interface switches to a graphical view of each drum sound's trigger row. In essence, each row of triggers represents the data created in the step grid, and vice versa.

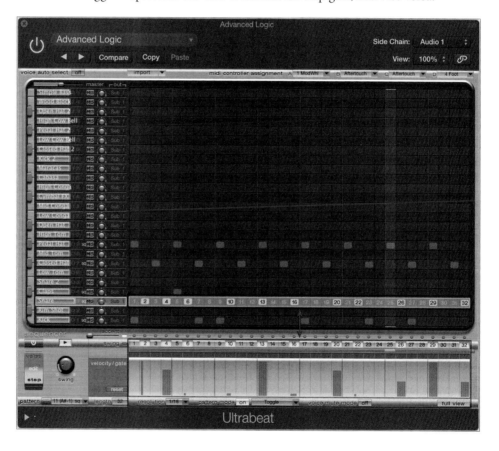

NOTE ▶ Although full view works great for creating triggers while referencing other sounds, you can adjust only velocity and gate time in the step grid.

2 In the step grid, Control-click the snare drum trigger row.

A shortcut menu appears containing sound-trigger editing commands.

Copy
Paste
Clear

Add Every Downbeat
Add Every Upbeat

Alter Existing Randomly
Reverse Existing

Shift Left 1 Step
Shift Left 1/2 Beat
Shift Left 1 Beat

Shift Right 1 Step
Shift Right 1/2 Beat
Shift Right 1 Beat

Create & Replace Randomly
Create & Replace Few
Create & Replace Some
Create & Replace Many

This menu contains many handy tools for quickly generating and editing step sequences for individual sounds.

3   From the menu, choose Alter Existing Randomly.

The snare pattern is altered, randomly dispersing the existing triggers to new positions.

4   Play the sequence, listening to the newly altered snare part.

5   If the randomly altered snare part is not to your liking, repeat the previous steps to create new results.

6   If necessary, further refine your part by turning individual steps on or off, adjusting velocity and swing values to your liking.

7   Play the A#-1 key on your MIDI controller to stop playback of the pattern.

8   Click the Full View button to turn off full view.

> **TIP** ▶ If you would like to edit Ultrabeat's patterns in Logic's many MIDI editors, drag the button immediately to the left of the Pattern menu to anywhere in the Tracks area. The pattern is copied as an individual region, ready for editing, processing, or looping.

Automating Parameters in Step Mode

Ultrabeat not only lets you program sound triggers via step sequencing, it also lets you do the same for each sound's parameters. This mode, called Step mode, provides step-by-step automation of any sound-shaping control in the synthesizer.

For this exercise, you will use Step mode to offset the pitch of the snare voice's Oscillator 1.

1   On the lower part of the Edit Mode switch (located in the lower left of the interface), click Step.

The sound-editing area dims, and yellow frames appear around all of the parameters that are available for automation. In addition, the step grid changes to display parameter offset instead of velocity/gate.

When in Step mode, you use the step grid to change the yellow highlighted parameters by offsetting the current sound settings.

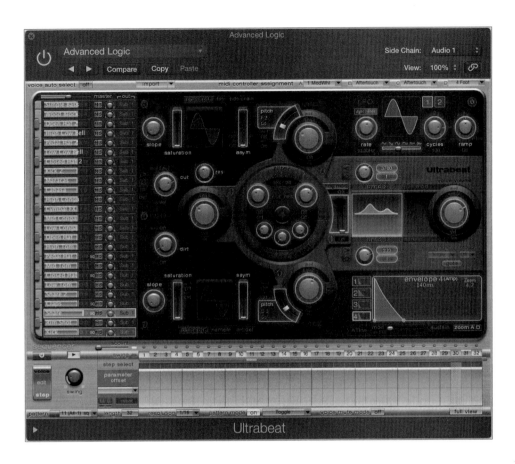

2   Click in the Step Select row for step 1, just below the trigger row.

3   Drag the Pitch slider for Oscillator 1 to G2.

NOTE ▶ When you drag a control, you define the target parameter for Step mode.

Notice that the Offset menu now reads Osc1 Pitch, and the step grid displays your adjustment as a positive offset (above the center line) to the original pitch (F2). This offset is expressed as a percentage.

TIP ▶ You can also drag the value bars up and down in the step grid to create offsets of the selected parameter's value.

If desired, Ultrabeat can randomize offsets for each trigger.

4   Control-click the step grid area, and from the Offset shortcut menu, choose Alter.

Small offsets are created for each trigger.

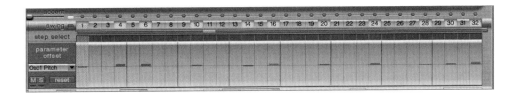

NOTE ▶ The Alter and Randomize selections in the Offset shortcut menu differ in how they randomize the offset values in the step grid. Alter randomizes all current parameters by a few percent of the current setting, essentially varying already-present input. Randomize creates new, random values, regardless of any already-present offset values.

5 Play the sequence, and stop playback when you've heard the results.

The pitch of the snare voice changes for the altered steps.

6 Click the Mute button located at the lower left of the step grid.

When enabled this control allows you to mute the currently displayed parameter offsets, thereby returning the part back to its unaltered state.

TIP ▶ When creating offsets in Step mode, you may decide that you want to make a quick change in the original drum sound. To do so without losing your creative momentum, press Option-Command to temporarily toggle Ultrabeat to Voice mode.

7 On the Edit Mode switch, click Voice.

8 From the preset menu, choose Save As.

9 Name the preset My Kit, and click Save.

TIP ▶ Ultrabeat can address multiple channel outputs (eight stereo and eight mono), just like the EXS24. You select these routings in the Assignment section, under the "out" column.

▶ **Drum Machine Designer**

Introduced in version 10.1, the new Drum Machine Designer in Logic excels in building custom electronic drum kits from a huge bank of drum and percussion sounds. Secretly lurking beneath its surface is Ultrabeat's sound engine, which provides the evocative sound sources for the new instrument via its powerful synthesis, signal processing, and modulation features. Drum Machine Designer builds upon these sound sources with extensive processing and creative signal routing to create an extremely powerful and flexible instrument.

When using Drum Machine Designer, you can see these relationships for yourself by clicking the All View button in the Mixer. Here you will find the various signal routings and processing used in each Drum Machine Designer preset (which sometimes use twenty or more multichannel outputs, each with multiple effects!). These complicated routings take up a lot of window real estate, but are hidden when using Tracks view.

Lesson Review

1. Oscillator 1 offers what modes of sound generation?
2. Oscillator 2 offers what modes of sound generation?
3. Source modulation routings appear in what color on the interface?
4. Via modulation routings appear in what color on the interface?
5. Routing to the filter and distortion circuit is done by enabling what?
6. Which feature in Ultrabeat is used to compose and play back patterns?
7. In order to define the target parameter for Step mode, you need to do what?

Answers

1. Oscillator 1 offers phase oscillator and frequency modulation synthesis (as well as side chain input).
2. Oscillator 2 offers phase oscillator, sample playback, and physical modeling.
3. Source modulation routings appear in blue.
4. Via modulation routings appear in green.

5. You can route to the filter and distortion circuit by enabling the Signal Flow buttons, located around each oscillator's Volume knob.

6. Ultrabeat's built-in step sequencer works in conjunction with the Logic project to compose and play back patterns.

7. You need to click a control first in order to define it as the target parameter for Step mode.

Editing

7

Lesson **7**

Working with the Arrangement

A computer-based system offers distinct advantages when developing and arranging musical material. First and foremost is being able to work with visual representations of sound, whether as audio waveforms or as graphical data (such as MIDI or notation). Using visual feedback, you can create detailed edits and work with arrangements by moving sections around as you would text in a word processor. This capability, coupled with the inherent nonlinear approach of digital audio workstations (DAWs), enables you to jump around in a composition, manipulating multiple aspects of a piece of music and playing back sections for instant feedback.

Many Logic Pro features are geared toward manipulating and developing musical material in a composition. This lesson focuses on techniques you can use to efficiently view, listen, organize, and move large chunks of data in a project.

Navigating the Arrangement

Before you can begin arranging, you must be familiar with the pieces that make up the overall project. Quickly creating a connection between what you see in the Tracks area and what you hear during playback is the first critical step before arranging a project.

You have many ways to position the playhead and initiate playback. While the familiar tape-style transport in the control bar is a good first choice, doing so doesn't really take advantage of the nonlinear feature of Logic Pro.

In this lesson, you'll try out the most useful playback and location features to familiarize yourself with the project, as well as greatly speed up your workflow when auditioning and arranging material.

Playing the Arrangement with the Bar Ruler

To understand the visual layout of the song in this project, you'll first need to get familiar with the project's sound. Rather than use traditional transport controls such as fast forward and rewind to move around, you'll try a variety of specialized playback functions to selectively audition parts of the project.

1   Choose File > Open.

2   In the file selector dialog, open Music > Advanced Logic X_Files > Lessons > **07_Anatomy of a Human Bomb_Start.logic**.

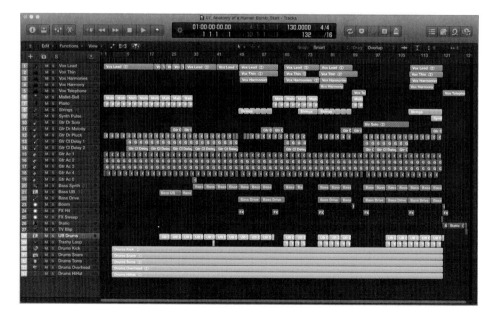

3   Start playback by double-clicking the lower half of the Bar ruler near bar 1.

As the song plays, take note of where it transitions from verse to chorus.

4   While playback continues, click anywhere in the lower half of the Bar ruler to move
the playhead.

The playhead jumps to your selected position and continues playing. This technique
works well for browsing throughout a project, allowing you to cue up sections of the
form without having to constantly start and stop playback.

5   Continue to click at various positions in the Bar ruler while exploring the content.

Be sure to listen to the song at bar 49 and 65 to become acquainted with both a chorus
and verse.

6   Double-click the lower part of the ruler near the beginning of the song.

Playback stops, and the playhead remains at its position where you double-clicked.

Isolating Material with Cycle Mode

Oftentimes, you will need to hear sections over and over when listening critically. Cycle
mode provides an easy way to temporarily repeat a section of a song. Setting a cycle area
has the added benefit of creating left and right locators you can use when editing.

In this exercise, you'll work with Cycle mode and learn several ways to set the locators
that will aid in auditioning material and set you up to perform edits.

1   In the Bar ruler, create a cycle area from 49 1 1 1 to 61 1 1 1.

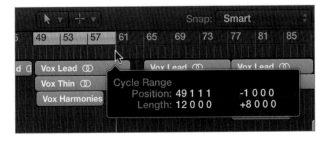

2   Play the project, listening to the entire cycle area.

At the end of the area, the playhead immediately jumps back to the start of the cycle area and repeats playback.

3   Click the bottom of the Bar ruler a few measures before the cycle area while playback continues.

The playhead jumps to the clicked location.

4   Continue listening until the playhead reaches the end of the cycle area.

The playhead returns to the beginning of the cycle area and continues repeating playback until you perform further action.

5   Press the Spacebar to stop playback.

You've observed one example of playback prioritization in Logic Pro. When Cycle mode is active, the playhead goes back to the start of the cycle area (left locator) when playback is engaged. This behavior is trumped by relocating the playhead by clicking in the Bar ruler.

Using Skip Cycle to Omit a Section During Playback

Cycle mode is an extremely useful feature for playing back just a project section, but you can also use it the opposite way. Using the skip cycle function, you can pass over a section during playback by swapping the left and right locator positions. Doing so allows you to create a quick arrangement that excludes a specific region during playback.

1   With Cycle mode still enabled, Control-click the cycle area, and from the shortcut menu, choose Swap Left and Right Locators.

The cycle area changes its appearance to indicate that it is now a skip cycle.

2   Double-click the bottom part of the Bar ruler a few bars before the skip cycle to begin playback. Observe what happens when the playhead reaches the skip cycle.

Playback starts from where you double-clicked, reaches the leftmost edge of the skip cycle, and immediately continues playback from the rightmost edge of the skip cycle, skipping the identified skip cycle area.

3   Control-click the cycle area, and from the shortcut menu, choose Swap Left and Right Locators again to turn off skip cycle.

4   Click the cycle area to turn off Cycle mode.

NOTE ▶ In addition to engaging skip cycle by using the shortcut menu, you can customize the control bar (see Lesson 1) to include a skip cycle button, or press the = (equal sign) key to turn the mode on and off.

Using the Marquee Tool for Playback

Although the Marquee tool is primarily thought of as an editing tool, it's also an efficient transport mechanism that lets you quickly position the playhead by clicking directly in the Tracks area.

NOTE ▶ In this project the Marquee tool has been configured as the Alternate (Command) tool for your convenience.

1   Hold down the Command key to bring up the Marquee tool, and then click just before the first region on the UB Drum track (track 28), around bar 20.

A light gray line appears at the position you clicked.

2   Click Play.

The playhead jumps to the marquee selection and playback begins.

NOTE ▶ If playback occurs for only an instant and then stops, you most likely slightly dragged the pointer when clicking with the Marquee tool, thereby creating a very short marquee selection. If the marquee selection is more than one pixel wide, playback will stop at the end of the selection. Use the Deselect All command (press Shift-Command-A) to clear your selection and try again.

3   While the song is playing, use the Marquee tool to click another position in the arrangement.

When you click in the arrangement, the playhead does not immediately jump to the new position. To move the playhead using this method, you must stop and then restart playback.

4   Press the Spacebar once to stop playback and once again to restart playback.

This time, the playhead moves to the new marquee position and playback begins.

5   Press the Spacebar to stop.

You can also use the marquee selection to play only a selected area of the project. This function is similar to Cycle mode, but more specific to auditioning actual objects (regions, notes, and so on) and areas in the Tracks area.

6   Using the Marquee tool, drag around the regions located on tracks 5, 6, and 7 (Vox Telephone, Mallet-Bell, and Piano), encompassing measures 88 1 1 1 through 93 1 1 1 (use the help tag as a guide).

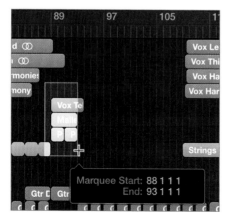

7   Click Play.

The playhead jumps to the marquee selection, playing the entire area and then stopping.

8   Press Option-Shift-D (Deselect All) to clear your marquee selection.

Using Specialized Playback Commands

In some instances it makes the most sense to initiate playback from a specific object using the Play from Selection command. When coupled with Solo, this feature is a quick way to audition a specific region in the Tracks area, or even specific notes in the editors.

1   Select the Mallet-Bell region (track 6) at measure 89 1 1 1 (one of the regions you selected previously using the Marquee tool).

2   In the control bar, click the Solo button.

3   Press Shift-Spacebar to enable Play from Selection.

Playback starts at the selected region.

4   Press the Spacebar to stop playback.

As mentioned previously, you can also use this command in the editors to start playback from an individually selected event or note.

5 Double-click the Mallet-Bell region you just auditioned.

The Piano Roll Editor opens, displaying the region's MIDI data.

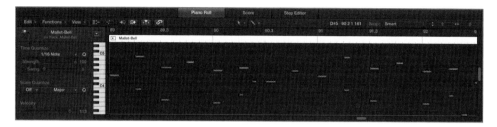

6 Use the mouse pointer to select any of the notes.

7 Press Shift-Spacebar (Play from Selection) to start playback at the selected note.

8 Stop playback.

9 Close the Piano Roll Editor.

10 In the control bar, click the Solo button to unsolo the region.

Once you get familiar with the playback key commands, you can combine them very effectively with zooming to quickly locate and audition material while editing. Let's experiment with an example that utilizes the Play from Left Window Edge command and allows you to start playback based on what you are viewing rather than what you are selecting.

11 Using the Zoom tool, drag around the regions on tracks 5, 6, and 7 at 89 1 1 1 to 94 1 1 1 (the Vox Telephone, Mallet-Bell, and Piano areas you selected earlier using the Marquee tool).

12 Zoom out horizontally a few times.

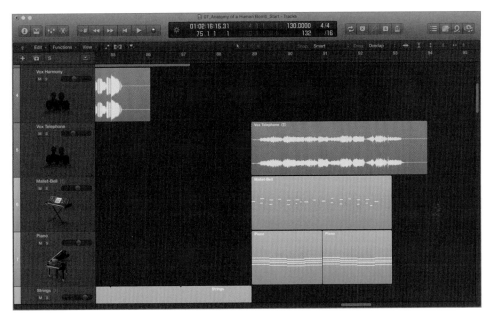

TIP While zooming, the displayed area of the window is justified to the current playhead position or to a selected region. When you want to zoom in to a specific playhead position, make sure that nothing is selected before you zoom. If you want to zoom in to an individual region, you must first select that region.

13 Press Shift-Enter to enable the Play from Left Window Edge command.

TIP To access the Enter key on a Mac portable keyboard, you also will need to hold down the Function (fn) key. If you use the Play from Left Window Edge command often, reassign this key command to a keyboard combination that fits under your fingers more comfortably.

Playback initiates from the left edge of the window, playing back the visible material.

TIP Try exploring more of the playback-oriented key commands such as Set Locators and Play, which allows you to quickly set the locators (and therefore the cycle area) and initiate playback.

Using Markers

Markers can serve multiple purposes in a project. They visually identify sections of a composition and also provide navigation points along the Bar ruler. Markers can serve as guides to help you quickly locate a project's sections for playback, editing, and arranging.

In this section, you will learn several techniques to efficiently create and edit markers that align with each of your project's major sections. Once the markers are in place, you'll name and color them to easily identify the form of the song, and use them as navigation points to quickly move around in the project.

Creating Markers

Markers are positioned and edited on the Marker global track. In this exercise, you'll use multiple techniques for creating markers via manual placement, or on the fly as you listen to the song.

1   In the track header, click the Global Tracks button.

Currently, the only global track configured is the Signature track, which you'll use later in this lesson.

2   Control-click the track header, and from the shortcut menu, choose Show Marker.

The Marker track is added in the Global Tracks area.

> **TIP** ▶ You can reorder global tracks by dragging the marker name to a new position; you can resize them by dragging the lower-left corner.

3   If necessary, locate the playhead to the beginning of the song.

In this project, the first verse starts immediately at bar 1 so you can use the Create Marker button to create a marker at the current playhead position.

4   In the Marker track header, click the Create Marker button.

A marker region named Marker 1 is created in the Marker track and continues through the end of the project. As you add more markers in the song, the first marker will automatically end where the next marker starts. The marker is gray to indicate that it is currently selected.

You're now going to create more markers at various song sections by positioning the playhead using a variety of techniques.

You can use the Period and Comma keys to move the playhead forward or back one bar.

5   Use the forward command by pressing the Period key (on the main part of the keyboard) until the playhead reaches 17 1 1 1. Then click the Create Marker button.

A new marker is created at bar 17. Holding down Shift while pressing the Period or Comma key moves the playhead forward or back in eight-bar increments.

6   Press Shift-Period twice to move the playhead to bar 33, and then click the Create Marker button.

The Go To Position command allows you to quickly navigate to anywhere in the project by entering a bar position or a SMPTE timecode.

7   Press / (slash), which is the Go To Position command.

In the Go To Position dialog, you can enter a specific measure number to which you want to locate.

8   In the Position field, enter *49* and press Return.

Now let's use a key command to create a marker.

9   Press Option-Apostrophe, which is the Create Marker command.

Oftentimes, playing the project and creating markers on the fly while listening to the song is faster and more intuitive.

10 To create a marker on the fly, begin playback just before bar 65 and carefully watch the Bar ruler and the counter in the Transport area. Either click the Create Marker button or press the Option-Apostrophe to create markers at the beginning of the major song sections located at bars 65, 77, 109, and 121.

Do not include a marker for the guitar solo—you'll be doing that later in the exercise. As long as you create the marker close to the desired location, Logic Pro will round the marker to the nearest bar. If you make a mistake, you can simply stop playback, press Command-Z to undo, and then try again.

So you don't have to wait long between each marker, you can click the lower part of the Bar ruler to jump just before the next marker position.

11 Click Stop.

TIP ▶ When working with material that doesn't align to the barlines, you need to set markers to locations that are not rounded to bars. In this case you can choose Options > Marker > Create Without Rounding (or press Control-Option-Apostrophe).

Another method of adding markers is to input them directly into the Marker track using the Pencil tool. For example, you might want to further divide the Chorus section into multiple parts for easier navigation.

12 Press T, and then choose the Pencil tool.

13 Position the mouse pointer to the middle of Marker 2. Hold down the mouse button and move the pointer until the help tag shows bar 25, and then release the mouse button.

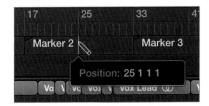

Notice that a new marker was added and all following markers are automatically renumbered.

14 Press T twice to change back to the Pointer tool.

Oftentimes, regions in your arrangement already denote song sections. You can use those regions to quickly create markers by dragging regions from the Tracks area into the Marker track.

TIP ▶ Moving the region into the Marker track without moving it horizontally in the timeline can be difficult. To combat this, press and hold down Shift after clicking to drag a region in only one direction.

15 Drag the Gtr Solo region into the Marker track, but don't release the mouse button until
you see a thin, white highlight around the Marker track, which shows that it's selected.

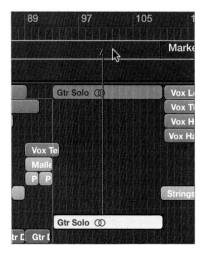

A new marker is created for the guitar solo, and it has taken the region's name and color.
You'll be naming and coloring the other markers you've created later in the lesson.

TIP ▸ You can also create markers from selected regions by choosing Create
Markers From Regions from the Marker pop-up menu in the Marker track header.

16 Press Option-Shift-D to deselect all regions, including the markers on the Marker track.

Now you can clearly see where the project's various sections begin and end.

Editing Marker Positions

Invariably, existing markers will need to be moved, edited, or deleted altogether. You
can edit markers as you would edit regions in the Tracks area, but with a few special
considerations.

To edit markers, you'll need to zoom in. Note, however, that pressing Control-Option will not produce the Zoom tool if the pointer is over the global tracks, so you need to start by dragging in the Tracks area.

1   Move the pointer over the Vox Lead track and Control-Option-drag from approximately bar 16 to bar 34 (encompassing Markers 2 and 3).

2   Hover the pointer over the upper part of the Marker track where the markers transition at bar 25.

The pointer turns into a Junction tool, letting you change where the transition between the markers occurs.

3   Using the Junction tool, move the transition point from bar 25 to 29.

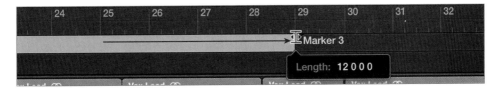

Now Marker 3 identifies a short four-bar interlude before the chorus at Marker 4.

4   Press Z to zoom back out and view the entire arrangement.

For the sake of this exercise, you're going to keep the project broken into simple song sections, so you won't need to identify the interlude at bar 29.

5   Using the Pointer tool, click various markers to see how they are selected.

6   Select Marker 3, and press Delete.

Marker 3 is deleted, leaving Marker 2 a bit short in length. You can easily lengthen markers as you would lengthen a region in the Tracks area.

7   Drag the right edge of Marker 2 to meet the left edge of Marker 3.

Naming and Coloring Markers

As you saw with the guitar solo, markers are more easily identified when they are named and colored. You will now customize the other markers so you can more easily identify sections of your project's arrangement.

1   Double-click Marker 1.

A field to enter the marker's name appears.

2   Type *Verse 1* and press Return.

3   With Verse 1 still selected, choose View > Show Colors, or press Option-C.

The color selection window appears.

4   Click a shade of blue for Verse 1. Leave the Color window open.

You may not see much change because the marker region is still selected. Once you select other markers, the color difference will be obvious.

5   Using the same technique, label and color each marker as follows:

Marker 2 – Chorus 1 (green)

Marker 3 – Verse 2 (blue)

Marker 4 – Chorus 2 (green)

Marker 5 – Verse 3 (blue)

Marker 6 – Chorus 3 (green)

Marker 8 – Chorus 4 (green)

Marker 9 – Outro (red)

Use bright colors to distinguish the marker regions from regions in the Tracks area. Reference the figure in the next step to see what you want to achieve.

TIP ▶ Hold down Shift and click to select multiple markers. You can then assign a single color to all the selected markers at once.

6   Select the Gtr Solo marker and color it a bright shade of purple.

7   Press Option-Shift-D to deselect all regions, including the markers on the Marker track.

8   Close the Color window.

9   Click the Global Tracks button to close the global track header.

Notice that the marker names and colors are superimposed over the lower part of the Bar ruler, making it very easy to see what part of the song occurs at which position in the timeline.

Locating with Markers

Now that you have a great visual reference for the primary sections of your song, you can use those markers to navigate the arrangement.

1   Option-click the Chorus 2 marker.

The playhead jumps to the beginning of the second chorus at bar 49.

The Next or Previous Marker commands let you quickly move between markers while keeping your hands on the keyboard.

2   Hold down Option while pressing either the Comma or Period key.

The playhead jumps backward and forward from marker to marker.

Using Marker Lists

Viewing a vertical list of markers provides a quick visual reference you can use to navigate to any project section, even when the entire timeline is not visible in the Bar ruler. The Lists area includes a Marker List for this reason.

1   In the toolbar, click the List Editors button, and then click the Marker tab.

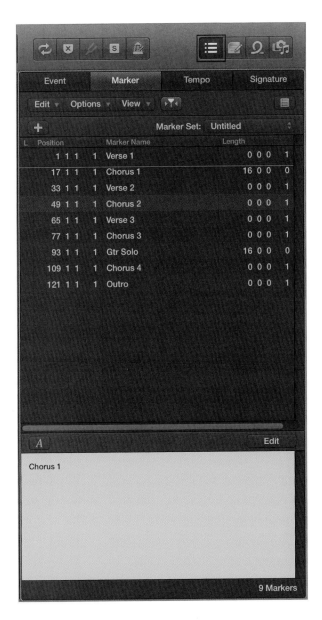

Here you see the markers you created earlier. The exact position of each marker is displayed next to its name.

NOTE ▶ The right column displays the length of each marker. Markers entered using the Create Marker button show a length of just one tick to indicate that they will extend to the next marker when viewed in the Marker global track.

2 Click the various markers in the list.

Clicking in this list does not move the playhead but does allow you to view the marker name and color in a text field at the bottom of the Marker List area.

TIP ▶ You can edit the text field to include extensive information such as production notes or lyrics. To edit the text, double-click the text field. Notes made here will also be visible inside the corresponding regions on the Marker track.

Although clicking the Pointer tool doesn't relocate the playhead, clicking with the Finger tool does. Option-click a marker in the list and the playhead will immediately jump to that position.

3 Try Option-clicking the markers in the list.

The playhead jumps from marker to marker.

4 Close the List Editors area.

TIP ▶ You can place a separate floating Marker List above the arrangement or as part of a two-monitor screenset. This window can be relatively small in size while still allowing you to click the markers in the list. To relocate the list, drag the Marker tab outside the List Editors area.

Saving Arrangements as Alternative Files

It is not uncommon to make several arrangements of the same project. These multiple arrangements can be quite disparate in scope and content (instrumental, extended or shortened form, and so on), even though they all use the same media assets. The new project alternatives in Logic Pro allow you to save multiple arrangements that tie into the same master project.

You've done quite a bit of work setting up your song for arranging by labeling relevant sections. Now it's a good idea to save what you've done at this stage as a "boilerplate" for future arrangements.

1 Choose File > Save As.

2 In the file selector dialog, name the file *07_Anatomy of a Human Bomb_Full*, and save it to the default location (the location of the lesson project files).

Now that you've saved the current state of your project, you can save as many project alternatives as you'd like.

3   Choose File > Alternatives > New Alternative.

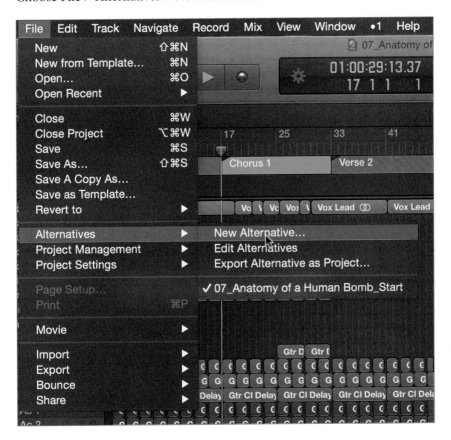

A window opens, prompting you to name the new file.

4   In the New Alternative Name field, type *07_Anatomy of a Human Bomb_Short*.

5   Click OK.

Look at the name displayed at the top of the main window. You can see that the project alternative is related to the **07_Anatomy of a Human Bomb_Full** project, as they are both listed, separated by a dash.

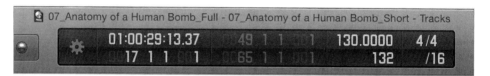

Using Global Edits

The ability to rearrange the structure of a composition is an essential part of composing and arranging. However, the seemingly simple task of cutting and repeating sections can become overly complicated, and achieving the desired results often entails multiple steps (dividing regions, selecting areas, cutting, pasting, and so on). Fortunately, Logic Pro offers several features that help with editing multiple regions over numerous tracks by combining multiple steps into single commands.

> **NOTE ▶** The commands used in this lesson can impact all tracks, including global tracks if the global tracks are open. This is a good thing—information in the global tracks such as markers, tempo, and time signature changes should generally be kept intact with the corresponding song sections.

To create these edits, you'll rely heavily on the use of both the locators and the playhead. Until now you've primarily used locators for defining cycle areas for playback. Now you will use locators to define edit points that impact the entire project.

Inserting Material into the Arrangement

You may have noticed that the song suddenly jumps a bit with Verse 1. In this exercise, you're going to add to the arrangement by creating a short intro section using some material from the first four bars of Verse 1.

Because global edits are performed with the aid of the left and right locators, you will first need to set these.

1   Drag in the Bar ruler to create a cycle area from 1 1 1 1 to 5 1 1 1 (four bars).

   If you were to perform a global edit now, all material in the locator area would be utilized. However, you can also be selective as to the included material in the edit by using locators in conjunction with selecting and copying regions.

2   Select the regions in the first four bars on the Mallet-Bell, Piano, and Gtr Ac 1-4 tracks.

3   Press Command-C to copy the selected regions.

4   Place the playhead at the beginning of the song.

5   Choose Edit > Cut/Insert Time > Insert Section at Playhead.

The regions you copied are inserted before Verse 1.

You can quickly create a marker for the new section by dragging the cycle area down into the Marker track. Doing so helps define locators for entire sections for future editing.

6   Click the Global Tracks button to display the Marker track.

7   Drag down the cycle area onto the Marker track.

A new marker is created for the first four bars of the song.

8 Using the technique you learned in the last exercise, rename the marker at bar 1 to *Intro* and change its color to red.

9 Play the song from the beginning.

This short intro works nicely, but you could augment it with some other material used later in the song.

10 Option-drag the Vox Telephone region at bar 93 to bar 1. Hold down Shift after selecting the region to prevent it from moving to a different track.

11 Turn off Cycle mode and play the project from the beginning to hear the results.

12 Click Stop.

Inserting Space in the Arrangement

The current song's form alternates between verse and chorus sections and eventually becomes a bit predictable. Adding an unexpected rest in the arrangement can add interest to the composition by catching listeners off guard. Play from bar 49 and pay particular attention to where the song transitions from Verse 2 to Chorus 2 and then stop.

You're going to add two beats of space between these sections; as before you'll need the help of locators to achieve this. This time you'll manually enter the locators using the locators display in the control bar.

1 In the LCD area in the control bar, double-click the left locator field. Enter *53* in the displayed field and press Return.

2 Double-click the right locator field. Enter *53.3* in the field, and press Return.

This number indicates that the right locator is positioned at bar 53, beat 3, or two beats after the left locator.

NOTE ▶ When entering positional values, you can use periods, spaces, or almost any nonnumeric character to separate bar, beat, division, and tick values.

Left locator

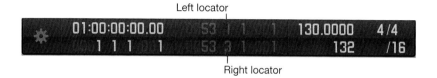

Right locator

The locators may be hard to see in the Bar ruler at this zoom level.

3   Zoom to show the area from approximately bar 50 to bar 60.

4   Choose Edit > Cut/Insert Time > Insert Silence Between Locators.

A dialog asks if you want to add a time signature change. Logic Pro recognizes that adding two beats of space into the arrangement would cause the musical downbeats of the song to fall away from the bar lines. Changing bar 53 to a measure of 6/4 will correct this problem.

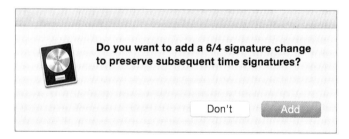

5   Click Add.

You can see the change reflected in the Signature global track.

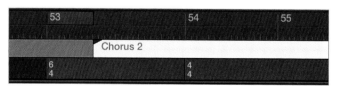

Although a bar of 6/4 meter takes up the correct number of beats, it usually infers compound time (two pulse notes, each divided into three). This is not the case, so let's fix that.

6   Press T and choose the Scissors tool. Click the second beat in bar 53, which is where you can see the right locator.

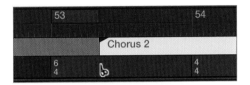

This corrects the time signature issue by creating a bar of 2/4 for the space you inserted.

7   Press T twice to return to the Pointer tool.

8   Control-Option-click to zoom back out to view the entire arrangement.

9   Begin playback near bar 49 and listen to the transition with the space you added.

10   Click Stop.

Removing Material from the Arrangement

Without using global edits, removing material from an arrangement can be a chore. You would have to delete material in the Tracks area and then drag the remaining material (and markers) over to fill up the space you created. Using the Logic Pro global editing functions to perform all of that in one step is far easier.

The song feels a bit too long, and it could be tightened up considerably by removing some material. In this exercise, you'll explore several ways to set locators quickly and perform the necessary global edits. Let's start off by shortening the length of the guitar solo.

1   In the Bar ruler, create an eight-bar cycle area in the middle of the guitar solo from 102 1 1 1 to 110 1 1 1.

2   Choose Edit > Cut/Insert Time > Cut Section Between Locators.

The regions in the locators are split automatically, and the selected material is removed from the arrangement. Notice that all the material following the locators, including the markers, were moved to the left, joining the material immediately preceding the locators.

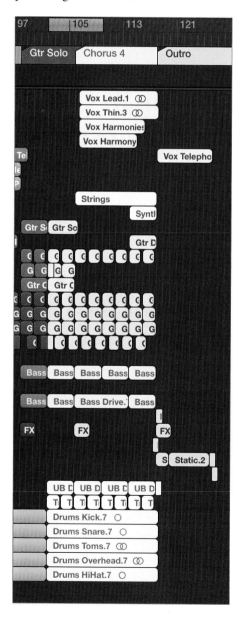

3   Turn off Cycle mode.

4   Audition your edit by playing the guitar solo section, and then stop playback.

Combining selection commands with global edits can be a powerful technique for quickly isolating and removing material from your arrangement. You can also remove the interlude after Chorus 2 to add some interest to the song by changing up the arrangement.

5   Select the Mallet-Bell region at bar 66.

This four-bar region encompasses the entire interlude coming out of Chorus 2. Let's use it to set our left and right locators. You can do so easily by using the Set Rounded Locators by Selection command.

6   Choose Navigate > Set Rounded Locators by Selection.

The left and right locators adapt to the length of the selected region.

7   Choose Edit > Cut/Insert Time > Cut Section Between Locators.

The four bars are removed, and the material immediately following the edit is moved to the left, joining the material immediately preceding the locators.

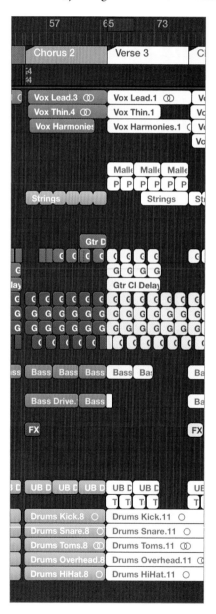

You can also quickly conform the left and right locators to a marker, which is especially useful when combined with global edits. Despite the cuts you already made, the song still feels a bit long. By removing the Chorus 3 section, you can use the energy coming out of Verse 3 to carry right into the guitar solo.

8   Press Option-Shift-D to deselect all regions, including the markers on the Marker track.

9   Select the Chorus 3 marker, and drag it up onto the top of the Bar ruler.

A cycle area is created that encompasses the entire length of the Chorus 3 marker. This time, you can try out a key command to make the cut.

10   Press Control-Command-X (Cut Section Between Locators).

The entire Chorus 3 section is removed (including the marker).

11   Turn off Cycle mode.

12   Audition your edit by playing the end of Verse 3 into the guitar solo section, and then stop playback.

Extending the Arrangement

In addition to removing material from your arrangement, it is also commonplace to add or repeat material to extend the form and add interest to a song. In this exercise, you'll repeat a portion of the last chorus to create a refrain. In addition, you'll extend the vocal regions in the section to create a more natural edit.

1   Using any of the techniques you've learned in this lesson, set locators from 86 1 1 1 to 94 1 1 1 (the first eight bars of the Chorus 4 section) and enable Cycle mode.

2   Start playback to familiarize yourself with the material in the locators, then stop playback. This area is the material you will repeat.

3 Choose Edit > Cut/Insert Time > Repeat Section between Locators.

The area in the locators is repeated, and the material immediately following is pushed to the right.

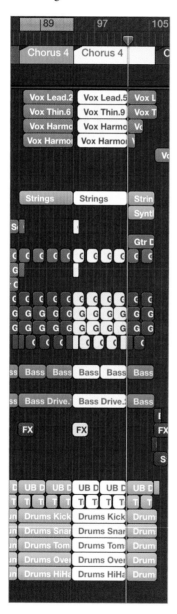

4   Turn off Cycle mode.

This edit copied the relevant material needed for the refrain, but it also created awkward phrases in the vocal tracks that overlap the barline.

5   Using the Zoom tool, select the top four tracks (Vox Lead, Vox Thin, Vox Harmonies, and Vox Harmony) from 86 1 1 1 to 106 1 1 1.

6   Solo the top four tracks.

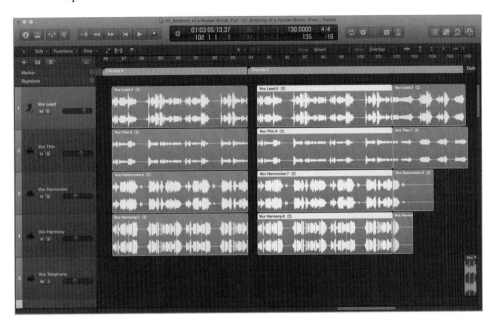

Starting around bar 86, you can see how the audio waveforms are cut off. You can hear this as well because the words of the vocal are interrupted at the end of the phrase.

7   Play from 86 1 1 1 to 106 1 1 1, listening to the vocal tracks, and then stop playback.

Because the audio recordings still contain the necessary material, you can alter the region length at the end of the first group of regions so the words are not cut off.

8   Select the regions residing in measures 86 to 94 of the four vocal tracks.

9   Choose Edit > Trim > Region End to Next Region.

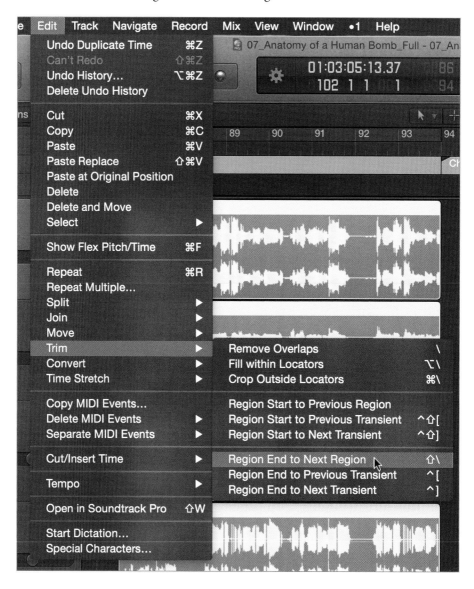

The regions' lengths adapt to meet the regions that follow them.

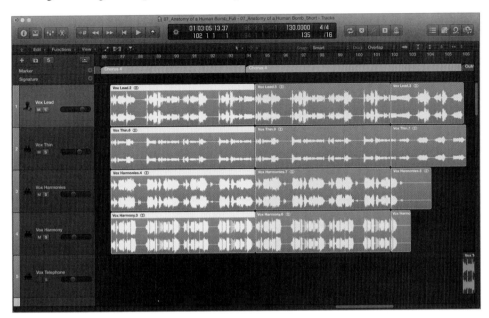

10 Play the project from bar 86 to hear your edit. Stop playback.

11 Unsolo the four vocal tracks.

12 Control-Option click in the Tracks area to zoom out to view the entire project.

Comparing Arrangements

Now that you've created an arrangement that is completely different from the first
version, you can save this revision to the project alternative you created earlier in the
lesson. Once you save the arrangement, you can toggle between project alternatives to
compare the results.

1 Choose File > Save.

2   Choose File > Alternatives, and look at the menu choices.

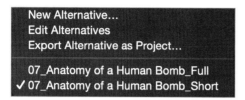

The menu lists all project alternatives associated with the project. The currently active alternative is selected. You can toggle between alternatives by choosing them from this menu.

3   Choose 07_Anatomy of a Human Bomb_Full.

This alternative is loaded with the original "boilerplate" arrangement.

4   Try toggling between the two arrangements, listening to the changes you made in this project.

Lesson Review

1.   How do markers aid in a production?

2.   Why is it helpful to change the text and color of markers in a project?

3.   Where are markers accessed?

4.   How can you initiate playback from the bar number displayed on the far-left side of the Tracks area?

5.   How are locators set?

6.   How do you simultaneously insert or delete sections across all tracks of a project (including global tracks)?

7.   How do you create multiple versions of the same project that enable you to compare several arrangements and edits?

Answers

1. Markers can identify section material or serve as navigation points.

2. Changing the appearance of markers (including production notes) helps you easily identify and navigate to sections in the arrangement.

3. You can access markers in the Bar ruler, Marker track, or Marker List.

4. Use the Play From Left Window Edge key command.

5. Set locators by dragging in the Bar ruler or by creating cycle areas for any region, event, or marker.

6. Set locators around the section to be added or deleted, and from the Edit menu, choose Cut/Insert Time commands.

7. Use Project Alternatives to create alternate versions of the same project, and access them by choosing File > Alternatives.

8

Lesson 8
Advanced Audio Editing

The flexibility of editing digital audio is one of the distinct advantages of working with nonlinear hard-disk recording systems. The user can precisely fix mistakes, adjust timing, rearrange section material, and combine elements in every conceivable way. What was once incredibly difficult or impossible to do with analog tape is now almost routine if you have the right set of tools and skills.

Modern production is both blessed with and plagued by this flexibility. On the one hand, it allows for sophisticated edits with great accuracy. On the other, falling into obsessiveness is all too easy, and you can worry a track to a lifeless lump of 1s and 0s.

That said, good editing techniques can take your material to another level, turning a raw performance into a polished piece of music.

In this lesson you'll pick up where you left off in Lesson 7 by further refining the audio recordings used in this song. Using the wide variety of powerful features in Logic, you'll not only learn how to fix problems out of necessity but how to edit creatively to bring new energy to songs.

Smoothing Transitions with Crossfades

Unwanted clicks and pops are an unfortunate byproduct of working with digital audio. These anomalies can occur when the audio waveform is interrupted in mid-cycle or cut off as a result of awkward region edits or recording takes. Clicks and pops can also occur in an otherwise great recording due to inappropriate buffer or clock settings on the audio interface at the time of recording. In this section you'll learn techniques to fix these issues with minimal fuss so you can focus on more creative endeavors.

Working with Crossfades

Crossfades are the easiest way to smooth over unnatural transitions between newly adjoined regions. Because the last lesson created so many new transitions, this exercise shows you how to apply crossfades en masse. First you'll get rid of the click between the two halves of the guitar solo to better understand the Logic crossfade features, and then you'll apply crossfades across all the drum regions to make their edits sound more natural.

1   Go to Advanced Logic X > Lessons and open **08_Anatomy of a Human Bomb_Start.logicx**.

The project opens zoomed around the Gtr Solo regions. A cycle area is already enabled, and the Gtr Dr Solo track is soloed.

Several audible clicks in the solo occurred for different reasons. To start with, the click at bar 82 is caused by the waveform being abruptly cut off where the regions transition.

2   Play the guitar solo and listen for the click at bar 82. Once you've located it, stop playback.

You can smooth this transition and eliminate the click by adding a crossfade between the adjacent regions.

As you add the crossfade, it's extremely helpful to see what's happening in the selected region's Parameter box. By default, the Fade parameters aren't visible in the Region Parameter box, so you'll need to disclose them.

3   Select the first Gtr Solo region to display its parameters in the Region Parameter Box. Then click the More disclosure triangle to reveal the Fade parameters.

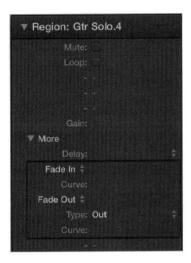

The Fade Out Type parameter displays Out, which indicates that the selected region is set to have a fade-out applied to it, but because it has no numerical value to the right of the setting, there is no audible effect.

For the next step, let's try a "hard-wired" key command to quickly access the Fade tool while using the Pointer (also see Lesson 1 section "Working with Hard-Wired Tool Menu Commands.")

4   With the Pointer tool, Control-Shift-drag from left to right to identify a selection area that overlaps the two regions by about a beat.

Upon releasing the mouse button, white shaded areas appear on each side of the region transition to illustrate the applied crossfade.

Notice in the Region Parameter box that the Fade type has been set to EqP (Equal Power) with a numerical value next to it. Equal Power uses logarithmic curved fades to keep the volume level from dipping during the transition. The value above represents the length of the fade in milliseconds.

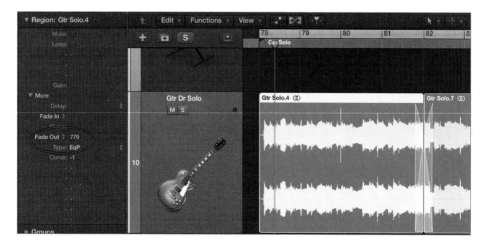

TIP ▶ Depending on where you dragged, you may see a value displayed in the Curve field. Logic centers the fade over the region transition, but it may have to change the curve slightly on one side or the other to compensate for a selection that isn't exactly equal. You can also adjust the Curve parameter independently to control the shape of the crossfade curves and provide more options for shaping the sound of transitions between sections.

5   Play the same section. The click at bar 82 is now gone.

Unless you're zoomed in closely, dragging a crossfade between regions often creates a crossfade area that is much bigger than is needed to remove the extremely brief clicks created by transitions. Long crossfades can also sound awkward because both regions can be audible at the same time, so keeping crossfades just short enough to eliminate the click is ideal. Instead of drawing them with the mouse, you can create small crossfades by typing numerical values in the Region Parameter box.

6   Double-click the fade time, enter *50*, and press Return.

The shaded area representing the crossfade resizes to reflect the change.

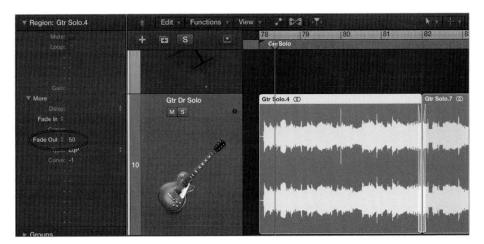

7   Play the transition.

With only a 50-millisecond crossfade, the click is inaudible with minimal audible impact on the material in the two regions.

8   Unsolo the Gtr Solo track.

9   Turn off Cycle mode.

Applying Crossfades to Multiple Regions

In Lesson 7, you rearranged many audio regions, which in their new order can create clicks or other noticeable glitches at transition points. To help smooth out abrupt edited transitions, you can apply a short crossfade to all edited regions at once.

1 Zoom out to view the entire arrangement.

2 Solo the drum tracks by dragging down the Solo buttons across all their track headers.

3 Play the song from the Chorus 2 marker, paying attention to the transition to Verse 3.

Although you don't hear a click or pop, the transition sounds a little abrupt. With further inspection, you'll notice a few more of these unnatural transitions throughout the drum tracks. You can use the crossfade technique to solve all these problems at once by multi-selecting the regions you want to fix, and then entering a short crossfade into the Region Parameter box.

4 Select all the drum regions except for the small regions at the very end of the song.

NOTE ▶ Crossfade settings need to be applied only to the region preceding a transition, which is why you don't need to select the last regions on each track.

5 In the Region Parameter box, change the Fade type to Equal Power Crossfade and set the time to *50*.

TIP The Fade In parameter is used only to create a volume fade-in at the beginning of a region when no preceding region has a crossfade value. In the event that a region with a crossfade value is located before a region with a Fade In value, the crossfade takes priority and the Fade In value is ignored.

6   Zoom on the drum regions at the end of the song to see that the crossfades have
    been applied.

7   Scroll over and listen to the transition between Chorus 2 and Verse 3.

    The transition still feels abrupt, even with the 50-millisecond crossfade. A longer fade
    time for this specific section can help to smooth the transition.

8   Select the drum regions during Chorus 2.

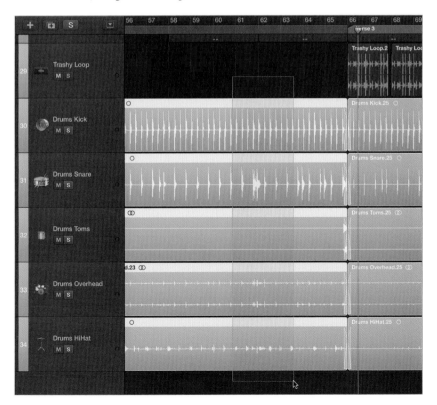

9   Set the fade value to *5000* and play the same transition again.

A setting of 5000 means the crossfade between the two sets of regions takes a full 5 seconds. This length allows for the cymbal crash in the Drums Overhead track (originally played coming out of Chorus 2) to be heard over the beginning of Verse 3, which sounds much more natural than when it was chopped off.

10   Unsolo all the Drums tracks by Option-clicking the Solo button on any of the Drums track headers.

11   Zoom out to view the entire arrangement.

Fixing Clicks in the Audio File Editor

Sometimes clicks and pops appear in the body of an audio region. These can be caused by clipping that occurred during their recording, sample rate clocking errors, or even by edited audio files that were bounced together without proper crossfades. When listening to the guitar solo, you might have noticed that just such a click exists in bar 80. In this exercise, you'll learn how to find clicks visually and audibly, and then literally draw them out of the region.

1   Double-click the first region of the original guitar solo at bar 78.

The Audio Track Editor opens displaying the Gtr Solo regions. Because you will be making changes to the audio file itself (and not just the region), you need to open the Audio File Editor.

2   Click the File tab to display the Audio File Editor.

3   Zoom out horizontally to view the entire region, if necessary.

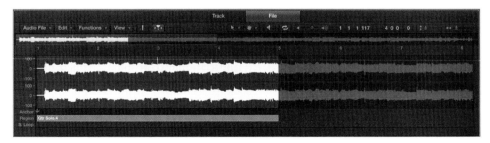

4   Click the Prelisten button to audition the region's audio file, and then click the Prelisten button again when you've identified the click.

An audible click occurs at bar 80. You can visually identify it by the sharp spike in the waveform on the left channel of the stereo recording.

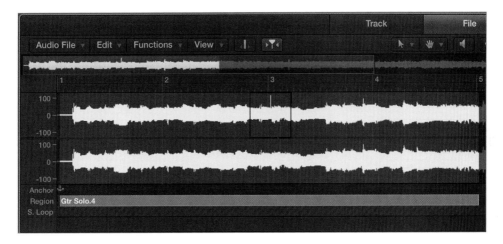

You can also audibly identify the click by scrubbing back and forth at varying speeds. This technique is useful to zero in on a click's location when it isn't clearly visible in the waveform.

5   Hold the mouse pointer in the upper part of the Bar ruler and drag left or right to scrub the audio around the click.

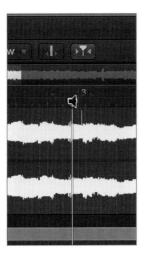

> **TIP** ▸ Double-clicking the Bar ruler starts and stops playback just as it does in the Tracks area.

6   Control-Option-drag around the click, zooming in so that the click is clearly visible.

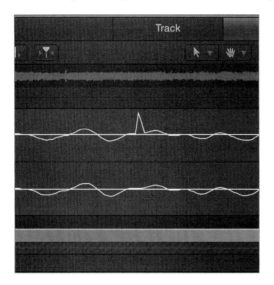

7   Change the alternate tool to the Pencil tool.

8   Using the Pencil tool, draw out the click.

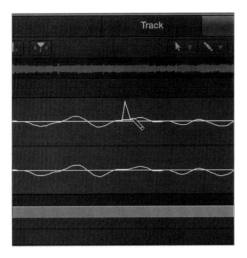

TIP ▶ The process of drawing out clicks can be hit or miss. After you draw out the click, if you still see a spike in the waveform, try to draw out the remaining spike. Sometimes you may inadvertently overwrite a good part of the waveform. In that event, press Command-Z to undo your change and try again.

Once the waveform looks good, make sure it sounds good. Use the scrub method you just learned to hear if the click is truly gone. Sometimes completely eliminating a click is impossible, but drawing it out may minimize the problem sufficiently in the context of the mix.

NOTE ▶ Because you're updating the actual audio file, the click will be removed from all regions that reference this audio file.

9   Close the Editor area, and then listen to the guitar solo with the rest of the tracks.

Creating New Parts from Existing Ones

One of the advantages offered by digital editing is the ease with which new parts are created from existing material through copying and pasting. In order to achieve a convincing result, however, it is of equal importance to use judicious edits to assemble the new part as well as create seamless transitions between the constituent building blocks.

In the previous lesson, you cut the guitar solo in half by removing the middle eight bars of the solo. Although the result sounds good, you might discover that combining various sections of the original 16-bar solo yields a better variation. Ideally, a new solo would be assembled through multiple takes that are comped in a take folder. However, you can still use the powerful Logic comp features with a single take by creating new regions from the same material, and then packing things into a new take folder for editing.

Packing a Take Folder

You're going to create a new 8-bar-long guitar solo using portions of the original 16-bar performance. To achieve this you'll begin by splitting the guitar solo in half, creating an A and B section. You'll then position the A and B sections on different tracks so that they start at the same time. Since you don't really want both parts to play simultaneously, you'll pack the A and B sections into a take folder, which you'll use in the next exercise to choose which parts of each section you want to hear.

1   Control-Option-drag around the Gtr Solo regions at bar 78. Zoom out horizontally and vertically until you can easily see about 16 bars.

2   Double-click the Gtr Dr Solo track header and rename the track *Gtr Solo (v1)*.

3   At the top of the track list, click the Duplicate Track button to create a new track, and then rename it *Gtr Solo (v2)*.

    This track will hold the new comp of the guitar solo you're going to create in the next exercise.

Now you need to copy the original guitar solo down to the new track.

4   In the Gtr Solo (v1) track, select the first region (Gtr Solo.4), and press Command-C to copy the region.

5   Place the playhead at bar 78.

6   With the Gtr Solo (v2) track header selected, press Command-V to paste the region.

You'll mute the original track so you can concentrate on the new comp you're building. You can revert to the original edit if you prefer it to the comp you're about to make.

7   Mute the Gtr Solo (v1) track.

Because the region is referencing only the beginning section of the original 16-bar guitar solo, you now need to expose the rest of the solo on the track.

8   Drag the lower-right corner of the copied region on the Gtr Solo (v2) track as far to the right as possible.

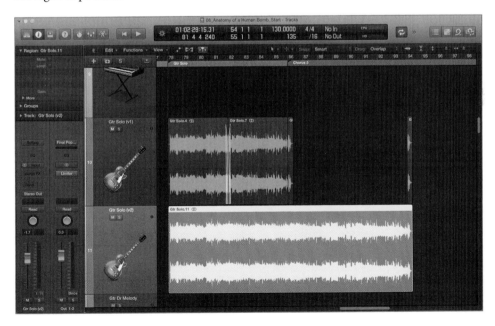

To intermix parts from the entire 16-bar solo, you need to make both halves start at the same point in time.

9 Press T, and then press 5 to select the Scissors tool. Click the region at bar 86 to divide it in half.

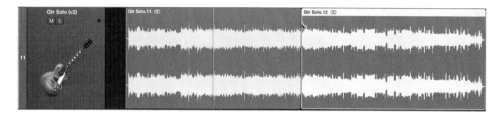

10 Press T twice to go back to the Pointer tool, and then drag the latter region (bar 86 to 94) to the Gtr Dr Melody track at bar 78.

> **NOTE ▸** Depending on your zoom level, you may need to zoom out vertically to see the Gtr Dr Melody track.

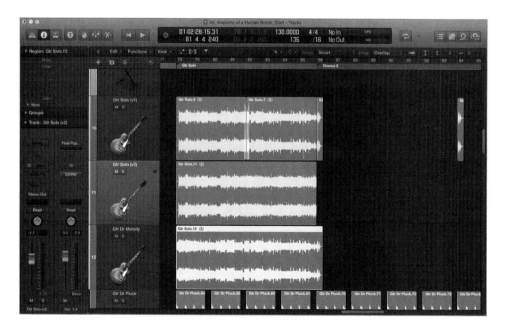

Putting the solo on the melody track is OK because it's only going to be there for a moment. Naming the regions will help identify which part you're hearing when you start to edit.

11 Use the Text tool to rename the region on the Gtr Solo (v2) track to *Gtr Solo A*, and rename the region you moved to the Gtr Dr Melody track to *Gtr Solo B*.

To easily identify which parts are playing, set each region to a different color.

12 Press Option-C to open the Color window.

13 With the Pointer tool, select the Gtr Solo A region. Choose a color from the Color window, and then apply a slightly different color to Gtr Solo B.

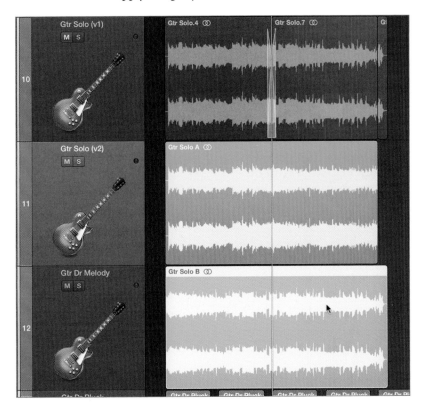

14 Close the Color window.

Now you're ready to pack the two regions into a single take folder.

15 Select the Gtr Solo A and Gtr Solo B regions on adjacent tracks. Control-click one of the selected regions, and from the shortcut menu, choose Folder > Pack Take Folder.

Gtr Solo B region is moved into a new take folder region named Gtr Solo (v2): Comp A, which also contains the Gtr Solo A region. (It is currently open.)

NOTE ▶ You may need to zoom out horizontally to view the open take folder.

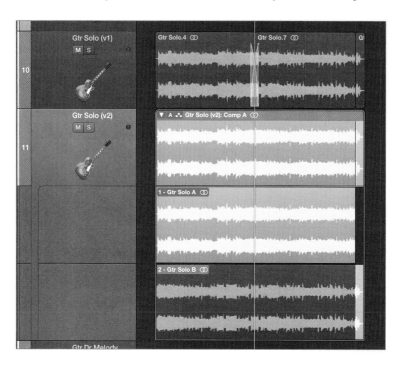

Creating a Comp

Now that you have both halves of the guitar solo packed into a take folder, you'll use Quick Swipe Comping to quickly create a preliminary edit that transitions between the Gtr Solo A and B performances. Although Quick Swipe Comping is very good at transitioning between two or more regions in a take folder, it doesn't allow you to move the parts forward and backward in time. This limitation can be problematic as you'll often need to move phrases around to fit into the overall arrangement. To overcome this limitation, you'll learn how to bypass Quick Swipe Comping so that you can freely reposition regions in a take folder using conventional editing tools.

1   Select the Gtr Solo (v2) take folder, and then press Z to zoom.

   The take folder shows the current composite on the track with two take lanes below. Take lanes are used to display the content of different regions that can be used to create your comp. Only one take lane can be heard at a time. Colored sections of a take lane indicate which parts of a region will be heard; dimmed areas are not heard. In this case Gtr Solo A is played in its entirety, but only the tail end of Gtr Solo B will be played. This transition is displayed in the comp above the take lanes, where the region changes colors at bar 86.

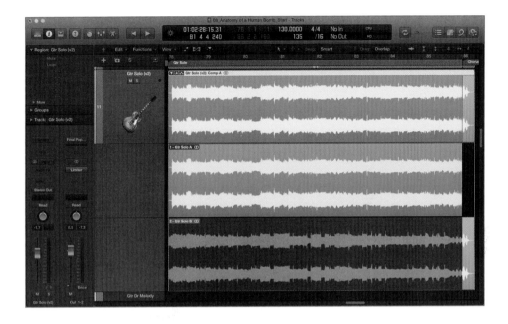

2   On the Gtr Solo (v2) track header, click the Solo button to solo the track.

3   Turn on Cycle mode.

4   Press Spacebar to begin playback.

Gtr Solo A plays with the last part of Gtr Solo B played at the end.

5   In the take folder menu (currently marked "A"), choose Guitar Solo B and play it to become familiar with that part.

Now you'll use Quick Swipe Comping to create transitions between the two takes.

6 Be sure the Guitar Solo B take is selected in its entirety.

7 In the Guitar Solo A track lane, drag from just before bar 80 to bar 82, and then play the transition.

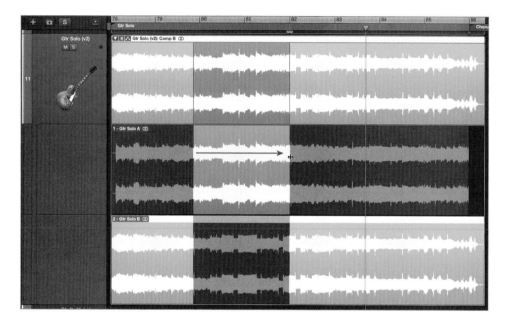

NOTE ▶ When using Quick Swipe Comping, Logic automatically assigns a cross-fade between adjacent regions. You can change the length as well as the curve of the crossfade (similar to the way you implemented crossfades earlier in this lesson) in Preferences > Audio > Editing.

You're going to keep the notes that begin Guitar Solo B, transitioning to the descending line that starts Guitar Solo A. To do this you must move the beginning part of Guitar Solo A in time. Moving parts in time is not possible with Quick Swipe Comping engaged, so you must first turn off Quick Swipe Comping mode.

8   In the upper part of the take folder, click the Quick Swipe Comping mode button to turn it off.

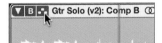

With Quick Swipe Comping mode turned off (Quick Swipe Comping button turns into a scissors icon), you're free to use all the Logic editing features to manipulate the regions in the take folder. Most importantly you can create new regions and move them in time.

9   In Gtr Solo A, Command-drag from 78 3 1 1 to halfway between it and 79 2 3 1 to select the area. Watch the help tag to confirm your exact positions.

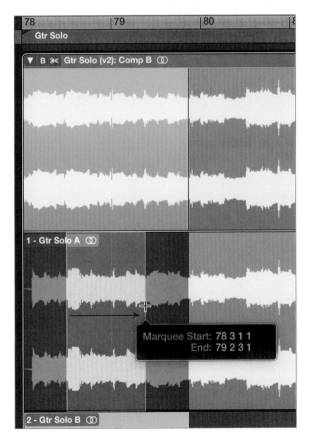

10 With the Pointer tool, click the marquee selection to divide the region at the selection borders, and then drag the new region to start at bar 79.

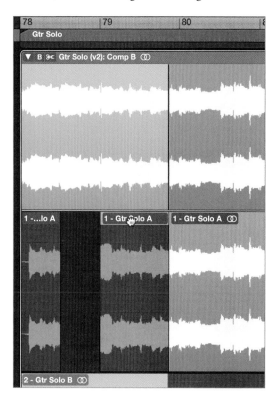

11 Turn on Quick Swipe Comping, and then select the newly moved region to add it to the comp.

12 In the track header, turn off Solo mode and then play the new version of the guitar solo with the rest of the tracks.

> NOTE ▶ When you edit the timing of regions in a take, all comps that reference the take are affected by the change, which can create unwanted changes to alternate comps.

13 Take a moment to experiment with creating other versions of the solo with and without using Quick Swipe Comping.

14 Close the take folder by clicking the disclosure triangle in its upper-left corner and turn off Cycle mode.

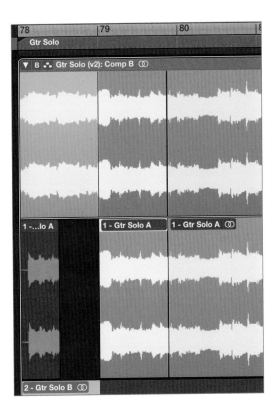

15 Zoom out to see the entire arrangement.

> **TIP** ▶ The take folder menu offers various tools for converting the content of a take folder back to conventional audio regions. Flatten will convert the current comp into discrete audio regions on the current track while deleting the takes used to create the comp. Unpack works in a similar way but retains the original takes by placing them on muted duplicate tracks.

Editing with Mixer Groups

Drums, background vocals, and layered guitar performances each comprise multiple tracks, but we often look at them as a single entity when making adjustments such as volume and, in this case, performing edits.

In this section, you'll use Mixer groups to organize the drum tracks into a group for editing. You'll also learn how to temporarily disable group editing when you want to edit individual regions in the drum group.

You'll also use phase-locked editing while performing edits on grouped tracks, which ensures that all the tracks in the group maintain their timing relationships down to the sample level.

Configuring an Edit Group

You can use Mixer groups to apply a variety of operations—volume, panning, and automation—to multiple channels at the same time. In addition, you can use Mixer groups to simultaneously edit tracks. In this exercise, you will use the Mixer group feature to place the drum tracks into an edit group and quickly make changes to the regions across all the drum tracks.

1   Choose View > Show Mixer.

2   Drag across the Drum tracks' names (tracks 31 to 35) to select their channel strips.

3   Click the Solo button on any of the selected channels to enable solo for the group.

4   Click the Group slot on any of the selected channel strips, and in the Group selection menu, choose Group 1.

The selected drum channels are assigned to Group 1.

Creating a group name helps you quickly identify groups in the project. These names are displayed in the Group slot. You can quickly access the Group settings in the inspector.

5   In the inspector, click the Groups disclosure triangle to open the Group inspector.

6   In the Group Settings window, double-click the Group 1 Name field, enter *Drums*, and press Return.

By default, channels within groups link only their volume and mute controls. In order to perform edits as a group, you need to activate the Editing setting.

7   Select Editing (Selection).

8   Close the Mixer.

> **NOTE ▶** Phase-Locked Audio is also selected. You'll learn about phase-locked audio later in this section.

Activating and Deactivating Groups Using Group Clutch

Now that your group is defined, an edit you make to any of the drum regions will be reflected on all the other drum tracks as a whole. To get a feel for this process, you'll first make a simple edit to mute the sound of unnecessary open mics at the beginning of the drum tracks. You'll see how to use the Group Clutch feature to temporarily disable groups when making an adjustment to an individual track. The Group Clutch works like an automobile's clutch, temporarily taking the group "out of gear" while letting you perform necessary adjustments on individual tracks without affecting the whole.

1   Use the Zoom tool to zoom in on the first group of drum track regions at bars 8 through 21.

2   Use the Scissors tool to snip the Drums HiHat region (track 35) at about 12 4 1 1.

All the drum regions reflect the same edit, dividing all regions at the same position.

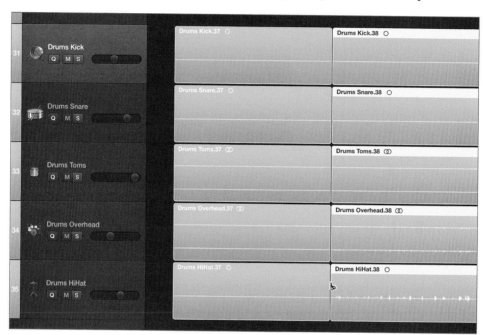

3   Using the Mute tool, click any of the regions to the left of where you split using the Scissors tool.

All the drum regions are muted at the same time.

Sometimes you need to temporarily bypass groups to make a change to an individual track in the group. In this case, you'll mute the snare drum in Verse 3 while leaving the other drum tracks in the group untouched.

4   Toggle the group clutch by pressing Shift-G.

All groups are bypassed, and the "Groups active" checkbox in the Group inspector is deselected.

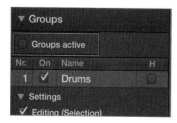

5   Scroll to Verse 3, and then click the Snare region at bar 66. Mute the region using the Mute tool.

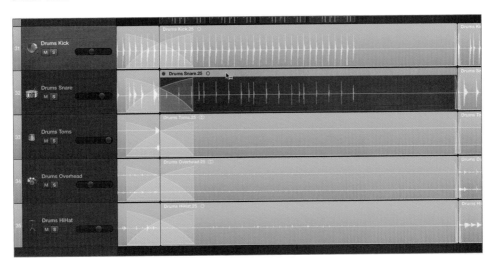

6   Press Shift-G (the Toggle Group Clutch command) to turn groups back on.

Editing Groups with Flex Editing

As you just learned, group editing is essential for keeping multiple regions locked together for region editing. Flex editing techniques also benefit greatly from groups by allowing you to perform operations (such as those you learned in Lesson 2) across multiple tracks.

When the phase-locked option is selected in the Group inspector, the timing relationship between all members of the group stay intact regardless of how any one track is moved, stretched, or quantized. This is especially important where there is some spill into all channels (especially the overheads). Without phase-locked editing, moving the snare on the snare track without also moving the corresponding section of the overhead track may produce unwanted doubling effects and phase cancellation that can smear the overall image.

In this exercise, you will use flex editing on all regions of the group at once while maintaining their phase relationships. For the sake of the demonstration, you'll move a snare beat a little earlier in time.

1   Scroll or locate to bar 102. Zoom into the drum regions from about bar 102 to about bar 104. Create a cycle area from 102 1 1 1 to 104 1 1 1.

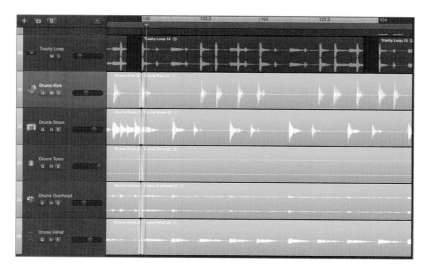

2   Turn on Flex view and on any one of the Drums tracks, set the Flex Mode to Slicing.

All tracks in the group go into Slicing mode.

3   In the lower half of the Drums Snare region, drag the snare hit at 103 2 1 1 to 103 1 3 1 (earlier by one sixteenth note).

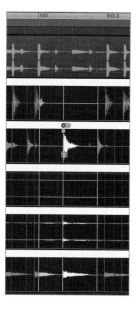

The snare is relocated a bit earlier across all the tracks (including the overheads, where you can see a visual waveform representing the snare).

4   Play the project and listen to the edit.

5   Press Command-Z to undo the edit.

6   Turn off Cycle mode.

Quantizing Drums with Phase-Locked Editing

Because phase-locked editing maintains the relative time of all tracks within the group, this feature is also ideal for quantizing audio across groups of tracks such as a drum kit. When phase-locked is selected in the Group inspector, a Q-Reference button is displayed in the track header of all the tracks in the group. Tracks with this button enabled lend their transients as reference points when using the quantize parameters found in the Region Parameter box. Because the kick drum is rhythmically rigid for this song, it will work well as the quantization reference track.

1   Zoom in on Chorus 2 so that you can clearly see the transient markers.

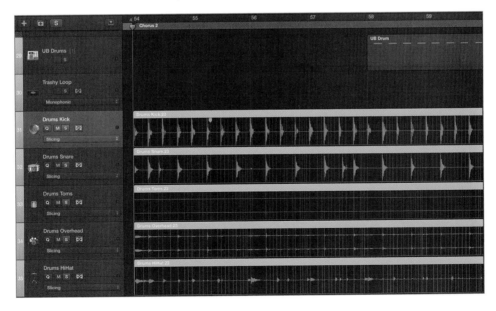

2   Deselect the Q-Reference button on the all the drum track headers except for Drums Kick.

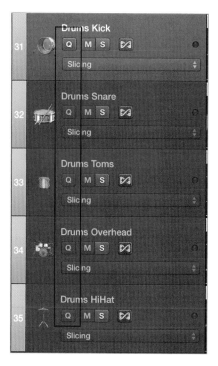

Now only the kick will be referenced when quantizing. You can confirm this visually by looking at the transient markers in each track of the group, all of which should align to the Drums Kick region.

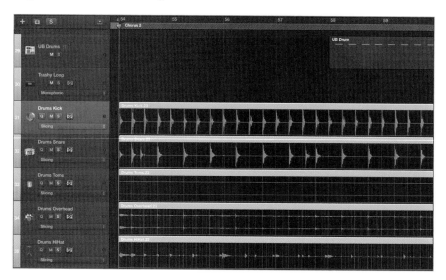

3   Select any of the drum regions (all in the group will be selected), and in the Region
Parameter box, set the Quantize value to 1/4-Note.

The drum regions display colored waveforms to indicate where timing shifts have
occurred. Notice that the colors for any particular beat are the same across all the
drum tracks, indicating that they have all been moved forward or backward in time
together to maintain their relative time relationship.

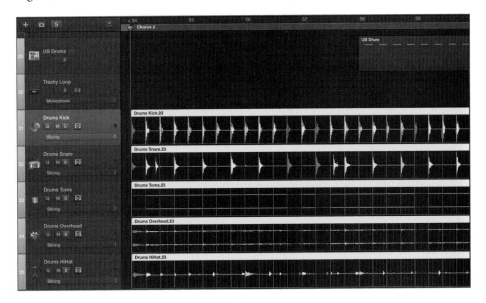

4   Turn off Flex view by clicking the Flex View button.

5   Turn off the Drums edit group by pressing Shift-G (Group Clutch).

6   Press Option-Shift-D to deselect all regions.

Repairing Drums with Marquee Transient

One of the snare drum hits in bar 60 was played softly compared to the others. In this lesson you'll replace the weak snare hit by replacing it with a better snare hit from elsewhere
in the same track. To speed up this workflow, you'll use marquee selection techniques that
use transients in the audio waveforms as a guide to quickly isolate selections for copying
and pasting.

1   Using the Pointer tool, select the Drums Snare region beginning at bar 54 and zoom in around measures 58 to 61 of that region.

2   Create a cycle area from 58 1 1 1 to 61 1 1 1.

3   Unsolo all drum tracks except for the Drums Snare track.

4   Play the project, listening for consistency in the snare hits.

The snare hit at bar 60 beat 2 wasn't played as hard as the others in the track. You can substitute in a good snare hit. The ability to snap transients in Logic Pro makes the selection and editing process easy.

5   Using the Marquee tool, click anywhere near the beginning of bar 58 to create a single-pixel marquee selection (mentioned in Lesson 7, "Using the Marquee Tool for Playback").

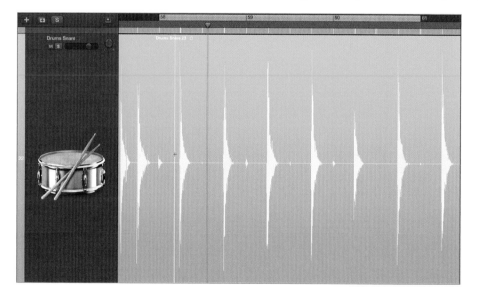

6   Press the Right Arrow key.

The marquee line snaps to the next transient in the snare region (58 2 1 1). You can use this snare hit to replace the weak one, and do so by having the marquee selection adapt to the next transient.

7 Hold down Shift and press the Right Arrow key once or twice until the entire snare hit is selected.

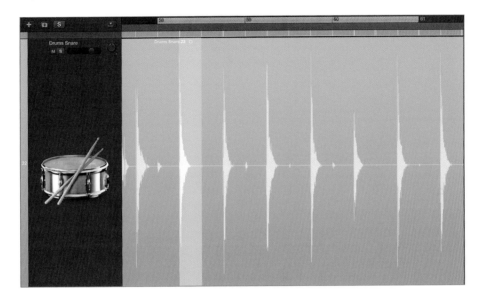

NOTE ▶ If you overdo the selection, continue holding down the Shift key and press the Left Arrow key to adjust the selection.

8 Copy the snare to the clipboard by pressing Command-C.

9 Press the Right Arrow key multiple times to locate the marquee line to the transient at the weak snare hit located at 60 2 1 1.

TIP ▶ If the marquee selection does not snap to the transients you want to reference, you can define the transient markers for a region using the Audio File Editor, as discussed in Lesson 2, "Editing Transient Markers in the Audio Track Editor."

Now you're ready to paste the good hit on top of the weak one. If you simply pasted the selection, you'd create an overlapping region, which could be problematic for visual identification and further editing. You can change the paste behavior by changing Drag modes.

10 From the Drag menu at the top of the main window, choose No Overlap.

11 Press Command-V to paste the good snare hit in place of the weak one.

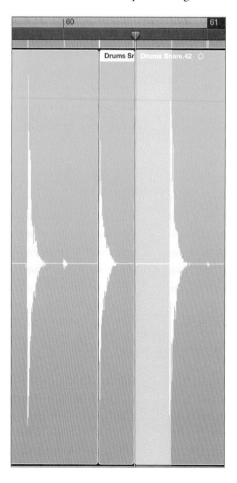

12 Listen to the repaired snare drum.

13 Stop playback.

14 Turn off Cycle mode.

15 Zoom out to view the entire arrangement.

16 Unsolo the Drums Snare region.

> **TIP** You can use the marquee selection techniques shown in this lesson with MIDI regions as well. The beginning or end of a MIDI note is used as the transient point that the marquee selection references.

Replacing Drums

The kick drum track in this song is, for the most part, a static four-on-the-floor pattern that is very popular in electronic music, but the acoustic sound of the drum doesn't lend itself to that style. You'll remedy this by turning each kick hit into a MIDI note message using the Drum Replacement/Doubling feature. Once converted, the resulting MIDI events will trigger an electronic kick drum sample to give the pulse of this song an even stronger foundation.

1 Close the Region Parameter box.

2 Solo the Drums Kick track.

Drum replacement/doubling works at the track level and not just the regions, so you need to be sure the desired track header is selected.

3 Click the Drums Kick track header to select it.

4   From the main window menu, choose Track > Replace or Double Drum Track.

A number of things happen all at once. The Drum Replacement/Doubling dialog appears. The Library opens to let you choose the type of drum sound you want to hear. The Drums Kick track automatically zooms in vertically to let you more easily identify the transient positions that are used to generate MIDI notes. Lastly, an entirely new software instrument track (using an EXS24 software instrument) called Drums Kick + is created along with a new region that contains MIDI notes for each detected drum hit.

NOTE ▶ The Drum Replacement/Doubling dialog is a floating window that will remain on top of the main window. You can still make adjustments such as zoom settings in the main window while the Drum Replacement/Doubling dialog is open. For the following exercise steps, you may need to move the Drum Replacement/Doubling dialog depending on your screen layout.

With all these options, you may feel like you don't know where to start. Begin by helping Logic determine where to create MIDI notes that represent the original kick drums.

In the Drums Replacement/Doubling dialog, the Instrument parameter is used as a preset to automatically choose a relative threshold, MIDI note number assignment, and EXS24 library presets for the sound to be used. In this case, the default Kick setting is appropriate.

The Relative Threshold value sets the minimum amount of amplitude needed to trigger a note. It contains a preset value, but you'll likely need to use the Relative Threshold control to tailor the selection based on the volume of transients on the recording. To see the effect on the regions, you must turn on Flex mode so you can see the transients.

5   Click the Show/Hide Flex button to show Flex Time.

Ideally you want one transient line for each kick that you see in the waveform, but you're zoomed out too far to visually confirm that the threshold setting is set to an appropriate value.

6 With the Drum Replacement/Doubling dialog open, zoom in on a drum region near bar 54 so that you can clearly see each kick transient.

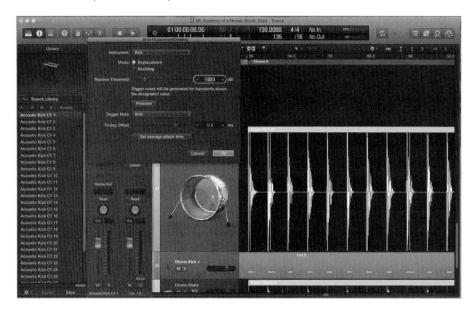

Now that you can more clearly see the transients of each kick drum, try gradually changing the Relative threshold value and observe the MIDI notes in the regions below the track. Different values will increase or decrease the amount of transients detected and will populate the associated MIDI region appropriately. Because the Relative Threshold setting impacts the entire track, you may need to scroll left and right to see if the setting is low enough to pick up all the kick hits.

7 Slide the Relative Threshold parameter to –22.

A problem with setting the threshold low enough to pick up all the kick hits is that it can sometimes detect unwanted material and create doubled notes on single instrument hits.

An unwanted double detection occurs on the first two kicks of bar 54 as well as elsewhere in the track. Generally, you'll want to set the threshold low and generate extra notes, because editing out unwanted notes is much easier than creating missing notes.

Now you can select the kick sound you want to trigger from the Library. By default, Logic brought up a palette of acoustic kick samples. You are not wed to these sounds, however, and can select other samples. To see your choices more easily, expand the Library to two columns.

8   Drag the Library's right-most edge toward the right to display two columns.

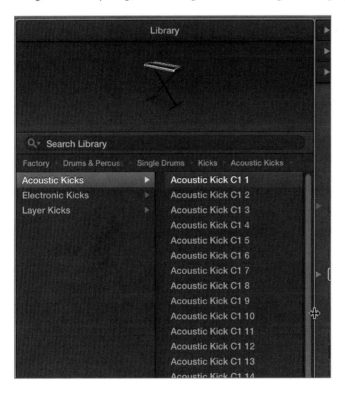

9   In the Library, click the Electronic Kicks folder and select Electronic Kick C1 55.

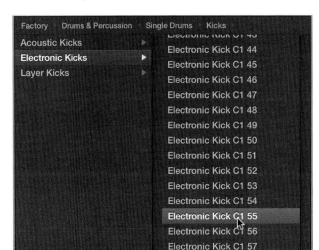

Now you need to hear in context the kick sound you selected. Although the Prelisten button in the Drum Replacement/Doubling dialog will accomplish this, it will begin playback based on the playback prioritization discussed in Lesson 7. Considering that you are at such a high zoom level, try setting the cycle area to keep things in frame.

10   Create a cycle area for bar 54 only.

11   In the Drum Replacement/Doubling dialog, click Prelisten.

The Drums Kick track is doubled by the new electronic kick sound you selected.

12   Click the Prelisten button again to stop playback.

Now that you've heard the results, you need to decide if you want to double or completely replace the original kick region.

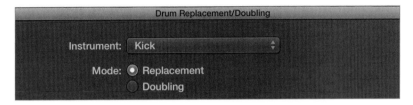

The only difference between replacement and doubling is that selecting the Replacement option will mute the original kick region. Since you're going for an electronic feel, let's replace the kick (default setting).

13 Select the Replacement option (if necessary) and click OK.

The original Drums Kick region is muted, leaving the doubled region you created intact.

NOTE ▶ Keep the Timing Offset parameter at 0.0 unless a noticeable delay occurs between the original and sampled drum.

To avoid confusion, you'll name the new region the same as the Drums Kick + track header.

14 Select the new region (Inst 8).

15 From the Tracks area local menus, choose Functions > Name Regions by Track Name.

16 Solo the Drums Kick + track and play the project, listening to the electronic kick you created. Stop the project.

Now you need to correct the problem of the doubled kicks. The Piano Roll Editor is an ideal place to address them.

17 Double-click the Drums Kick + region to open the Piano Roll Editor.

NOTE ▶ When Logic did the drum replacement, it not only detected the timing of each hit, but it also translated the relative amplitude to velocity.

In the Piano Roll Editor, you can clearly identify the doubled notes created by the drum replacement process transient detection.

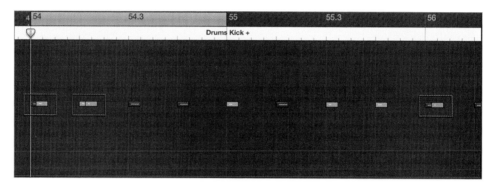

18 Using the Eraser tool, click each doubled note (the rightmost note of each pair) to erase them one by one.

NOTE ▶ The Trigger Note assignment in the Drum Replacement/Doubling dialog determines the MIDI note number to be used. If this parameter is set to Auto, the value of the drum type selected in the Instrument parameter will be used to automatically generate an appropriate note number that corresponds with the General MIDI drum map.

Lesson Review

1. How can you smooth transitions between edited regions?
2. How can you eliminate clicks and pops in an audio file?
3. How can you create new parts from existing material?
4. How can you simultaneously edit multiple tracks of a drum recording?
5. How can you quantize an acoustically recorded drum kit?
6. How can you quickly replace bad sections of audio with good sections?
7. How can you replace the sound of a drum instrument?

Answers

1. You can smooth transitions with crossfades. To do so for large numbers of regions, set crossfade parameters in the Region Parameter box.
2. In the Audio File Editor, zoom in on the waveform and draw out the click using the Pencil tool.
3. Pack a take folder of selected regions, and then use Quick Swipe Comping to edit the parts together.
4. Using Mixer groups, create an Edit group with phase-locked editing enabled.
5. Assign drum tracks to a phase-locked edit group, and then enable quantization parameters in the Region Parameter box.
6. Cut and paste material using marquee selections that are precisely tuned using the Snap to Transient commands.
7. Apply the "Replace or Double Drum Track" command to convert audio tracks into a MIDI track that will trigger sampled instruments.

9

Lesson Files	Advanced Logic X_Files > Lessons > 09_Anatomy of a Human Bomb_Start
Media	Advanced Logic X_Files > Media > Anatomy of a Human Bomb
Time	This lesson takes approximately 60 minutes to complete.
Goals	Utilize aliases to repeat performances in other parts of the project
	Edit regions by applying playback parameters
	Use quantization techniques to change the rhythmic feel
	Use specialized selection techniques to edit MIDI events
	Modify MIDI data using the Transform window
	Split multipart MIDI regions into individual parts for editing

Advanced MIDI Editing

At its heart, MIDI is a command protocol consisting of status messages that indicate when and how events are performed. While digital and analog audio represent actual sound, MIDI data numerically represents the actions that create or control sound generation. As a result, MIDI editing can be somewhat counterintuitive.

Logic provides similar editing tools and parameters for both MIDI and digital audio recordings, especially at the region level (for example, for copying and dividing). However, editing the two differs significantly at the finer, note level.

Even considering the powerful digital audio tools in Logic Pro, MIDI still has a distinct advantage when it comes to editing: offering extreme flexibility through real-time and nondestructive processing of all data.

In this lesson, you will use several methods of creating expressive musical parts out of existing material, and you will learn selection and editing techniques that enable you to work efficiently at the note level.

Using Aliases

An alias in Logic functions much as it does in the Finder: It is a reference to another region. It does not contain any actual data but refers to the content of the original item from which it was created. Like the repeated segments of a looped region, aliases update themselves when the original region is modified, but aliases have added flexibility in that you can freely move them anywhere in the timeline or even to other tracks independent of the original region.

In addition, you can set most region parameters on alias regions independent of the region they reference, which allows you to assign unique playback properties while maintaining their connection to the original.

In this exercise you'll use aliases through a variety of editing functions to layer the string part with another sound.

1   Go to Advanced Logic X > Lessons and open 09_Anatomy of a Human Bomb_Start.logic.

The project opens with a cycle region around Chorus 3 with the Strings region at bar 86 selected. Notice that the looped region repeats the 2-bar Strings region until the end of Chorus 3.

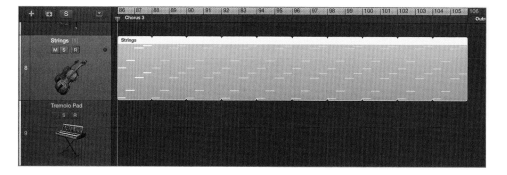

2   Play the song in Chorus 3 and solo the Strings track header on and off to listen to the Strings region by itself and with the rest of the tracks.

To have more editing flexibility with the Strings region, you'll now convert the loops into aliases.

3   In the main menu area, choose Edit > Convert > MIDI Loops to Aliases.

Notice that the name and information displayed in the alias is italicized. The information listed after the arrow in the alias refers to the region name and track number from which it was derived.

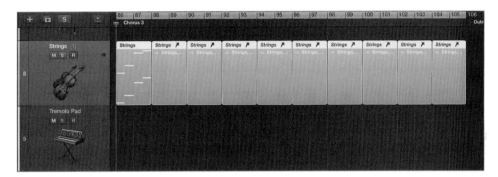

4   Press Option-Shift-D to clear the current selection.

You create new aliases from regions by simply Option-Shift-dragging a region to the destination.

5   Option-Shift drag the original Strings region at bar 86 down to the Tremolo Pad track while watching the help tag, which reads "Make Alias."

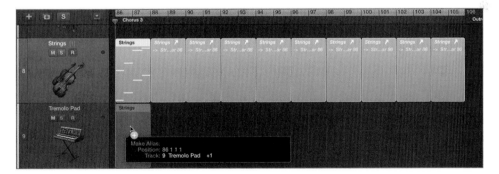

6   Choose Edit > Repeat Multiple, and in the Number of Copies field, enter 9. Click OK.

NOTE ▶ Because the region being repeated is already an alias, it doesn't matter in the dialog window whether you select Copies or "Aliases or Clones."

7   Use the Solo buttons on the Strings and Tremolo Pad track headers to listen to the tracks by themselves as well as in context with the rest of the mix.

The string part consists of four notes that ascend in pitch; however, the pitch of the last two notes of the phrase stand out a little too much in the mix. You can quickly resolve this issue by editing the notes of the original region, while also altering the notes for all the aliases.

8   Double-click the original Strings region to open it in the Piano Roll Editor.

The Piano Roll Editor opens in the bottom of the main window.

9   In the Piano Roll Editor, select all four notes in bar 87 and then drag them down one octave (–12 notes).

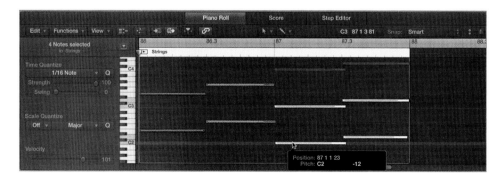

10 Close the Piano Roll Editor, and play the song.

All the aliased Strings regions on both the Strings and Tremolo Pad track reflect the change you just made and play the last half of the phrase in a lower octave.

11 Unsolo the String and Tremolo Pad tracks and listen to the new part with the rest of the song before clicking Stop.

As you can see, aliases are extremely effective when you want to repeat a theme throughout a project but retain the ability to make changes to that theme later in production.

Working with Region Parameters

MIDI regions are data containers that hold various types of MIDI events. The events in a MIDI region can be altered individually using one of the MIDI editors (Piano Roll Editor, Score Editor, Step Editor, Event List Editor, Transform window, and so on) or altered all at once using the Region Parameter box.

The Region Parameter box gives you access to a variety of parameters that affect the data in MIDI regions. These functions invite experimentation, as they are entirely nondestructive, and the MIDI data can be returned to an unaltered state at any time. Think of these parameters as filters you can apply to single or multiple MIDI regions in varying degrees of intensity, without permanently altering the data.

In this series of exercises, you'll be making changes to region parameters on the fly so you can instantly hear the result of your work. Start and stop playback and solo tracks as you feel the need.

Transposing Regions

You can transpose note events in any MIDI region all at once by changing the Transpose parameter in the Region Parameter box.

You'll add a bit of energy leading up to the outro by transposing the aliased String and Tremolo Pad regions up one octave, which you can easily do all at once by a change in the Regions Parameter box.

1 Select the regions on the Strings and Tremolo Pad tracks from bar 102 through 105.

Four regions on two tracks are selected.

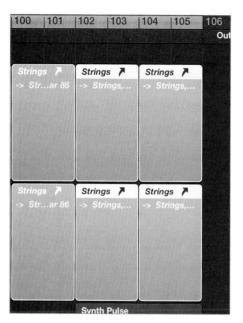

You can apply region parameters to single regions and also to multiple regions simultaneously. The Region Parameter box displays the number of selected regions that will be affected by the parameter adjustments. In this case, instead of displaying the name of the individual selected region, the box displays "4 selected."

2   In the Region Parameter box, place the mouse pointer just to the right of the Transposition parameter and drag up until the value reaches +12, or click the double-arrows to the right and from the octave menu choose the same value.

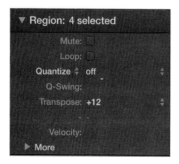

3   Play the song just before the selected regions and listen for the transposed strings.

> **TIP** ▶ You can also apply the settings in the Region Parameter box to incoming MIDI signals by changing settings without a region selected. (The box reads "MIDI Thru" instead of a region name.) When the recording is completed, the resulting region inherits the same parameter settings as MIDI Thru.

Modifying Velocities in a MIDI Region

In Lesson 8, you converted an audio recording in the Drums Kick track to MIDI data, which in turn triggered a sampler. This created varying velocity values for each drum hit that resulted in more dynamic change than in the original performance. In this lesson, you'll limit the range of velocity values for the kick drum notes to control the dynamics while still providing a degree of expression that reflects how the drummer played the part.

The Velocity and Dynamics parameters provide a fast way to alter all note velocity values in a region. The Velocity parameter simply offsets note velocities. The Dynamics parameter also acts on MIDI note velocities; but instead of adding or subtracting a fixed value, it scales the difference between the highest and lowest velocity values. It functions similarly to the way a compressor or expander acts on the dynamics of an audio signal by increasing or decreasing the dynamic range for the selected MIDI region. When applying a value larger than 100 percent, the differences between "soft" and "loud" notes are increased (as they would be by an expander), and they are decreased with values of less than 100 percent (as they would be by a compressor).

1   Scroll down to display the Drums Kick + track, and then Option-click the Solo button on the Drums Kick + Track to turn off all other solos.

2   Play from the beginning of Chorus 3.

3   Click the Drums Kick + region to select it. Click the More disclosure triangle in the Region Parameter box to view the additional settings.

4   In the Region Parameter box, from the Dynamics menu, choose Fixed (click the arrows to the right).

Fixed sets all note velocities to 64, producing a consistent timbre and volume.

5   Play the project listening to the kick sound. Stop the playback.

6   Change the Dynamics setting to 50%.

Now the difference between the highest and lowest velocities is half of what it was before, thereby creating a kick part that maintains the accents and nuances of the original performance but keeps the volume and tone more consistent.

Although the kick part is also more consistent, it is quite a bit quieter. As with the makeup gain in a compressor, you can correct this by raising the velocity values with the Velocity parameter.

7   Drag the Velocity parameter up to +20.

8   Unsolo the Drum Kick + track.

9   Play the project to listen to the affected region in context. Adjust the Dynamics and Velocity parameters to your liking.

> **NOTE** ▶ Settings in the Region Parameter box, with the exception of Loop and Quantize, aren't reflected in the editors. The changes are applied during playback. However, you can also write these changes permanently to the region: In the Track area's local menu bar, choose Functions > MIDI Region Parameters > Apply All Parameters Permanently.

Using Delay to Adjust the Feel

The Delay parameter is used to move a region forward or backward in time. By choosing a positive value, you can delay the playback of a region, achieving a laid-back or dragging feel. Negative values push the region earlier, creating a rushing or driving feel in relation to the beat.

The current project's musical material warrants a driving rhythm, especially in the drums. You can set Delay on the Drums Kick + region to further push the energy of the song.

1   Play the project, listening to how the Drums Kick + works with the rhythm section.

Delay settings are displayed in ticks (the smallest possible bar subdivision or system quantization), note values, and milliseconds.

2   In the Region Parameter box, click the arrows to the right of the Delay parameter, and from the pop-up menu, choose 1/192 = +20 ticks (9.6 ms).

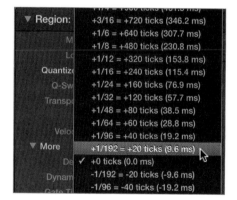

> **TIP** Logic automatically converts musical time increments (like you just saw in the Delay pop-up menu) into milliseconds based on the tempo of your project. Therefore, projects with different tempos will show different millisecond values. To further refine the delay setting, you can adjust in half-millisecond intervals by dragging up or down in the blank space to the right of the Delay parameter.

By selecting this value, you are advancing the playback of the Drums Kick + region by a 1/192 note, or 9.6 milliseconds.

3   Play the project from Chorus 3, and listen to the kick drum in the arrangement so you can continue to adjust the delay parameter to your liking.

TIP ▶ The Delay parameter always displays in musical values in addition to ms or ticks, ranging from 1 bar of delay to a 1/4 note of advance. This is especially useful for creating echo effects between regions of similar content on separate tracks.

Using Gate Time to Alter Articulation

The Gate Time parameter directly affects the length of MIDI events, but not in the way you might expect. Instead of uniformly decreasing or increasing the length of all MIDI events in a region, the Gate Time parameter changes notes by a percentage of their lengths, thereby allowing you to adjust the articulation of a performance from, say, staccato to legato.

The first region on the Bass Synth track needs a little tightening up because the longer notes sustain a bit too long and bleed into the shorter ones. By adjusting their lengths with the Gate Time parameter, you can modify the length of notes to change the articulation of the performance.

1   Scroll up and select the Bass Synth track, which in turn selects all the Bass Synth regions in the already enabled cycle area (Chorus 3).

2   Solo the Bass Synth track.

    To clearly hear the effect of the Gate Time parameter, you can audition it using an extreme setting.

3   In the Region Parameter box, click the arrows to the right of the Gate Time parameter, and from the pop-up menu, choose Fixed.

4   Play the project to audition the results. Stop playback.

Each note is played with the shortest possible duration, creating an extremely staccato performance.

5   From the Gate Time pop-up menu, choose 50%.

All events are adjusted to 50 percent of their length, creating an articulate performance.

6   Play the project to hear the results. Stop playback.

Now you'll create a legato feel.

7   From the Gate Time pop-up menu, choose Legato.

Each note's duration extends to the beginning of the next note, creating a fluid bass line that sounds appropriate for this part of the song.

8   Play the project to hear the results. Stop playback.

9   Turn off Solo mode by Option-clicking an active track solo button.

10   Turn Cycle mode off.

Correct and Modify Rhythm with Quantize

Just as musical rhythm is expressed in relation to the grid formed by beat and meter, sequencers map MIDI event timings to a grid determined by a base resolution provided by the software application. To ensure that the placement of an event in time is as accurate as possible, Logic offers a resolution of a 1/3840 note (one tick).

This resolution allows for a vast range of rhythmical placement, but on occasion you will need to adjust the accuracy of events in relation to note lengths (eighth notes, sixteenth notes, triplets, and so on). You can do so by applying quantization, which compares events to a chosen resolution and then corrects their time placement by moving them to the nearest position on a beat/time grid.

Logic offers multiple methods for quantizing events, including adjusting the data in the Region Parameter box. In this exercise, you'll check out the effect on note events when quantizing by correcting the timing of the Mallet-Bell region that plays in the intro.

1   Scroll up to track 6 (Mallet-Bell), and in the control bar, click the Go To Beginning button.

2   Double-click the Mallet-Bell region at bar 1.

The Piano Roll Editor displays the contents of the Mallet-Bell region.

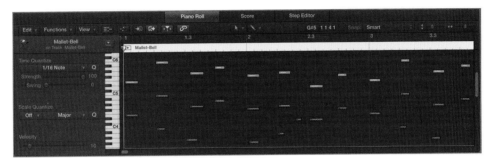

Adjustments to Quantization parameters are visually reflected in the editors, so keep your eye on the Piano Roll Editor to see how the changes you're about to make affect the note positions.

3   Solo the Mallet-Bell track, and if necessary, turn on Cycle mode.

4   Press U to set the locators around the Mallet-Bell region. Play the project.

You can hear the rhythmic unevenness in the Mallet-Bell part.

To more easily see the changes you're going to make, you'll need to zoom in a little closer.

5   In the Piano Roll Editor, zoom in on the notes that play in the first two measures.

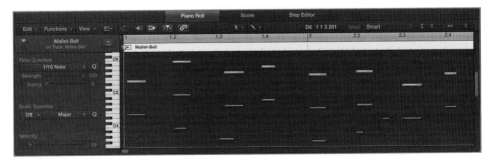

Notice that most of the notes are played late and clearly not aligned to the grid lines that represent quarter-note divisions.

Although the Mallet-Bell line is primarily playing a quarter-note pattern, a few eighth-note pickups are played, so you will need to choose an eighth-note quantization value to avoid having those pickups rounded to quarter-note positions.

The eighth-note quantization settings have many variations, and all but one are intended to swing the eighth-note feel.

6   While keeping your eye on the Mallet-Bell part in the Piano Roll Editor, in the Region Parameter box, click the Quantize menu and choose 1/8 Swing F.

You can hear and see that the pickup notes in bars 2 and 4 have been shifted later in time to create a swing feel.

TIP ▶ Swing settings for both eighth and sixteenth note feels are available with letters from A to F that respectively increase the swing feel. Another way to get finer control over the intensity of the swing feel is to choose a Quantize parameter without swing and adjust the Q-Swing parameter. Values above 50% move every alignment grid line more to the right, and values below 50% move them more to the left.

In this case the part needs to be played with a straight feel.

7   Change the Quantize parameter to 1/8 Note.

The Mallet-Bell part now plays perfectly in time.

In some instances you may want to tighten the rhythm of a part, but you'll also want to preserve some of the human feel. You can do so by correcting only those notes that are the most out of time. This is easily accomplished using the Q-Strength parameter.

NOTE ▶ The Q-Strength and other advanced quantization parameters are located in the More section of the Region Parameter box. If you don't see them, click the More disclosure triangle to view these settings.

Q-Strength lets you choose just how much the Quantize setting pulls the start of each note to the timing grid. A value of 0% means that quantizing has no effect; higher percentages create tighter timing. If no value is displayed next to the Q-Strength parameter, it is considered to be at 100%, and the notes will be perfectly aligned to the timing grid.

8   Double-click the blank space to the right of the Q-Strength parameter and set the value to 50%.

The notes move to a position that is half the distance between the eighth-note grid lines and the notes' original positions, tightening up the rhythm but still maintaining a human feel.

Using the Q-Range parameter, you can also include or exclude notes from quantization based on how close a note is to the quantization grid. This can be helpful when you want to quantize only the notes that were played the farthest out of time.

It's easiest to understand how Q-Range works by first looking at the region without the effects of quantization.

9   Turn the Q-Strength value down to 0%.

The notes revert to their originally played position.

A three-note chord plays at bar 1 beat 3. The lowest note in the chord is fairly close to the beat grid line, but the top two notes are played considerably later.

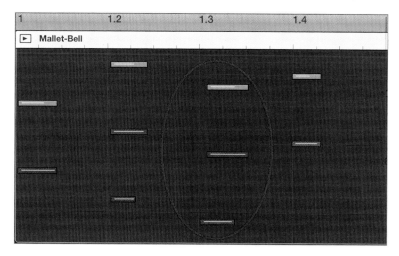

10 From the Q-Range pop-up menu, choose –1/32 = –120 (–57.7 ms).

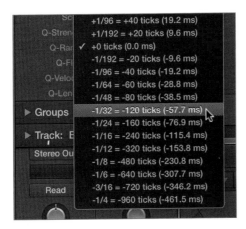

You won't see any change just yet because the Q-Strength is still set to 0%.

11 Change the Q-Strength parameter back to 75%.

Only the top two notes in the chord move closer to the beat grid line. The lowest note is not affected.

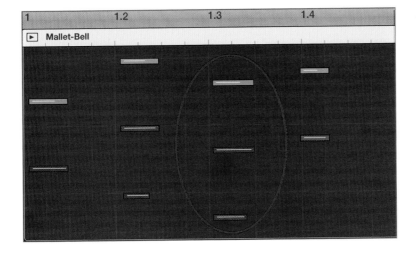

Because the setting has a negative value, only notes that were more than 1/32nd note away from the quantization grid line are selected for quantization. If you had set the Q-Range settings using a positive value, only the notes that were less than 1/32nd note of the quantization grid line would be selected for quantizing.

TIP▶ You can adjust Q-Range values in single-tick increments by dragging up or down in the space next to the Q-Range parameter.

Now that you understand how the Quantize, Q-Strength, and Q-Range parameters work and relate to each other, you can adjust these settings to create the feel you want for the Mallet-Bell region.

12 Adjust the Quantize, Q-Strength, and Q-Range settings for the Mallet-Bell region to your preference, and then click Stop.

13 Unsolo the Mallet-Bell track.

Arpeggiating Chords with Q-Flam

The term *flam* is typically associated with hitting a drum with one stick just a moment before hitting it with the other to create a fatter sound. In Logic, you can use the Q-Flam region parameter to create a similar effect when multiple notes are positioned at the same exact point in time. Small values create subtle timing offsets between notes of a chord, and larger values create arpeggio effects.

The Piano region at the beginning of the song plays blocks of chords. Because the notes were step recorded, you'll use Q-Flam to break the chords apart.

1 Solo the Piano track (below the Mallet-Bell track).

2 Select the first two Piano regions at the beginning of the song. Play the project to start auditioning the material, letting it continue to play while you make the following adjustments.

In the Piano Roll Editor, you can clearly see that all the notes in each chord are played at the same time.

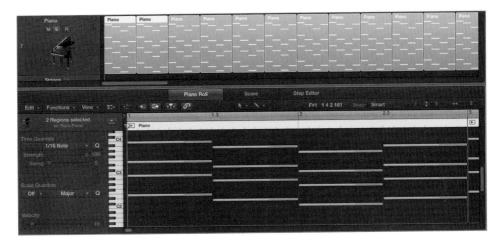

For Q-Flam to function, a quantize value must be selected in the Quantize parameter even when notes are already aligned.

3   In the Region Parameter box, set the Quantize parameter to 1/4 Note.

4   Open the Q-Flam menu and choose 1/64 = +60 ticks (28.8 ms).

The chords sound more "rolled," and as you can see, each note in the chord plays a 1/64th note after the previous one. Positive Q-Flam values create an ascending arpeggio (low notes play first) of the notes, while negative values create a descending arpeggio.

5   Change the Q-Flam value to –1/8.

6   Unsolo the Piano track. Listen to the new part with the rest of the mix.

    Now the piano part plays a descending eighth-note pattern that works nicely in the intro.

7   Stop playback.

Using Template Parameters

In Lesson 2 you learned how to create groove templates from audio regions. In fact, all the quantization settings are based upon similar premade templates that include timing as well as note velocity and length information that can be applied to the content of regions. You can tailor these templates to better match the region content by adjusting the Q-Velocity and Q-Length parameters.

The Q-Velocity and Q-Length parameters let you choose how closely you want those values in the selected region to match those of the groove template. These values are expressed as percentages, where 100 means that the velocity or length matches the template exactly.

In this exercise you'll adjust the settings of an eighth-note Synth line that was step recorded resulting in a lifeless feel. Using the Q-Velocity and Q-Length parameters, you'll modify the line to include rhythmic and dynamic accents.

1   Go to bar 102, scroll downward, and solo the Synth Pulse track (track 10).

2   Select the Synth Pulse region at bar 102, and then press U to set the locators around the region. Play the project to audition the material, letting it continue to play as you work on the next few steps.

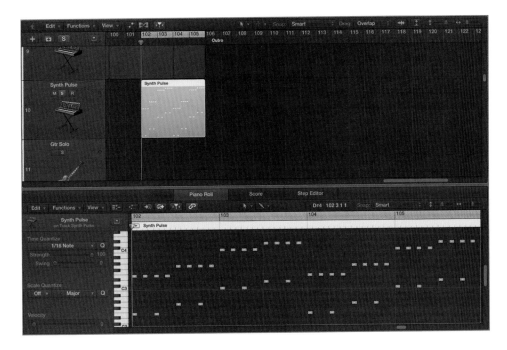

Although the notes are already aligned to the grid, you must first choose a Quantize parameter setting to serve as the map to which velocity and note lengths conform.

3   In the Region Parameter box, set the Quantize parameter to 1/8 Note and raise the Q-Velocity parameter to 100%.

As you raise the value, you can see in the Piano Roll Editor how the original note velocities gradually change to the velocities provided by the 1/8 Note template. It's clear that the 1/8 Note template accents notes that fall directly on each beat.

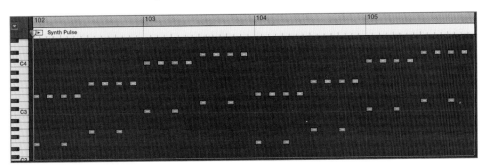

4   Raise the Q-Length parameter to 100%.

Notice how the 1/8 Note quantize template contains longer notes on the quarter-note positions compared to the eighth-note positions.

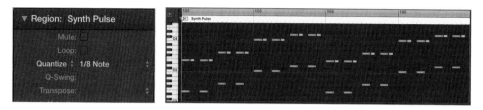

5   Stop playback.

Selecting MIDI Events for Editing

Let's continue developing the Synth Pulse line by editing at a finer level: individual MIDI events. You can do this in any of the MIDI editors, but the Piano Roll Editor works particularly well for quickly selecting and viewing region contents.

You'll be using a variety of specialized menu commands that work particularly well for music production workflows because they can quickly select and edit information based on musical context.

The Synth Pulse part is an eighth-note pattern that alternates between an octave interval and single note. Your goal is to create a part that consists entirely of individual notes that toggle between an upper and lower pitch. You'll achieve this by using specialized commands to select and delete the top notes in each octave interval.

1   Choose Edit > Select > Lowest Notes, or press Shift-Down Arrow.

The lowest note of each octave interval is selected, as are the single notes played between the intervals.

The notes you want to delete are, in fact, the notes that aren't currently selected, so you can simply invert your selection.

2   Choose Edit > Select > Invert Selection (or press Shift-I), and then press Delete.

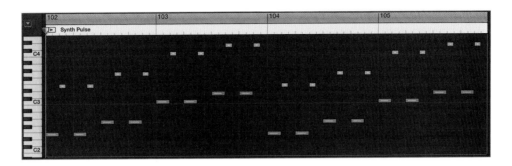

The Synth Pulse alternates octaves in a rhythmically active part.

Now you'll make the phrasing sound more interesting by lengthening some of the upper notes.

3   Shift-click the second and fourth green notes in bar 102 to select them.

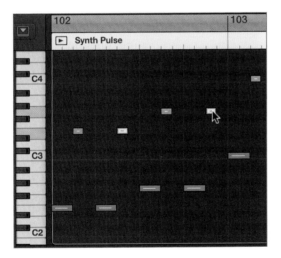

The goal is to select the remaining notes of the region that happen in the same relative bar positions, which can be tedious to do manually. The Select Same Subpositions command is a powerful tool that selects any other notes in the region that occur at the same position relative to the barline.

4   Choose Edit > Select > Same Subposition, or press Shift-P.

Now that the correct notes are selected, you can apply additional operations to change their lengths, and so on.

5   Choose Edit > Trim > Note End to Following Notes (Forced Legato).

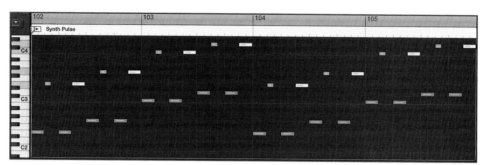

The length of each of the selected notes is extended so that each note ends as the next note begins.

6   Unsolo the Synth Pulse track, and listen to the edit in the context of the mix.

NOTE ▶ The selection and force legato functions mentioned in the previous exercise are also available from any editor's local Edit menu.

Using MIDI Transform Functions

MIDI Transform functions are powerful selection and processing tools that allow you to manipulate all types of MIDI information in almost all conceivable ways. Each function employs a set of conditions and operations to specify exactly what data is selected and how it will be manipulated.

The functions can range from simple to complex. In this section, you will learn how to use one of the many preset transform functions, and you'll also create a custom transform set to use in your projects.

Working with MIDI Transform Sets

MIDI transform sets are essentially transform function presets you can access in the MIDI Transform window or in the local menus of any editors that can manipulate MIDI information. You'll familiarize yourself with how transform functions work by first working with a premade MIDI transform set.

Earlier in the lesson, you used the Q-Flam parameter to arpeggiate piano chords in the intro. You'll now give those regions a more human feel.

1   Select and audition the two Piano regions in the intro by soloing the track and creating a cycle region from 1 1 1 1 to 5 1 1 1.

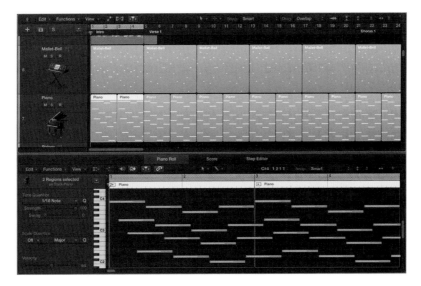

2   In the Piano Roll Editor's local menus, choose Functions > MIDI Transform > Humanize.

The Transform window opens.

The Humanize function applies a slight randomization to events to create a looser and more natural-sounding performance.

The Transform window is divided into three main sections: Select Events by Conditions, Operations on Selected Events, and Operation on Byte 2. Although these headings might sound a little confusing, their operations are easily understood.

Basically, to use the transform functions on MIDI data, you must indicate exactly what you want to affect in the Select Events by Conditions section. Here, you specify the criteria of the desired target, whether you want a simple selection based on event type (or status) or a complex selection with multiple conditions (for example, events that have a specific length, position, and value).

The Operations sections indicate how you want to modify the selected MIDI events. This can be almost any kind of MIDI transformation you can dream up, even converting one type of event to another for further processing. With the Humanize transformation, for example, selected notes are randomized in position, velocity value, and length. Each transformation has a specific extent assigned to it, which can be anything from a single number or note to a range of operations. Here, the position, velocity, and length of the selected note events are randomized within a positive or negative range of 10 ticks.

The Operation on Byte 2 section is a graphical representation of the transformation itself and directly depicts the values for byte 2 of the MIDI event chosen in the Status column. (A MIDI channel voice message consists of a status byte followed by one or two data bytes.) In the case of note events, byte 2 is velocity; for controllers, it is the value for the assigned controller.

All of this translates to a function that slightly varies note events, imparting a looser, more human feel.

3   At the bottom of the Transform window, click "Select and Operate."

The note events displayed in the Piano Roll Editor change slightly in position, length, and velocity.

You can repeatedly click "Select and Operate" to further increase the amount of humanization that is applied. It's best to listen as you add more humanization, so this time let's play the part while making the changes.

4   Play the project and continue to click "Select and Operate" while listening to the effect.

NOTE ▶ If you feel as if you've applied too much humanization, you can press Command-Z to undo the most recent operations.

5   Stop playback.

Creating New Transform Functions

When navigating through the Transform menu, you probably noticed numerous preset transform functions. These functions efficiently accomplish many common MIDI editing tasks. However, at times you will need to create your own transform set to address a specific need, whether it is quick selection of specific MIDI data for editing, or selecting and performing an operation on the MIDI data via a single step.

For this exercise, you will create a transform function designed to humanize only notes that are above the root note of the piano chords that begin at bar 5. Having the lowest note of the chord anchored directly on the beat helps to preserve the tightness of the track, even though the upper notes will be humanized and slightly out of time.

In the previous exercise, you may have also noticed that after you humanized the piano too much, notes with high velocities tended to stick out, and lower velocities weren't loud enough. To address this, you'll configure your transform set to randomize only the velocities between a defined upper and lower range.

1   In the Tracks area, select the Piano region at bar 5, and adapt the cycle area to the region by pressing U.

2   Play the project to audition the material.

Creating a new transform set is done in any open MIDI Transform window, whether opened in a MIDI editor or from the main Window menu.

3   In the open MIDI Transform window, click the disclosure triangle next to the Presets menu and choose **Create Initialized User Set!**.

A dialog appears, asking if you'd like to create a new transform set or rename the current one.

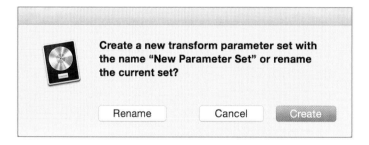

4   Click Create to open a new, blank transform set.

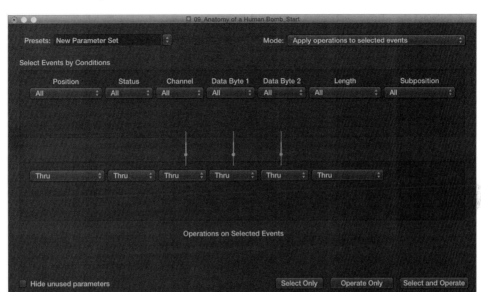

Notice that many more parameters are accessible via pop-up menus than when you opened the Humanize preset. Preset transform functions open with unused parameters hidden from view, presenting only the relevant parameters for selection or operation.

> **TIP** ▶ Preset transform functions will display all parameters if you deselect the "Hide unused parameters" checkbox in the Transform window. Displaying all parameters allows you to further extend the preset's capabilities by adding more selection and operation data.

5   Select the text in the Presets menu ("New Parameter Set") to edit it, and enter *Custom Humanization*. Press Return.

A dialog appears, asking if you'd like to rename the current, empty set or create a new one.

6 Click Rename.

When you create a new transform set, start off by defining just what you want to transform. In the Select Events by Conditions area, All is displayed by default for every parameter, signifying that no discrimination is made when selecting MIDI data (all event types, positions, and channels will be selected). To narrow the focus of the selection, you need to specify the relevant parameters instead of leaving them in their default states.

Start defining selection criteria by choosing the MIDI event type from the Status menu.

7 From the Status pop-up menu, choose = (equal sign).

In the new menu that appears just below your chosen option, you can specify the event type.

8 From the new pop-up menu, choose Note.

By specifying Note as the Status parameter, you exclude all events but MIDI notes from the selection. Even so, this selection is still far too general. The goal of the transform function is to select only those MIDI notes that have a pitch equal to or higher than F2. To do so, you need to define more criteria in the selection parameters.

9 From the Pitch pop-up menu, choose >= (greater than or equal to).

A value field appears below the menu. Entering a number in this value field defines a selection greater than or equal to the inputted number.

10 Double-click the number in the value field and enter *F2*. Press Return.

Now that your selection criteria are defined, you can specify what will happen to the selected data when the operation runs. You do so by choosing operations from the parameter menus in the "Operations on Selected Events" area.

11 In the Velocity column in the "Operations on Selected Events" area, click the pop-up menu to view the list of operations you can perform (but do not choose anything yet).

As you can see, you have many ways, simple and complex, to transform MIDI data.

MORE INFO ▶ The Logic Pro X User Manual provides definitions of the available operations.

12 From the Velocity pop-up menu, choose Random.

Two value fields appear below the Random menu. Rather than randomize within a certain range from a note's current velocity value (as with the +– Rand setting used in the Humanize transform set), a randomly selected value between these two numbers will be applied irrespective of a note's original value. In this case, you want a low number that will still produce a loud piano note, and a high number that still won't trigger the fortissimo samples (which would stand out too much).

13 Double-click the Random value fields. In the upper (lower value) field enter *70*, and in the lower (higher value) field enter *115*.

14 In both the Position and Length column in the "Operations on Selected Events" area, choose the +– Rand setting.

15 Change the value fields for both parameters to 20 ticks.

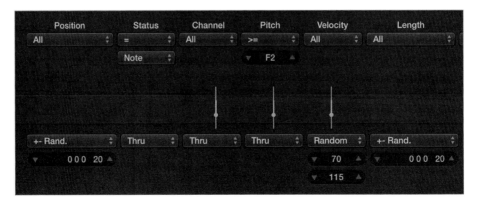

You have now created a new transform set that, when activated, will humanize the start and length of each note within 20 ticks of the current value, and randomly assign velocity values between 70 and 115 on any notes at or above F2.

16 Click Select and Operate.

All MIDI notes at F2 or higher are humanized without risking that the velocities are too low or too high.

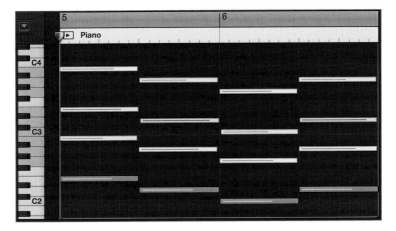

17 Play the project, listening to the newly transformed MIDI data.

> **NOTE ►** If you want only to select specific MIDI data without processing it, click the Select Only button. Likewise, you can choose to only process previously selected MIDI data by clicking the Operate Only button, thereby bypassing the selection criteria altogether.

Applying New Transform Sets

All newly created transform sets are immediately available in both the MIDI editor windows, as well as the Tracks area via the Functions > MIDI Transform menu. This puts your transform set creations within easy reach whenever you are editing MIDI data.

1 Close the Transform window, turn off Cycle mode, and in the Tracks area, select the Piano region at bar 7.

For this operation, you want to apply the newly created MIDI transform set to all regions that follow the selected one on the Piano track.

2 Choose Edit > Select > All Following of Same Track.

3   Choose Functions > MIDI Transform > Custom Humanization.

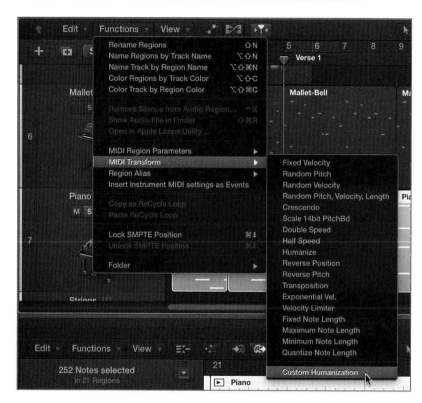

The Transform window opens, displaying the transform set you created earlier.

4   Click "Select and Operate."

All MIDI notes with velocity at or above F2 are humanized.

5   Close the Transform window.

6   Unsolo the Piano track.

7   Play the project from the beginning, listening to the newly transformed material in the context of the project.

> **TIP** ▶ Newly created transform functions are saved in the project file itself. To use your newly created transform functions in other projects, you must first import them by choosing File > Project Settings > Import Settings and then selecting a project file that contains the MIDI Transform function(s). With the Transform Sets checkbox selected, click Import.

Separating MIDI Events

It is not unusual to record MIDI drum parts by triggering multiple sounds in a single pass, creating a single region containing both the kick drum and snare parts. This technique can help create a track that locks into a groove. Having the kick drum and hi-hat on the same track, on the other hand, can make it more difficult to edit the parts using techniques learned in this lesson, and there's less flexibility when mixing.

Because a MIDI file transmits a stream of commands with discrete events, it allows for some fancy editing functions. One such function is Separate MIDI Events, which enables you to break out a MIDI region into components based on specific criteria to separate regions on separate tracks. You can try this on the bass drum and hi-hat part, splitting them into separate tracks for independent editing.

1   Zoom out horizontally until you can see the entire length of the project.

2   Scroll down and click the UB Drums track (track 29) header to select all the regions on that track.

3   In the Piano Roll Editor, click the Collapse Mode button.

The Piano Roll Editor shows the upper hi-hat line with kick drum hits.

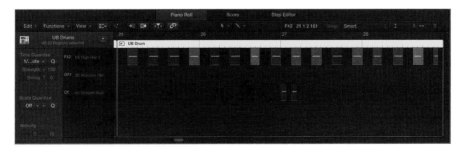

To separate the kick drum from the hi-hat, you must first combine all the UB Drum regions in the project into a single region; otherwise, a new pair of tracks will be created for each of the current UB Drum regions.

4   Choose Edit > Join > Regions, or press Command-J.

When using the Separate MIDI Events By Note Pitch function, a new track and a new region are created for every note number found. In addition, the newly created tracks are automatically assigned to the same instruments as the original MIDI region.

5   Choose Edit > Separate MIDI Events > By Note Pitch.

A new track is created for each of the notes contained in the UB Drums region, and the UB Drums track is now empty and no longer necessary.

6   Select the now-empty UB Drums track header, and press Delete.

For easier identification, name the new tracks and regions with their corresponding instruments.

7   Double-click the Track header that contains the newly created regions. Rename the first track *UB Kick* and the second *UB Hi-Hat*.

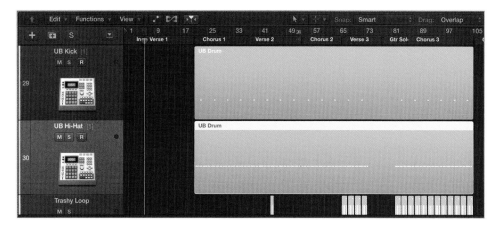

8   Select both of the newly created regions and choose Functions > Name Regions by Track Name.

Lesson Review

1. How are aliases used?

2. What does the Region Parameter box do?

3. How can you quickly modify the timing of a MIDI region?

4. What are the Q-Velocity and Q-Length parameters used for?

5. What does the Invert Selection command do in a MIDI editor?

6. What does the Select > Same Subposition command do in a MIDI editor?

7. Where can you access the transform functions?

8. How are the transform functions useful?

9. What do the Separate MIDI Events functions do?

Answers

1. Aliases duplicate material that needs to automatically update when the original is edited.

2. The Region Parameter box allows real-time control over various playback parameters, enabling you to transpose and adjust the feel of events in a MIDI region.

3. Select a Quantize setting to determine the timing grid to which notes will be aligned. Use Q-Swing and Q-Strength to further refine how the notes are placed in relationship to the grid.

4. You can use Q-Velocity and Q-Length to conform MIDI notes to the length and velocity values defined in a quantization template you select using the Quantize parameter.

5. The Invert Selection command selects all regions (in the Tracks area) or events (in a MIDI editor) that are not currently selected and deselects any regions or events that are selected.

6. The Select > Same Subposition command selects all regions or events with a similar bar or beat relationship to the selection.

7. Access the transform functions via the main Window menu, or via the Functions > Transform menu in all MIDI editors.

8. The transform functions contain many helpful operations for processing MIDI data, such as humanizing performances.

9. The Separate MIDI Events functions separate combined parts recorded in a single MIDI region into individual regions for further editing.

Mixing

10

Lesson **10**

Managing the Mix

Logic provides dedicated channels for MIDI, audio, and software instruments. These channels are accessed via the integrated Mixer, which shows them in an organized display.

Each channel offers a set of controls for working with the signal throughput (volume, pan, sends, and so on). You can link these controls together so that groups of channels respond to the manipulation of a single control.

In this lesson, you will use the Mixer to efficiently view and access the Mixer channels, as well as navigate plug-ins in the insert chain. In addition, you will utilize groups to link controls of multiple channels, thereby streamlining your mix process.

Importing Channel Strips and Data

Logic can import track content, channel strip configuration (including plug-ins and routings), and automation data from one project into another. With the import function, you can easily transfer mix and region data from sessions recorded at a separate place and time.

In this first exercise, you will open the project file you'll use throughout the lesson, and import additional data from another project file, adding it to the mix.

1   Choose File > Open.

2   In the Music > Advanced Logic X_Files > Lessons folder, open 10_Midnight Wonder_ Start.logicx. The project file opens.

3   Play the project to familiarize yourself with the material. Click the Stop button when you are finished.

A double-tracked guitar riff was recorded in a separate project in another studio. You can use the Logic import features to add these tracks, including the channel strips and automation, into the open project.

4   Choose File > Import > Logic Projects.

5   In the Music > Advanced Logic X_Files > Lessons folder, select 10_Midnight Wonder_ Guitar.logicx.

6   Click Import. The Browsers area opens, displaying all the channels available for import from the selected project file.

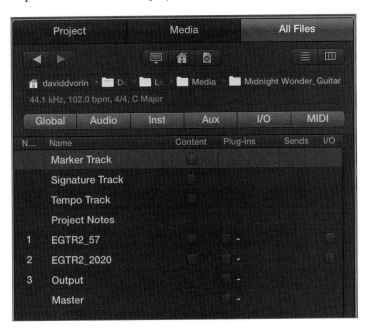

In the All Files Browser, you can select the data you want to bring in from the imported tracks. This includes Content (region data and placement), Plug-ins, Sends, I/O, and Auto (automation data).

7   In both the EGTR2_57 and EGTR2_2020 rows, select Content, Plug-ins, I/O, and Auto. (You might need to scroll over to see the latter column.)

NOTE ▶ The Sends checkbox is dimmed because the imported channel strips from this project do not have an active send setting. If sends are imported, Logic will also create an aux that reflects the bussing of the original track, complete with inserts.

8   Click Add.

The EGTR2_57 and EGTR2_2020 tracks and channel strips are added to the project and displayed in the Tracks area.

9   Close the Browsers area.

10   Select the EGTR2_57 and EGTR2_2020 tracks one by one in the track list, looking at their channel strips in the inspector. Each channel strip is imported with both insert effects and volume information intact.

> **TIP** ▶ Importing channel strips and data from one project file to another is a great way to rebuild a project that has been corrupted, and it helps to resolve issues with "problem" projects.

Working with the Mixer

The Mixer has three display modes that access the channels of a mix: Single view, Tracks view, and All view. Understanding how the three differ will help you navigate through your mix more efficiently.

Using Tracks View

The Mixer's Tracks view is often referred to as an adaptive mixer. In this display mode, Logic creates a Mixer setup adapted from the Tracks area's track list, reflecting aspects such as order, names, and assigned colors. The Mixer's Tracks view will reflect the Tracks area's track list, even when new tracks are created and reordered.

Tracks view (the default) will probably be the view you use most often when mixing because it allows you to focus on those elements that are directly involved with the project's musical arrangement.

With the project open, you can observe firsthand the relationship between the Tracks area and the Mixer's Tracks view by rearranging the track order for a more ergonomic mixing setup.

1   Click the Mixer button to open the Mixer area.

2   Press the Up and Down Arrow keys on your keyboard.

When a channel is selected, it is highlighted in the Tracks area and in the Mixer. This adaptive relationship also holds true when shuffling track order.

3   In the Tracks area, Command-click the EGTR2_57 and EGTR2_2020 tracks to select them.

Note that the channels are located next to the lead vocal channel (LVOX). A more convenient location would be in the Mixer next to the other electric guitar tracks (EGTR1_57 and EGTR1_2020). You can move the track in the Tracks area while observing the changes in the Mixer.

4   Click the track icon for either of the two selected tracks (the pointer switches to a
hand), and drag them downward, placing them after track 19 (EGTR1_2020).

The track order changes in the Tracks area and the Mixer, and both the EGTR2_57
and EGTR2_2020 tracks are inserted after the EGTR1_2020 track.

Tracks area track list

Mixer

Using the Channel Strip Filters

The channel strip filter buttons, located at the upper-right side of the Mixer, define the
types of channels displayed in the Mixer. The buttons can be selected singly or in combination. When you use the filter buttons in Tracks view, the display shows only those tracks

in the Tracks area that are of the selected types defined by the filter buttons. Limiting the displayed channels can be helpful when concentrating on a specific aspect of the mix, or when screen real estate is in high demand. By default, all the filter buttons are selected, thereby displaying every type of channel available in a given view.

To better understand this functionality, let's look at the channels in their entirety. Screenset 2 is configured to display the Mixer window alone.

1   Press 2 to open screenset 2.

2   Click the Audio channel strip filter button (it is currently active) to deselect it.

All audio channels in the arrangement are hidden, leaving a single instrument channel plus the aux, output, and master channels used by the Tracks area tracks.

3   Click the Audio button again.

All channel types are now active, and the complete arrangement is visible.

Using All View

The Mixer's All view displays all the channels available in the project, grouped by type (audio, software instrument, aux, and so on) and organized in ascending order (Audio 1, Audio 2, Audio 3, and so on).

Because the channels displayed in All view correspond to type and not to tracks in the Tracks area, you can use this view to look at channels—such as output and master channels—that are not otherwise contained in your arrangement. As in Tracks view, channels in All view are displayed via the channel strip filter buttons. The channel strip filter selections made for the Tracks and All views are independent, and they remain intact even when you toggle between the display modes.

Rather than use All view to display multiple (or all) types of channels, dedicate All view to a single type of channel, such as output channels. All view then becomes an "alternative" Mixer that provides quick access to a frequently used channel type in a mix.

In this exercise, you will set up All view as a dedicated output mixer.

1   In the Mixer menu bar, click the All button.

By default, all filter buttons are turned on and display all channel types available in the project's Environment. To view only channels of a specific type, you need to disable all channel strip filter buttons for channels you do not wish to view. This can be time-consuming, but Logic supplies a single-action shortcut.

2   In the menu bar, Option-click the Output button.

All channels disappear and are replaced by the output channels (four stereo channels) available to the project.

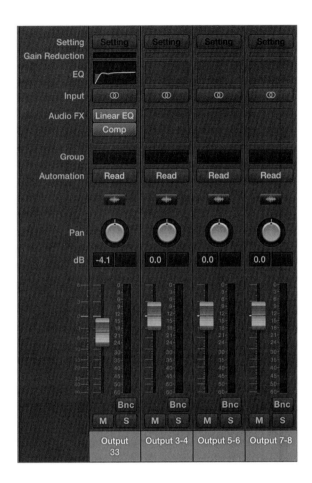

NOTE ► You need an audio interface with at least eight outputs for the output channels to appear active (having a fader, pan control, inserts, and so on). Otherwise, the output channels will be labeled but blank.

Option-clicking a channel strip filter button displays only that selected channel type. You can add other channel types to the view by clicking additional filter buttons.

3   Click the Master button to enable it. The master channel is added to the Mixer.

4   Click the Tracks and All buttons to toggle between the view of the output and master channels (All view) and the tracks used in the arrangement (Tracks view).

Notice that the display modes remember the channel filter settings you last assigned, even when switching between Tracks view and All view.

This setup enables you to conveniently access individual outputs on your audio interface as you adjust volume levels, apply signal processing, or perform bounces.

The channel strip filter settings are saved in the screenset, so you can make them a part of your permanent Mix setup.

5   Unlock, and then lock the screenset, which saves your changes.

Using Single View

Single view essentially limits the Mixer display to a single selected channel and all channel strips that are a part of its signal path. This view offers an effective display in which to trace the signal flow from track to output, including all send destinations (aux channels). You can leave Single view enabled as you select source channels via the Tracks area's track list, but toggling it on and off while you're mixing in the other views makes more sense, especially when working with just the Mixer window in the screenset. Doing so allows you to quickly focus in on, and make adjustments to, a single channel's signal flow and then return to working on the total mix.

1   In the menu bar, click the Tracks button if it's not already selected.

2   Click the BANJ2020 channel strip (track 12).

3   Click the Single button.

The complete signal flow stemming from the BANJ2020 channel is displayed, including the send destination (Chamber) and the output and master channels.

4   Click the Tracks button to return to the overall mix.

Creating Production Notes

In Logic, you can quickly create production notes to comment on takes, indicate mix settings, and save session information along with the project file. Notes can be created in a dedicated Notes area adjunct to the Tracks window, as well as in the Mixer window.

1   Press 1 to open screenset 1.

2   In the Tracks window, click the Note Pads button. The Notes area opens.

As you can see, project information was already entered in the Notes area under the Project tab. The Notes area also has a Track tab that allows you to enter notes associated with a selected track.

3   Click the Track tab.

4   In the Tracks area, select the Kick track (track 32).

5   In the Notes area, click the Edit button.

6   In the Notes area, enter *Kick needs more low end*.

NOTE ▶ You can change the font, size, and style of the note text by clicking the Fonts button.

7   Close the Notes area by clicking the Note Pads button.

As mentioned earlier, you can create and view track notes in the Mixer window.

8   Press 2 to open screenset 2.

Notes are displayed on the channel strip via the Channel Strip Components menu.

9   Choose View > Channel Strip Components > Notes. The Mixer expands vertically, revealing the Notes area beneath the channel strips.

Panning Stereo Tracks

The Mixer channels offer true stereo functionality without requiring you to dedicate two tracks (a left and a right channel) for playback. This feature enables playback of inter-leaved stereo files, stereo software instruments, and stereo busses through a single mixer channel, providing ease of use when working with stereo sources.

On stereo channels in the Mixer, the Balance control balances the relative levels of the stereo track's left and right channels. Adjusting the balance of a stereo track reduces one side in favor of the other.

For example, imagine a stereo drum overheads track that has the hi-hat on the left side of the stereo field and the ride cymbal on the right. If the track's Balance control is turned to the left, the right side of the signal diminishes in volume, losing the ride. If the knob is turned to the right, the opposite happens, reducing the hi-hat signal in favor of the ride.

While this stereo balance function is easy to use, it also represents a limitation when placing a sound in a mix's stereo field. It is often necessary to reposition the center of a recorded stereo signal in the mix while changing the spread (stereo width). Fortunately, Logic offers a handy plug-in, the Direction Mixer, that does this for any stereo track. The plug-in produces a more focused sound, as you are truly panning a stereo signal instead of adjusting the signal level of the left and right channels.

1   Select the Piano channel strip (track 20). Then click the third Insert slot, and from the pop-up menu, choose Imaging > Direction Mixer > Stereo. The Direction Mixer plug-in window opens.

TIP ▶ You can also click a plug-in name in the pop-up menu to insert it, rather than choosing the format (mono, stereo, or 5.1) in the subsequent menu. When doing so, Logic automatically selects the format that best matches the channel.

The Direction Mixer plug-in offers panning functionality via the Direction parameter. Graphically, the Direction knob is quite different from the Pan control used on mono tracks. Values in the range of –90 to +90 degrees represent the full stereo field; greater and lesser values (from +90 to +180 or from –90 to –180 degrees) bring the middle of the signal back toward the center, but with the left and right sides reversed. At +180 (or –180) degrees, the signal is dead center, but with the left and right sides inverted.

2   Drag the Direction knob up to set a value of about +22, thereby placing the center of the Piano signal slightly to the right side of the mix.

In addition to positioning the middle of the stereo signal across the stereo field, you can use the Direction Mixer plug-in to widen or tighten the spread of the stereo base by adjusting the Spread parameter. A setting of 1.0 maintains the width of the original signal. Lower settings bring the sides toward the center, decreasing the spread.

3   Drag one of the Spread sliders to set a value of 0.8.

This tightens up the stereo signal so that it doesn't take up quite as much width in the stereo mix.

4   Click the Solo button for the Piano channel.

5   Press Shift-Spacebar (Play from Selection) to play the project from the beginning of the Piano part.

NOTE ▶ Although the Tracks area is not displayed in the current screenset, you are actually selecting the region information when clicking the channel strip. As another example of the link between the Tracks area and Mixer, this functionality enables you to select track material and play using the Play from Selection command without leaving the Mixer.

6   While the project is playing, toggle the Bypass button on and off to hear the Piano track with and without the Direction Mixer.

Notice that with the Direction Mixer active, the piano sounds as if it's sitting slightly to the right, but the stereo image is not compromised. If you had used the main Balance control to do the same thing, you might have lost the sound of the low notes on the piano, because they are normally heard in the left side of the stereo image.

7   With the Direction Mixer plug-in active (bypass is off), stop playback and close the Direction Mixer window.

8   On the Piano channel, click the Solo button to unsolo the channel.

9   Play the project again, this time listening to how the Piano track fits in the stereo mix. Stop playback when you are done.

NOTE ▶ The Direction Mixer plug-in also decodes MS (middle-side) mic'd stereo recordings. Once the MS mode is engaged (by clicking the MS button), you can alter the stereo signal with the Spread and Direction controls as you would with standard left-right stereo signals.

Switching the Contents of the Plug-in Window

Accessing the multitude of active plug-ins in a project can be a clumsy process requiring the opening and closing of each plug-in window. By linking plug-in windows, you can create a simple way to navigate around the active plug-ins and view their contents in the same window, regardless of their channel locations.

This navigation technique also helps when you're copying presets from one location to another and identical processing is required. The two acoustic guitar tracks are a good example, since they could both benefit from similar EQ and dynamics processing. In this exercise you'll navigate from the ACGTR channel to the ACGTRDBL channel using the plug-in window menus, while copying and pasting settings from one plug-in to another.

1   In the Mixer, look at the two adjacent acoustic guitar tracks (tracks 14 and 15).

    Notice that they have identical plug-ins at the same Insert slots in the channels. However, the ACGTR plug-ins have customized settings, which you will copy to ACGTRDBL.

    To use this technique, you need to have an open plug-in window.

2   In the ACGTR channel (track 14), double-click the Channel EQ plug-in to open the plug-in window.

    The EQ curve indicates a steep high-pass filter at around 100 Hz, a subtle dip at around 295 Hz, and a smaller boost at around 2350 Hz.

3   Click the Copy button.

Doing so copies the EQ plug-in settings from ACGTR, which you can now paste into the Channel EQ in the ACGTRDBL channel. By enabling Link, you can view the Channel EQ setting for ACGTRDBL in the same plug-in window.

4   Click the Link button.

5   Click the Channel EQ located in the first Insert slot on the ACGTRDBL channel.

The ACGTRDBL Channel EQ settings (default) are now displayed in the plug-in window (evidenced by the text at the top of the plug-in window).

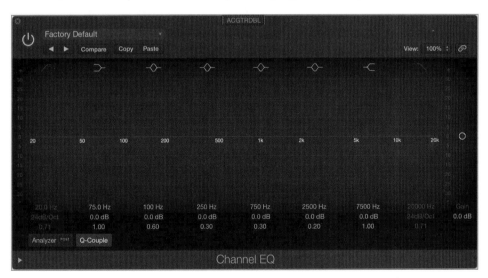

6   Click the Paste button. The plug-in settings from ACGTR are pasted into the Channel EQ of ACGTRDBL.

Let's move on to display the Compressor plug-in, located in the second Insert slot for the ACGTR channel. You'll use its settings to copy and paste into the other channel's Compressor plug-in.

7   In the second Insert slot on the ACGTR channel, click the Compressor.

The Compressor interface now appears in the plug-in window.

8   Click the Copy button.

9   Click the Compressor located in the second Insert slot on the ACGTRDBL channel.

The Compressor inserted in the second Insert slot on the ACGTRDBL channel is displayed in the plug-in window.

10   Click the Paste button.

The Compressor plug-in setting from ACGTR is pasted onto the Compressor of ACGTRDBL.

11   Close the plug-in window.

Changing Plug-in Locations

Where you place an effect in the signal flow is as important as which effect you place. Inserting effects at different orders in the signal chain can lead to different results depending on the processing involved.

Changing effect placement is easily done in the Mixer by dragging with the Pointer tool. You can try this by changing the order of the lead vocal signal chain (track 1), placing the EQ after the Compressor.

1   In the Mixer, select the LVOX (track 1) channel, and then solo the channel.

2   In the first Insert slot on track 1 (the LVOX channel), click the middle of the Channel EQ and drag downward to place it between Insert slots 2 and 3 (a line will appear between Insert slots 2 and 3).

The signal chain reflects the new order, inserting the Channel EQ (including the settings) after the Compressor.

NOTE ▶ When dragging plug-in locations, pay special attention to the area where you release the mouse button, as this affects placement in the signal chain (top to bottom). A light rectangle or line appears to help you place the plug-in. With careful placement, you can put plug-ins above or below the others (indicated by a line) in the signal chain, and even swap locations (the target slot will be indicated by a rectangle).

3   Press Shift-Spacebar to play the project and listen to the lead vocal channel with the new plug-in order.

4   While it's playing, drag the Channel EQ plug-in back to the first Insert slot. The plug-in changes position, even when the project is playing.

5   Stop playback.

TIP ▶ This technique also works for dragging Insert plug-ins from one channel to another. If you do this, make sure to keep format (mono, stereo, or 5.1) compatibility between the two channels in mind. You can even copy plug-ins from location to location by pressing the Option key while dragging.

Using a Plug-in's Extended Parameters

Many of the Logic plug-ins (both instruments and effects) have extended parameters that are hidden from the standard interface by default. These settings are worth exploring and are easily accessed by clicking the disclosure triangle at the lower left of the plug-in interface.

The Tape Delay parameters on the LVOX channel sound great but could benefit from a little coloration to make the result sound more like the pleasing harmonic distortion associated with tape-based saturation. You can add this coloration using the Distortion Level parameter located in the Tape Delay's extended parameters.

1   In the LVOX channel (track 1), double-click the Tape Delay plug-in to open the plug-in window.

2   At the lower left of the Tape Delay's interface, click the disclosure triangle. The extended parameters appear at the bottom of the plug-in window.

3   Drag the Distortion Level slider to the right to a setting of 3.000 db. While subtle, this adjustment introduces gentle audio clipping, emulating a vintage tape delay system or echo unit.

4   Unsolo the LVOX channel, and then listen to the effects processing applied to the track in the context of the mix.

5   Close the Tape Delay window and stop playback.

Using Mixer Groups

A group is used to link similar controls (panning, volume, and so on) in different channels. This creates a direct relationship among all the channels in the group assignment. As a result, when you adjust the parameters on one channel, the same parameters are adjusted in all the group's channels.

Assigning Channels to Groups

In this exercise, you will assign the backing vocals to a group using the same process you learned in the "Editing with Mixer Groups" section in Lesson 8. This time, instead of using this function for editing, you will be linking together specific properties to control in the Mixer.

1   Drag the pointer over channels 4 through 11 (all the backing vocal tracks) to select them.

With multiple tracks selected, you can create an ad-hoc group, which allows you to temporarily do simple things like assign busses.

2   Click the first bus slot of any of the selected channels, and choose Bus 1 (Chamber).

This method is very efficient when performing simple tasks, but it requires that the desired channels be selected to perform an operation. This requirement can be a bit of a hassle, especially when you are currently working on other channels or selecting tracks for editing. By assigning channels to groups, you can link the channel controls whether they are selected or not.

3   Click the Group slot on any of the selected channel strips, and from the pop-up menu, choose Group 6: (new).

NOTE ▶ The Groups list contains a few groups that were created earlier for editing purposes. All are currently inactive.

A faint number 6 appears in the Group slot for all the selected channels to indicate that all groups are currently inactive. Let's now set up the new group's settings and enable it.

4   Click the Group slot again, and from the pop-up menu, choose Open Group Settings.

The Group Settings window opens.

In this window, you can set the channel properties you want to link.

5   In the groups list, scroll down to view slot 6. Click in the Name column, and type *BVOX* for the group name. Press Return.

6   In the Group Settings window, select Solo and Send 1 to link the Solo button and topmost Send knob for the group.

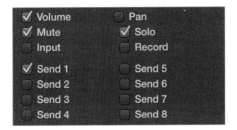

7   At the top of the window, select the "Groups active" checkbox.

8   Close the Group Settings window.

   6: BVOX now appears in the Group slot for each track, which signifies that the channels are assigned to Group 6.

9   Click the BVOXJ channel strip (track 4), selecting it only.

Now that you have assigned the eight channels to a group, you can adjust all tracks simultaneously, including the solo and send controls you specified in the Group Settings window.

In this mix, the harmony vocals need reverb processing to create a more reflective sound. You previously assigned the sends for Bus 1 (Chamber).

Because the channels are similar in character and material, you'd like to have the same send level for all channels sent to this reverb. Because Send 1 was selected in the BVOX Group Settings window, changing any channel's Send 1 value will also cause the others to change.

10   Click the Solo button for the BVOXJ (track 4) channel. The Solo button becomes engaged for all channels.

11   Press Shift-Spacebar to play the project. While listening to the playback, drag up the Send knob on any of the backing vocal channels, applying reverb to your liking. All Send knobs move as you adjust any one.

12   When you are finished setting the reverb level for the channels, stop playback.

Disabling a Group Temporarily

Oftentimes, you need to adjust individual channels of an assigned group without affecting the entire group. At these times, you can temporarily disable the group by using the group clutch, similar to how you used it in Lesson 8 (in the section "Activating and Deactivating Groups Using Group Clutch"). In the current project, the female backing vocals (BVOXS and BVOXS2 channels) could use a bit of a boost in volume to blend with the other parts. To change the faders without affecting the other channels, you need to engage the group clutch, make an adjustment, and then reengage the group by turning off the group clutch.

Previously, you accomplished basically the same thing by selecting the "Groups active" checkbox in the Groups Settings window. This method can be cumbersome because you must open and close this window repeatedly. When mixing, using the group clutch key command (Shift-G) is much more convenient. You will probably be performing this task most often during playback, so the keyboard shortcut makes for a more ergonomic mix process.

1   Play the project, listening closely to the BVOX group.

2   Press Shift-G (the group clutch key command).

The group display dims, indicating that the group clutch is engaged.

3   Drag the BVOXS and BVOXS2 faders up to about –13.0 (dB).

4   Press Shift-G again.

The group display turns from dimmed to yellow (active), indicating that the group clutch is disengaged.

5   With the song still playing, turn off soloing for the BVOX group by clicking any channel's Solo button for the group. You can now hear the entire arrangement.

6   In one of the BVOX group channels, drag the fader to adjust the level of the group in relation to the mix.

All faders move in tandem, maintaining the relative gain between them.

7   Stop playback when you are happy with the volume level of the harmony vocals in relation to the overall mix.

NOTE ▸ Because the part you are playing is at the end of the song, you might run out of material to listen to while doing the mix moves. If necessary, just stop and initiate playback again using the Play from Selection key command (Shift-Spacebar).

Lesson Review

1.   What track data can you import from one project to another?
2.   Explain the difference between the Mixer's Tracks, All, and Single views.
3.   Notes can be created for both the project and what?
4.   Which insert plug-in aids in accurate stereo placement in a mix?
5.   A plug-in window's Link button allows what?
6.   How do you link the controls of multiple channels while mixing?
7.   How do you temporarily disengage a group?

Answers

1. You can import track content, channel strip configuration (including plug-ins and routings), and automation data from one project into another.

2. The Mixer's Tracks view adapts to the Tracks area's track list, and vice versa. The All view displays all the channels existing in a project's Environment, and it can be used to create an alternative mixer with commonly accessed channels. The Single view displays the entire signal flow from a selected channel, including send channels and output.

3. Notes can be created for both the project and tracks.

4. Stereo tracks can be accurately balanced and their images adjusted by means of the Direction Mixer plug-in.

5. The Link button allows navigation from plug-in to plug-in in the same window, making it easier to copy and paste settings between plug-ins.

6. Use groups to link the controls of multiple channels while mixing.

7. Engage the group clutch (press Shift-G).

11

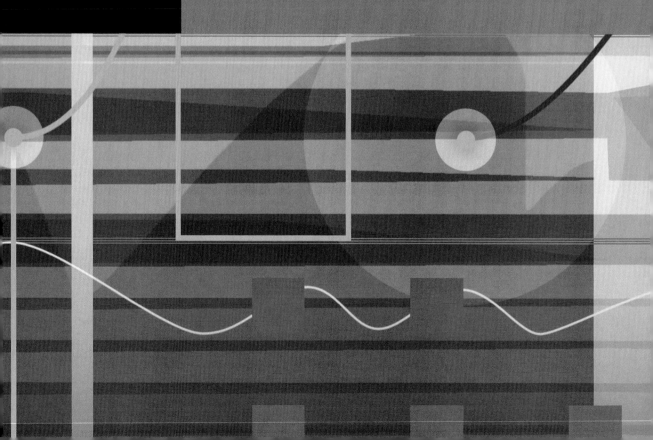

Controlling Signal Flow

In the software world of Logic, a signal is routed from one channel to another via the sends and input/output fields of each channel. Signals are often sent to multiple destinations simultaneously and can even interface with external devices by leaving the audio interface and coming into it again.

In this lesson, you will configure the Mixer to route audio signals to accomplish specific mixing tasks such as side chaining, sending post-pan or pre-fader, parallel processing, and submixing. You will also create bounces of individual regions and tracks that take into account the signal flow of their respective channels. In addition, you will learn how to integrate external effects processors into your signal flow, interfacing the physical world with the virtual one.

Using Side Chain Effects

Side chaining processors is a valuable mixing technique wherein the signal from one channel is used to control an effect on another channel. When side chaining with Logic, the plug-ins involved and how they are routed can take many forms, depending on the desired result.

In this exercise, you will explore a side chain technique employed by mix engineers to add low-end to a kick drum by using a gated sine wave oscillator triggered by the kick drum signal itself.

1   Choose File > Open.

2   Open Music > Advanced Logic X_Files > Lessons > 11_Midnight Wonder.logicx.

3   In the Marker track, drag the first Chorus marker (bar 33–48) upward onto the bar ruler to create a cycle area that encompasses the Chorus section.

4   In the track list, select the Kick track (track 33). Solo the Kick channel, and play the project, listening to the Kick track.

    The kick has a lot of beater sound but could use a bit more low-end body.

5   Press 2 to open screenset 2 (Mixing).

6   Choose Track > New Audio Track.

    A new channel (Audio 29) appears next to the original Kick track.

7   Double-click the name area of the new track, and enter *Kick Osc* to rename it. Press Return.

    By default, Logic created a stereo audio track. To maintain compatibility with the kick drum channel, you need to change it to mono.

8   Change the Channel mode for the Kick Osc track from stereo to mono.

9   On the new Kick Osc channel strip, click the top Insert slot, and from the pop-up menu, choose Utility > Test Oscillator > Mono.

The Test Oscillator plug-in window opens.

NOTE ▶ Your plug-in window may open with Link active. For the purpose of this exercise, disable it so you can see more than one plug-in window at the same time.

The Test Oscillator generates raw waveforms at a set frequency. You will use this to generate the sine wave that will supply the low-end for the kick sound you are trying to create.

By default, when you open a Test Oscillator on an audio track, it will start producing a constant signal. Because the Kick track is still soloed, the Kick Osc channel is muted. You'll be hearing the signal shortly, but for now let's use this advantage to finish setting up the signal chain without the Test Oscillator's incessant sound.

10 In the new Kick Osc channel strip, click the second Insert slot, and from the pop-up menu, choose Dynamics > Noise Gate > Mono. The Noise Gate plug-in window opens.

The Noise Gate allows a signal to pass through only when it is above a set threshold, thereby opening the "gate." When the signal is below the threshold, it reduces the gain by a specified amount, thereby closing the gate.

Because it is placed after the Test Oscillator in the signal chain, the Noise Gate plug-in receives the generated sine wave signal in series. By using a side chain for input, you can have the Noise Gate "listen" to another channel's signal level to open and close the gate instead of the Test Oscillator's, which allows the sine wave to pass through only when the side chain signal is above the set threshold. Using this technique, you can use the original Kick channel (Audio 1) to open and close the gate in time to the kick drum.

11 In the Side Chain menu at the upper right of the Noise Gate plug-in window, choose Audio 1 - Kick.

NOTE ▶ The list displayed in the Side Chain pop-up menu corresponds to the channel type and number, not to the channel order in the Mixer. Channel type and number are displayed in the Mixer at the top of each channel strip.

12 Unsolo the Kick channel (track 33).

13 Solo the Kick Osc channel (track 34).

14 Play the project briefly, and then click Stop.

You should hear an incessant high-pitched sine wave, generated by the Track Oscillator. At the moment, the Noise Gate isn't doing its job—opening and closing in time to the kick drum signal routed to the side chain. The threshold level must be set to close the gate at a higher gain setting, when the original kick signal level falls after the initial transient.

15 Play the project. While listening to the oscillator, raise the Threshold slider to about –13 dB.

The sine wave now triggers in time with the original kick track. Whenever the signal rises above the threshold level, the Activity indicator lights and the gate "opens," allowing the Test Oscillator to be heard. The result is a sine wave playing in time to the kick drum.

The frequency of the sine wave is much too high to supply the needed low end that is the goal of the exercise. You can change the frequency of the Test Oscillator's generated sine wave using the Frequency knob.

16 While playing the project, drag the Test Oscillator's Frequency knob down to about 50.000Hz.

TIP ▶ You can further shape the generated sine wave using the Noise Gate's Attack, Hold, and Release knobs, extending or shortening the envelope characteristics of the sound for different effects.

You can monitor the side chain signal coming into the Noise Gate by selecting the Monitor option in the Side Chain section. This is an excellent way to troubleshoot the signal flow if you are experiencing any problems.

17 In the Noise Gate window, select the Monitor checkbox.

The original Kick track now sounds through the Kick Osc channel, routed in via the side chain. You probably noticed the spillage of the toms picked up by the kick drum mic. As this signal is used to open and close the gate, the toms might cause undesired triggering. Fortunately, the Noise Gate's Side Chain section also contains controls to limit the side chain input to a specific frequency so you can key into a specific frequency range for the trigger. Because the kick drum signal is lower in frequency than the toms, you can filter out most of the toms signal from entering the side chain input.

18 Drag the High Cut slider all the way to the left to 200 Hz.

As you can hear via the side chain monitor, most of the toms signal is cut out, leaving a strong kick drum fundamental. Although it doesn't sound stellar, this result provides an effective trigger for the Noise Gate.

19 Deselect the Monitor checkbox.

Now that you've created your routing, you'll balance the two signals and blend them to create a single kick sound.

20 Close the Noise Gate and Test Oscillator plug-in windows.

21 Solo the Kick channel (track 33).

22 While playing the project, reduce the Kick Osc channel's volume so that it is barely noticeable (around –17 db or lower), supplying a bit more low end to the original kick drum sound.

23 Unsolo both the Kick and Kick Osc channels.

24 Listen to the newly layered kick drum sound in context of the mix. Stop playback.

▶ **Side Chain Techniques**

Side chaining is used for many tasks. Try using some of the following techniques for both mixing and sound-generation purposes:

▶ Use a Noise Gate on a bass track set to receive side chain input from the Kick drum, opening the gate only when the kick sounds. Doing so tightens the timing of the two parts, locking them together.

▶ Use a Compressor on a rhythm instrument or entire mix set to receive side chain input from a vocal track, "ducking" the sound when the vocal signal is present.

▶ Use the side chain input on the EVOC 20 PS Vocoder Synth to route a vocal (or other) track in as the analyzed signal.

▶ Use the side chain input on the ES1, ES2, or Ultrabeat to route audio signals into the synthesizers. Use the filters, envelopes, and modulation sections to shape the sound.

Positioning Sends Pre or Post Channel Strip Controls

In Logic channels, signal flows from the inserts to the volume fader, followed by the pan control. You can configure send controls to route signals at various points in the channel strip's signal chain. When you first open a send on a channel, it routes the signal post-volume and post-pan, which means that the signal routed to the busses will change along with both the volume fader movements and the pan control. This default behavior is the standard setup for mixing when sending signals to reverbs and delays that are inserted on aux channels.

However, sometimes more flexibility is required, such as the ability to send a signal pre-fader. In this exercise, you will try out both default and custom settings, using post-pan sends for parallel compression on the drum channels, as well as setting up a headphone mix using pre-fader sends.

Creating Parallel Compression Using Post-Pan Sends

Parallel compression is a mixing technique that applies compression to a channel's signal via a bus instead of using a channel insert. This setup is often utilized to layer a heavily compressed signal with the original one, providing the sonic coloration of aggressive compression while maintaining the dynamic characteristic of the original channel's signal.

When you use this technique with a group of channels, make sure you maintain the pan relationship of the original channels when you send to the aux channel for processing. By sending post-pan, the panning of the individual tracks is retained, and it is reflected in the stereo bus.

In this exercise, you will apply parallel compression to the drum channels using post-pan sends to maintain the stereo image.

1   In the Mixer, drag over the track names of the drum channels (channels 27–34).

2   On any of the selected drum channels, click the next available Send slot and choose Bus > Bus 7.

All selected channels now have a send assigned to Bus 7, and a new aux channel is created with its input set to Bus 7.

3   Press and hold down the mouse button over any of the newly created Bus 7 sends and look at the menu.

By default, Logic creates a post-pan send when instantiated. When sending a signal post-pan, you are also sending post-fader. As a result, both the panning and the volume levels for each channel are maintained when sending to the bus. For this reason, you should set all send levels to the same setting (unity gain, or 0 dB, is best) when applying parallel compression because the levels hitting the compressor should reflect the volume levels set in the faders.

4   On any of the selected channels, Option-click the Send level knob to set all levels to unity gain.

NOTE ▶ The Send knobs are displayed in green when configured post-pan.

5   On any of the selected channels, double-click the Send slot (Bus 7).

The Mixer automatically locates to a newly created aux channel (Aux 7). This channel will be used to apply parallel compression to the signal sent from the drum channels. It helps to differentiate this specialized channel by assigning it a color and name.

6   Choose View > Show Colors, and color the Aux 7 channel red. Close the Colors window after you've assigned a color to the channel.

7   Double-click the channel's name, and enter *Drm Comp*. Press Return.

When creating new aux channels, Logic assigns the format (mono, stereo, surround) of the new aux channel based on the channel from which you assigned the send. In this instance, Logic created a mono Aux because the source channels are all mono. You need to change the Aux channel to stereo in order to maintain imaging for the drums.

8   On the Drm Comp channel, click the Channel Mode button, and from the pop-up menu, choose Stereo.

9   On the Drm Comp channel, click the top Insert slot, and from the pop-up menu, choose Dynamics > Compressor > Stereo.

A compressor is instantiated and ready for use. As stated earlier, the bus compressor in parallel compression is usually set to a fairly aggressive setting, creating a heavily compressed signal to mix in with the original one.

10 In the Settings menu, choose Compressor Tools > VCA Smashed.

Next you'll test the parallel compression routing.

11 Solo the Drm Comp channel.

12 Play the project. You hear the drum channels signal, heavily compressed. Stop playback.

Because the signal is being sent to the bus post-fader (in addition to post-pan), any change in volume levels of the source channels will change the level of the compressed signal. This situation can be a handicap when trying to blend the signals during a mix because one is dependent on the other.

Apple Pro Training Series: Logic Pro X: Professional Music Production discusses how to use summing track stacks to create a submix by routing the signal output of selected channels to a single aux channel. You can use this same technique to submix the signals from all the drum tracks, which allows you to adjust the volume level of the entire drum kit while leaving the independent channel volume faders in place.

Track stacks can only be assigned in the track list.

13 Press 1 to open screenset 1.

14 Command-click each of the drum tracks (tracks 27–34) to select them.

15 Choose Track > Create Track Stack.

16 In the Track Stack dialog, select Summing Stack, and click Create.

The tracks are placed into a new summing track named Sum 8.

17 Double-click the summing track, and rename it *Drm Sub*. Press Enter.

18 Click the disclosure triangle on the Drm Sub summing track to hide the subtracks.

This channel will be your submix fader for the unaffected drum signal. Now that the submix is created, let's finish the job in the Mixer.

19 Press 2 to open screenset 2.

Let's test your signal routing and fine-tune the relationship between the heavily compressed bus (Drm Comp) and the original channels (Drm Sub).

20 Solo the Drm Sub channel. (You previously soloed Drm Comp channel.)

21 Play the project.

You now hear the signals from the original drum channels layered with the heavily compressed Drm Comp channel.

22 While listening to the mix, blend the Drm Sub channel signal with the heavily compressed Drm Comp channel by adjusting their volume faders.

23 Option-click any of the active Solo buttons (to unsolo all channels) and listen to the parallel compressed drums in relation to the entire mix.

24 Stop playback.

> **TIP** ▶ With Logic's compressor plug-in on a submix channel, you can create a similar parallel compression effect by adjusting the compressor's Mix control. However, the approach used in the exercise provides more flexibility because sends can be used to precisely control how much of a particular instrument is included in the compressed chain.

Creating a Headphone Mix Using Pre-Fader Sends

If you have an audio interface with more than two outputs, you can create an independent headphone mix for tracking sessions to provide recording artists with custom mixes for tracking. You can do this by using sends on each channel to pass a signal to an aux channel set to output on a different pair of audio outputs than your main mix.

To make the control room's mix independent of the headphone mix, however, you need to configure the sends pre-fader, and send the signal before it reaches the volume fader in the channel strip. This setup lets you adjust the control room mix normally (by adjusting the faders) and adjust the headphone mix via the send levels.

1   In the Mixer's local menus, choose Edit > Select All (Command-A). All channel strips are selected.

2   On any of the selected *stereo* channels (Piano, Drm Sub), click the Send slot third from the top (the narrow one at the bottom) and choose Bus > Bus 9. All channels (including the reverb returns and submixes) now have a send assigned to Bus 9.

3   Hold down the mouse button over any of the newly created Bus 9 sends and choose Pre Fader.

NOTE ▶ When Pre Fader is selected, the send knob relocates to the left of the send field to represent the change in signal flow.

4   In any selected channel, double-click the Send slot (Bus 9) you just created. The Mixer automatically locates to a newly created aux channel (Aux 9).

5   Using the technique you used earlier in the lesson, color the channel purple and name the channel *Phones*. Press Return.

The Phones aux channel is now set to output to the main stereo outs. To create an independent headphone mix, however, you need to assign the output of the bus to a spare pair of outputs on your audio interface (connected to a headphone amplifier box and headphones).

TIP ▸ Some audio interfaces have built-in headphone amplifiers you can assign separately from the other inputs and outputs. Using them eliminates the need for an external headphone amplifier box.

6   On the Phones aux channel, click the output field and select an available pair of outputs on your audio interface.

NOTE ▸ If your system configuration does not include at least four outputs, you can still follow along with the exercise by using output 1-2 for the Phones channel, and assigning all other channels to No Output.

Each channel's send level dictates how much signal will be sent to the bus (regardless of the channel fader settings), and allows you to create an entirely independent mix for headphones using the send controls on each channel.

7   Play the project.

8   While listening to your headphones, adjust the send amount to Bus 9 on all channels, one at a time, creating a headphone mix.

NOTE ▸ The Master channel's fader position affects the volume of all outputs, including any headphone cues.

9   Stop the project.

TIP ▸ You can create as many headphone mixes as you have free pairs of audio interface outputs. For each headphone mix, you will need to create a pre-fader send. This allows independent mixes to be created for each artist tracking.

Labeling Your Audio Interface's Inputs and Outputs

In a studio environment built around Logic, the audio interface is the hub for all audio input and output (I/O) signals moving through the computer. Keeping track of signal flow is vital, especially when you need to integrate external gear such as preamps and reverbs into your setup.

Fortunately, Logic lets you assign tags to any input, output, or bus channel using a method similar to physically labeling a patch bay. These definitions are global, which makes the labels accessible to any project file or template.

In this exercise, you will set Logic to use the audio interface's default labeling as provided by the manufacturer, and you'll create your own custom label for connecting an external processor.

> **NOTE ▶** Ideally, your system configuration should include at least six inputs and outputs to create the following routing without decoupling the headphone mix created in the previous exercise. However, if your system configuration includes only four inputs and outputs, you can still follow along with the exercise by assigning all track channels to Stereo Output, and the Phones channel to No Output, thereby freeing up a pair of channels to use for the following exercise.

1   Choose Mix > I/O Labels to open the I/O Labels window.

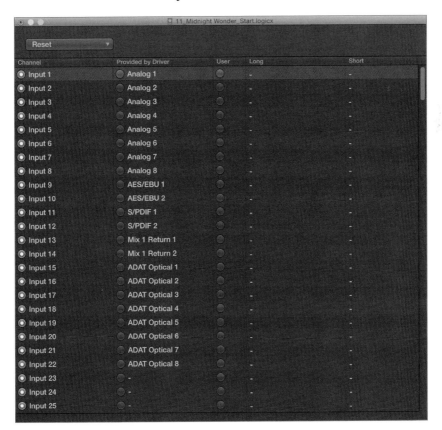

On the left are the default labels for each physical input and output of the audio interface. Immediately to the right, in the "Provided by Driver" column, are corresponding
labels supplied by the audio interface's driver.

NOTE ▶ This window corresponds to the unique setup for the audio interface hardware you are using. Therefore, the figures shown here may differ slightly from what
you see on your system.

The labels supplied by the audio interface's driver more accurately describe the type
of connection than the default labels. Enabling these is a good idea, if they are not
already enabled.

2   Choose Edit > Select All (or press Command-A) to select all I/O assignments in the
I/O Labels window.

3   Click any radio button in the "Provided by Driver" column to enable it.

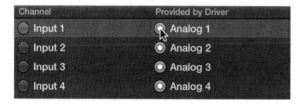

All labels in the "Provided by Driver" column are enabled.

These labels may suffice for generic channels, but for the purpose of connecting a
specific piece of outboard gear, such as an external reverb processor, you are better off
creating a custom label so you can easily identify the processor channel in the Mixer.

4   Scroll down the I/O Labels window to view the stereo choices (Input 1-2, 3-4, and so on).

5   In the User column of the Input 5-6 row, click the radio button to enable it.

6   In the Long column, double-click the data field and enter *PCM92*. Press Return.

7   In the Short column, double-click the data field and enter *PCM92*. Press Return.

8   Scroll down in the I/O Labels window and rename Output 5-6 as in the following figure.

You are now set up to view the new labeling the next time you access the input and output fields in the Mixer.

9   Close the I/O Labels window.

Incorporating External Effects Processors

Although software effects processors can offer distinct advantages over external processors, having high-quality hardware processors in the signal chain can uniquely improve the sound. External effects processors are easily incorporated into the Logic Mixer with a "helper" plug-in that manages the flow to the processor from the audio interface's inputs and outputs.

Using the I/O plug-in, you can treat the external processor almost as if it were itself a software plug-in, inserting it into a channel or applying it as a send effect in the Mixer. To illustrate this technique, you will insert an imaginary hardware reverb unit as a send effect.

To enable the integration in this exercise, you need to physically send a signal from your audio interface to your hardware processor and back again. This is done by connecting an open pair of outputs from your audio interface to the stereo inputs of the hardware reverb, and connecting the stereo outputs of the hardware reverb back to an open pair of stereo inputs on the audio interface.

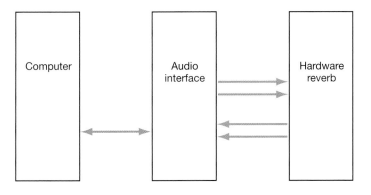

If you have a hardware reverb processor, try this by connecting the equipment according to the preceding diagram, using inputs 5-6 and outputs 5-6 of your audio interface. If not, follow along with an "imaginary" external processor connected.

Once this physical cabling is completed, you need to create a new aux channel to feed the external hardware.

1   Choose Options > Create New Auxiliary Channel Strip.

A new aux channel (Aux 10) appears in the Mixer, with its input set to 1-2. To use this as an effect send and return, you must set the input to a bus.

2   In the Input field, select Bus 10.

3   Double-click the track name for Aux 10, and rename it *Ext verb*.

TIP ▶ Clearly name aux channels that feed external hardware to differentiate them from the Logic internal send effects.

If this channel is to function as a send effect, you'll need to route to the external effects processor. This is done via the I/O plug-in.

4   In the Ext verb channel, click the top Insert slot, and choose Utility > I/O > Stereo. The I/O plug-in window opens.

The next step is to assign the appropriate inputs and outputs of the audio interface to access the hardware processor. This is done via the Input and Output menus.

5   Click the Output menu and choose 5-6 (PCM92).

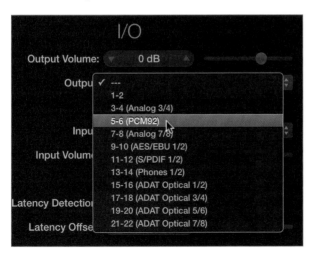

6 Click the Input menu and choose 5-6 (PCM92).

You can now send signals to the hardware reverb inserted on the Ext verb channel just as you would for any send effect by using the channel Send menu.

7 In any channel, click the next available Send slot, and from the pop-up menu, choose Bus > Bus 10 (Ext verb).

NOTE ▶ As when reverb plug-ins are inserted as bus effects, the wet-dry ratio on the external hardware reverb should be set to 100% wet.

8 Turn off Cycle mode.

9 Play the project. While the project is playing, on the channel you are sending to the external reverb, drag up the Send knob to adjust the amount of signal sent to the hardware reverb on Bus 10.

10 Raise the return level by dragging the Ext verb channel fader up until you can hear the effect.

NOTE ▶ Because all external hardware processors are different, you might need to adjust the send and return levels in Logic to achieve optimum gain staging. You can also apply additional signal gain going to and from the external effects processor by dragging the Output Volume and Input Volume sliders on the I/O plug-in. When using this setup, do not change the Logic master channel strip fader or master fader in the Transport bar because doing so changes the volume level of all output channels, and therefore, also changes your send levels to the external hardware.

11 Stop the project playback.

TIP ▶ You can also use the I/O plug-in as an insert effect, sending signals to and from external effects processors such as hardware compressors, EQs, stomp boxes, and so on.

Bouncing in Place

Logic can bounce both regions and tracks "in place," or in their original position on the timeline, which is extremely useful for "rendering," or creating a version of the data with all channel strip processing applied, saving CPU resources. The Logic Bounce in Place features provide a great deal of flexibility when producing the new file, enabling you to bounce the channel's audio signal with or without plug-ins, effect tail, and volume and pan automation.

> **NOTE ▶** You cannot perform an in-place bounce of a region routed to a MIDI channel strip.

1   Open screenset 1.

2   In the track list, select the BKWD BANJ (track 14) track. The regions at the end of the Chorus sections are selected.

3   Use the Zoom tool to zoom in on the first of the selected BKWD BANJ regions (bars 46–47).

4   Solo the BKWD BANJ track.

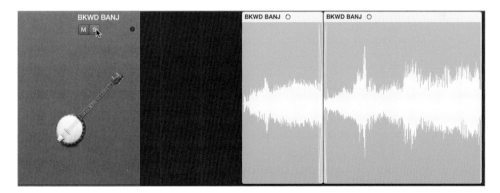

5   Press Shift-Spacebar to play the project from the selected regions, stopping after you've had a chance to listen to the selected BKWD BANJ region.

6   Unsolo the BKWD BANJ track.

7   In the Inspector, look at the track's channel strip.

As you can see (and hear), the channel has plug-ins inserted, applying EQ and Enverb (set to create a backward reverb effect) to the selected region. In this exercise, you will use the Bounce in Place feature to create a new version of both BKWD BANJ regions, with signal processing applied, at the exact same point in the timeline.

8   Choose File > Bounce > Regions in Place to open the Bounce Regions In Place dialog.

You have a few things to consider before performing the bounce. One consideration is whether or not to create a new track (and channel strip) for the bounced region, and what to do with the original region after the bounce is performed.

9   In the Destination section, select New Track, if necessary.

10   In the Source section, select Mute, if necessary.

Enabling these settings creates a bounced region on a new track, and automatically mutes the original region.

Another thing to consider when bouncing is whether or not to apply the channel's active inserts, printing the effect to the new file. To do this, you need to deselect the Bypass Effect Plug-ins option.

11 Deselect the Bypass Effects Plug-ins option, if necessary.

Clicking OK at this point would create a new file without the full decay—or "tail" of the reverb plug-in inserted on the channel—because it lasts longer than the length of the original region.

The "Bounce in Place" feature can compensate for the added time incurred by the tail by creating a new recording that allows the tail to die out naturally without clipping it short.

12 Select "Include Audio Tail in File" and "Include Audio Tail in Region." Deselect "Include Volume/Pan Automation," if necessary.

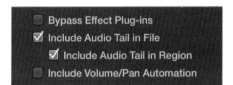

If "Include Volume/Pan Automation" were selected, Logic would render a new file with the existing volume and pan automation data. This isn't necessary in this instance because the new track will contain the original track's automation.

NOTE ▸ If "Include Audio Tail in Region" is deselected when bouncing, a new audio file is created, including the added time incurred by the tail. This time, however, the region length is preserved, and does not adapt to include the added time. In effect, Logic will not play the tail, but you can still make it available by dragging the region borders.

13 Zoom out horizontally and vertically so you can see both the original and newly created regions.

14 Click OK.

A new track and region (BKWD BANJ_bip) are created underneath the BKWD BANJ track, and the original region is now muted. Note that the newly created channel does not have any plug-ins instantiated, but it does have the same volume setting and send assignments as the original channel.

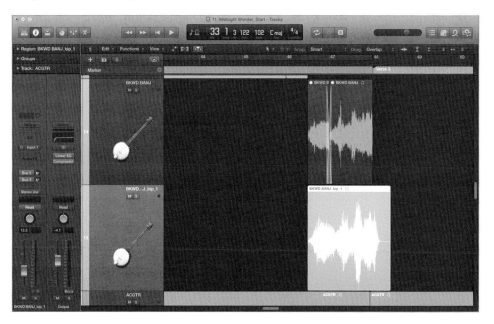

15 Play the project from about bar 44, listening to the newly created region and channel. It sounds exactly the same as the original. Stop playback.

NOTE ▶ Once the original region and channel is no longer necessary, you can delete the channel and region to conserve valuable CPU power.

Rendering Software Instrument Tracks as Audio

Bouncing in place also works great for rendering software instruments into audio tracks for additional editing, processing, or even exporting to another software application.

1 Press 1 to open screenset 1 again.

2 In the track list, select the Piano track (track 22).

3   Solo the Piano track.

4   Click the Show/Hide Automation button to view the automation data for all tracks.

5   Note the automation and channel strip plug-ins for the Piano track.

The goal here is to replace the original software instrument track with an audio track that has the same signal chain, including the inserted plug-ins and volume automation. This enables you to work with the piano as audio, while still being able to do any additional mixing tweaks you deem necessary.

6   Choose File > Bounce > Track in Place.

The Bounce Track In Place dialog appears.

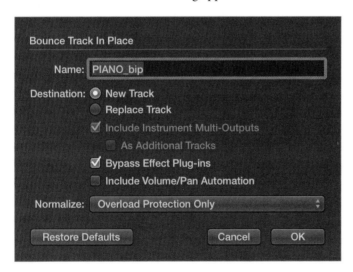

NOTE ▶ This dialog is virtually identical to the Bounce Regions In Place dialog, but it leaves out the Source and Include Audio Tail options.

7   In the Destination section, select Replace Track.

NOTE ▸ When bouncing software instruments that have multi-output capabilities (such as EXS24 and Ultrabeat), you can choose to include the signals from all outputs into the bounce. To do so, select Include Instrument Multi-Outputs. You can also bounce each separate output as an individual track by selecting As Additional Tracks.

8   Select the Bypass Effects Plug-ins option, if necessary.

9   Deselect the Include Volume/Pan Automation option, if necessary.

TIP ▸ In addition to providing standard normalization when bouncing the new file, the Normalize menu also offers downward normalization via the Overload Protection Only item. This acts as a safety net, avoiding clipping when levels rise above 0 dB.

10   Click OK. A new track and channel, PIANO_bip, are created with the signal flow and automation intact, replacing the original.

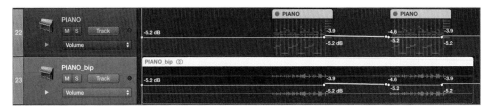

Lesson Review

1.   What is the most efficient way to apply effects processing to multiple channels at once?

2.   Side chaining plug-ins allows you to do what?

3.   Sends can be configured in what three ways?

4.   How do you insert an external effects processor into the signal chain?

5.   When bouncing regions or tracks in place, a channel's audio signal can be rendered to a new audio file with and without what?

Answers

1. Use aux channels as submixes to apply effects processing to multiple channels.

2. Side chaining plug-ins allows you to control an effect on one channel by the signal from another channel.

3. Sends can be configured post-fader, pre-fader, and post-pan.

4. Insert external effects processors into the signal chain using the I/O plug-in.

5. When bouncing regions or tracks in place, a channel's audio signal can be rendered to a new audio file with or without plug-ins, effect tail, and volume and pan automation.

12

Lesson 12
Controlling the Mix

A good mix is a performance of sorts. Like an instrument in an ensemble, each element of a mix speaks its part clearly and expressively, complementing the other elements. This is a dynamic process, frequently involving the continuous adjustment of individual signals as a project progresses.

To create a dynamic-sounding mix, you have to be able to control audio signals over time. Adjusting volume, panning, or even plug-in parameters through the course of a project is an important part of breathing life into a mix.

The comprehensive track-based automation system in Logic allows you to change over time the settings of virtually all channel-related software controls. You can record these movements offline or make them in real-time by using a mouse, dedicated hardware MIDI control surface, or MIDI controller. Whichever entry method you use, you can easily edit and manipulate the automation data after the initial input, giving you control over all the sonic elements in a composition.

In this lesson, you will learn various methods for efficiently tackling specific automation editing tasks, focusing on techniques that get the most from the data you have already entered. In addition, you will learn how to assign MIDI knobs and faders to plug-in parameters and volume and pan controls, transforming your MIDI controller into a powerful control surface.

Editing Automation

When automation is shown, you can easily create offline automation in the Tracks window by clicking in any visible track's automation lane. Live automation, on the other hand, is created by dragging a mouse or manipulating a hardware control surface to send control messages to Logic. However the messages are entered, it is essential that you edit the automation data to control your mix as effectively as possible.

In this exercise, you will automate the mutes for the doubled acoustic guitar channels to create an articulate performance. After a basic shape is made in the automation curve, you will use editing to populate the automation data throughout two related tracks.

> **NOTE ▶** This lesson assumes that you are familiar with the basics of creating and editing automation in Logic. If you need a refresher, see "Automating the Mix" in David Nahmani's *Apple Pro Training Series: Logic Pro X Professional Music Production*.

1   Choose File > Open.

2   Select Music > Advanced Logic X_Files > Lessons > **12_Midnight Wonder.logicx**.

3   Create a cycle region from bar 88 to bar 95. Enable Cycle mode.

4   Use the Zoom tool to drag over the ACGTR and ACGTRDBL regions approximately around the bars defined by the cycle area.

5   Drag-select the Track Solo buttons for both the ACGTR and ACGTRDBL tracks (tracks 16 and 17, respectively), soloing them.

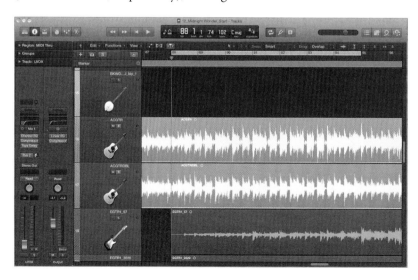

6   Play the project while listening carefully to the two tracks for the length of the cycle. Stop playback.

The doubled guitar parts, while sounding pretty tight with each other, could use more articulation to create a staccato feel at times during the strumming pattern. You can do this by toggling the mutes of each channel at specific points, effectively turning their output on and off.

Snapping Automation Data to the Timeline

You could automate the channel mutes in real time by clicking the mute buttons while in Touch, Latch, or Write mode. However, this live method is not as precise as adding offline automation, wherein you create the data by clicking in the automation lane.

To more easily place the automation data at a musically relevant position (bars, beats, and so on), you can enable Snap Automation. When Snap Automation is turned on, all created nodes and edits are snapped to the grid.

1   Press Command-Right Arrow (the Zoom Horizontal In key command) to zoom in far enough to see only bars 88 and 89.

2   Click the Show/Hide Automation button to reveal the automation data for the project.

3   In the ACGTR track header, from the Automation parameter menu, choose Main > Mute.

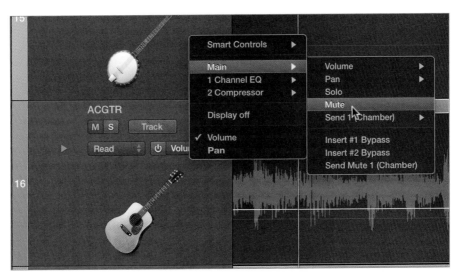

4   In the Tracks area, choose Snap > Snap Automation.

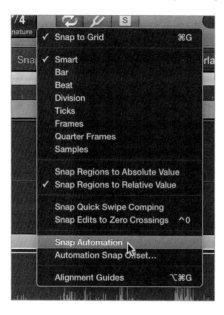

5   Double-click in the lower half of the ACGTR automation track as close to 88 4 2 1 (second sixteenth note of beat four) as possible to create an automation node.

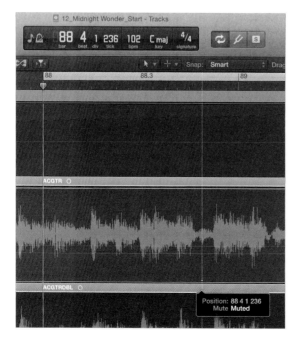

When looking at the help tag, you probably noticed that the node was created slightly earlier (88 4 1 236). This might seem odd at first because you are using Snap Automation, which should align nodes precisely to the grid. However, this placement is correct, due to a setting in the Automation preferences. Let's take a quick look at those preferences before any further editing to understand what is happening here.

6   From the Snap menu, choose Automation Snap Offset to open the Automation Preferences window.

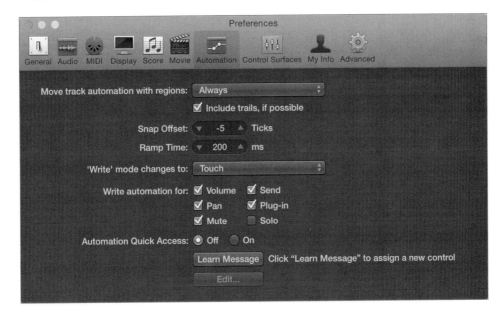

The Snap Offset setting in Automation preferences governs the behavior you just noted, allowing a specific number of ticks to be added or subtracted to the snap automation. Setting the Snap Offset to slightly early (by using negative values) can be advantageous for the acoustic guitar parts because they're slightly ahead of the beat.

7   Close the Preferences window.

8   Double-click in the upper half of the ACGTR automation track as close to 88 4 3 1 (second sixteenth note of beat four) as possible to create an automation node.

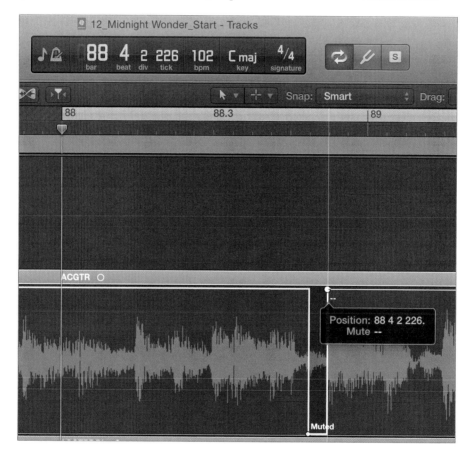

The new automation node is created at 88 4 2 226, slightly earlier than the third sixteenth note of the beat.

Copying Automation

Now that you've created a single mute event (on and off) in the automation track, you could continue the laborious process of adding notes where needed. Copying the existing automation data throughout the automation track, however, is far easier. You can do this one of two ways: by Option-dragging or using copy and paste commands.

1   Shift-drag around the mute automation you created earlier on the ACGTR track, selecting both nodes.

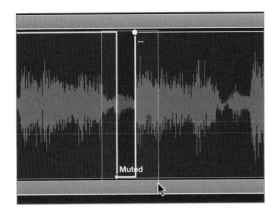

2   Option-drag the lower selected node to the right, thereby copying the automation data to 89 1 3 236 (note the similar waveform).

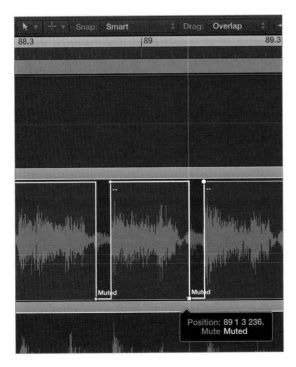

While Option-dragging works well for quick copies, it is sometimes easier to copy the automation data into the buffer, and then paste it at positions specified by the playhead.

3   Choose Edit > Copy to copy the selected automation data (the newly copied automation is still selected).

Before pasting, you must first select the track header of the destination track.

4   Click the ACGTR track header to select the track.

5   Position the playhead at 89 3 1 1.

6   Press Command-V to paste the automation data.

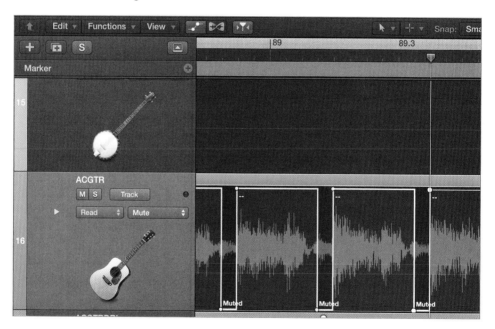

The automation data is pasted at the same relative position.

7   Using the same method, paste the copied automation data at the following positions:

▶   90 1 4 1

▶   90 3 2 1

▶   90 4 4 1

▶   91 3 2 1

▶   91 4 4 1

▶ 92 2 2 1

▶ 92 4 4 1

▶ 93 2 2 1

▶ 93 3 4 1

8   Press Control-Shift-Z (Zoom to Fit Locators) to look at the automation data for the
entire section.

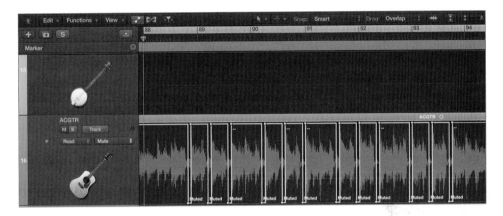

9   Unsolo the ACGTRDBL track.

10 Play the project and listen how the mutes accentuate the articulation of the acoustic
guitar part. Stop playback.

Now that you've created the automation for one acoustic guitar part, you can copy
and paste the data onto the doubled part, precisely placing the mutes in time with
each other.

To make selecting only the relevant data (instead of the entire track) easier, as well
as pasting it at a rational position, start by placing a node in the ACGTR automation
track on the downbeat of a bar.

11 Double-click at the top of the ACGTR automation track at 88 1 1 1.

12 Using the Pointer tool, Shift-drag over the remaining automation nodes (bars 88 through 93) to select them.

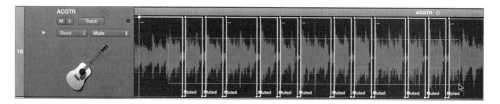

13 Press Command-C to copy the automation.

14 Click the ACGTRDBL track header to select the track.

15 Position the playhead at 88 1 1 1.

16 Press Command-V to paste the automation data onto the ACGTRDBL track.

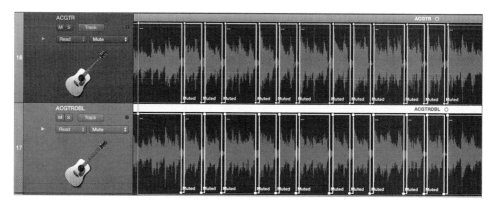

TIP ▶ You can also copy automation data from one parameter to another in a single track by holding down the Command key while choosing parameters in the Automation Parameter menu. Logic will then prompt you to convert (or copy and convert) the data, thereby allowing you to either transfer the automation of one parameter onto another, or copy the data while retaining the original automation.

Bending Automation Curves

Entering offline automation with a mouse generally produces linear automation shapes that possess straight lines and sharp angles. This linearity tends to sound rigid and mechanical in comparison to online automation created by physical gestures. In addition, offline automation fails to scale values from minimum to maximum wherein the data is weighted toward one side or the other (think convex or concave curves), a desirable way to make the automation sound more natural.

Fortunately, Logic offers a way to adjust the offline automation by manually "bending" the line between two automation nodes to create just this sort of "live" gesture. The Banjo part could benefit from this technique to organically create a swell in volume automation, underlining the dynamic change at the end of the Instrumental section.

1   Scroll upward until the BANJ2020 track (track 13) is visible.

2   Zoom out horizontally until you can see bars 88 through 98. Adapt the cycle area to encompass the same bars.

3   Solo the BANJ2020 track.

The Banjo part is displaying volume automation (the yellow line). Let's start by creating a simple crescendo for the last part of the instrumental section leading to the Chorus.

4   Click the automation curve for the BANJ2020 track at 88 1 1 1, thereby creating an automation node.

5   Create additional automation nodes at 97 1 1 1 and 97 2 1 1.

6   Drag the automation node at 97 1 1 1 upward to a value of about –6.6 db.

7   Play the project and listen to the increase in volume automation. Stop playback.

You now have a straight, linear increase in volume of about 4 db. Let's improve on this by creating a surge in volume level that is weighted toward the latter half of the passage. You can do so by bending the automation curve using the Automation Curve tool to create an S-shape. But instead of choosing the tool from the tool menu, let's use one of the hard-wired key commands mentioned in Lesson 1.

8   Control-Shift-click the automation curve between the nodes positioned at 88 1 1 1 and 97 1 1 1, and drag to the right while continuing to hold down the keys.

The automation curve bends into an S-shape.

9   Play the project, listening to the new volume automation curve. Stop playback.

10 Unsolo the BANJ2020 track.

Applying Automation to Multiple Tracks at Once

Channels that are grouped in the Mixer can share automation modes, and also mirror automation written to any of the tracks when the group is active (that is, when group clutch is off). Any edits made to individual automation tracks in a group is reflected in the other tracks as well, which enables you to quickly create offline automation, and to edit real-time automation for groups while working on a single track.

In this exercise, you will add and alter automation data to an entire group of drum tracks at once, creating a surge in volume leading out from the Instrumental section into the last Chorus.

1 Press 2 to open screenset 2.

2 In the Mixer, scroll to the far right to view the drum tracks.

As you can see, the drum tracks were previously assigned to Group 1: Drums. Currently, the groups are inactive (because group clutch is enabled).

3 In any of the tracks, click the Group slot, and from the pop-up menu, choose Open Group Settings. The Group Settings window opens.

You can link (or unlink) the automation mode setting of the group's channels by enabling the Automation Mode checkbox in the Group Settings window. Automation Mode is selected by default.

4 Select the "Groups active" checkbox to enable groups in the Mixer, or disable group clutch by pressing Shift-G.

5   Close the Group Settings window.

6   Press 1 to open screenset 1.

7   In the track list, Shift-click tracks 30 through 36 (OHL through KICK) to select them.

8   Press Z to zoom the selected tracks.

9   Click the Show/Hide Automation button. All drum track volume automation is displayed (currently without data).

10 In any of the selected drum tracks, click in the track automation area around measure 94. New automation nodes are created in each track.

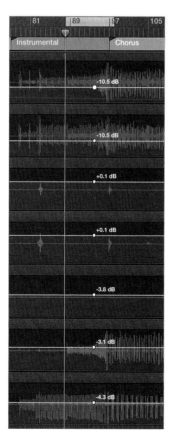

11 Create another automation node at measure 97.

12 In the Kick track, drag the newly created automation node at measure 97 upward to about –1.3 dB (about 3 dB higher than the previous node).

> **TIP** You can alter Volume and Send automation nodes in 0.1 dB increments by holding down the Control key while you change the value.

Notice that each track's automation node also increases in value by 3 dB, reflecting the changes made to automation on any track in the group.

Using VCA Groups

Brand new to Logic Pro 10.1 are console-style VCA groups. These are similar in function to the pre-existing folder track stacks, wherein the stack master fader controls the subtracks as one unit without changing audio routing (as summing track stacks do).

However, VCA faders provide distinct ergonomic functionality, allowing you to place them anywhere in the Mixer without first grouping channels in a folder. They are also ideal for use with live automation, as they put the associated channels underneath your fingers for easy control.

In this exercise, you'll assign the lead vocal track to a VCA group and write automation for the channels all at once.

1 Press 2 to open screenset 2.

2 In the Mixer, scroll to the far left to view the three lead vocal channels.

3 Drag over the three lead vocal channels (LVOX, LVOXDBL, and LVOXTPL) to select them.

4 In any of the selected channels, click the VCA field and choose Create New VCA for Selected Channel Strips.

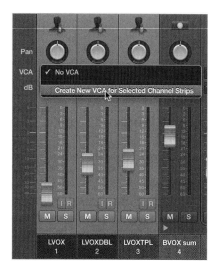

The Mixer automatically scrolls to the right, creating a new VCA 1 fader that is placed immediately to the right of the Master fader.

The goal is to use the VCA fader to write automation and control the channels that are assigned to it. To make the job easier, add the channel to the track list so you can view and edit the automation in the Tracks area. In addition, the VCA is in a less-than-ideal position, as it is quite far from the channels it is controlling. Not to worry, Logic will change its placement when you add the VCA to the Tracks list.

5   From the Options menu, choose Create Tracks for Selected Channel Strips. The VCA channel moves next to the LVOX channel.

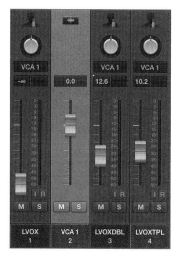

TIP ▶ Like VCA channels, aux channels are not represented in the Tracks area where offline automation is performed. To perform the offline automation of a channel control or plug-in inserted on an aux channel, you must add it to the Tracks area's track list just as you added the VCA channel by choosing Options > Create Tracks for Selected Channel Strips.

You're now ready to use the VCA to control all three lead vocal channels. Let's try it out on the last Chorus section by riding the volume levels to keep the vocal clear and present above the rest of the arrangement.

6   Press 1 to open screenset 1.

7   Drag the last Chorus marker (bars 97 to end) upward onto the bar ruler, creating a cycle area.

8   Press Control-Shift-Z (Zoom to fit Locators) to zoom in on the selected cycle area.

9   Click the Show/Hide Automation button.

10 In the Inspector, click the Automation Mode menu on the VCA 1 channel and choose Latch.

11 While playing the project, drag the VCA 1 fader up and down to create volume automation, listening to the results. When you've reached the end of the song, stop playback.

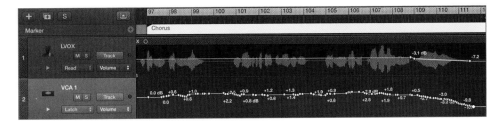

12 Press 2 to switch to screenset 2.

13 From the Automation Mode menu on the VCA channel, choose Read.

14 Play the project while observing the VCA and lead vocal channels.

The output of the three lead vocal channels is attenuated. Note that the VCA fader moves along with the automation curve, but the individual lead vocal channels do not, thereby keeping their same relative levels.

15 Stop playback.

Using Trim Automation to Scale Existing Values

In the basic APTS Logic book, you used the offline trim function to change values for all nodes on an automation curve exponentially by dragging the Automation value. Logic Pro 10.1 also allows you to trim existing automation in real time, scaling the values with a fader as you are listening. This technique is advantageous when using a hardware control surface (covered in the next section) because it puts the ability to attenuate values under your fingertips.

1 Press 1 to switch to screenset 1.

2 Press Control-Shift-Z (Zoom to fit Locators) to zoom in to the selected cycle area.

3 Click the Show/Hide Automation button to see the volume automation you performed with the VCA fader.

   Note that the automation curve you created is quite nuanced, reflecting the movement of your fader-changing values. Using trim automation, you can raise or lower automation values while maintaining the level of detail and contours of the original pass. Think of this as an additional layer of automation, augmenting or diminishing what is already present.

4 In the track header of the VCA 1 channel, from the Automation Mode menu, choose Trim.

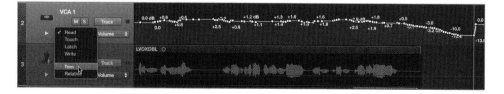

   Now that you've put the VCA 1 channel into Trim mode, you need to select how you want to write the new automation pass.

5 From the Automation Mode menu, choose Touch.

In addition to displaying "T-Touch" in the automation menu, the VCA 1 channel's fader now displays a yellow line underneath the fader that represents the original volume automation, and it changes dynamically as values increase or decrease. Before you write the new trim automation layer, let's observe this behavior.

6   Play the project while observing as the yellow line changes to reflect the contours of the automation curve. Stop playback.

Now let's add the trim automation layer.

7   Play the project, alternately watching the fader value and the automation track itself as you drag the VCA 1 fader up and down. When you've reached the end of the song, stop playback.

While writing, the trim automation layer is displayed as a red line over the original volume automation.

After playback is stopped, Logic calculates the resultant automation curve and displays the changes you made. The original contours are still in evidence, with some alteration dictated by the trim layer.

8   From the Automation Mode menu on the VCA channel, choose Read.

9   Play the project, observing the VCA and listening to the results.

To prepare for the next series of exercises, get the VCA channel out of the way in the track list.

10   In the track list, drag the VCA 1 track to the bottom.

11   Name the project *12_Midnight Wonder_Done*, and save it to Advanced Logic X_Files > Media > Completed.

> **TIP** ▸ Relative mode acts much like Trim mode. However, instead of combining both passes into a third new pass, it keeps the trim layer intact, allowing you to do further editing. Use this mode when you want to keep your options open, including enabling you to delete just the trim layer itself or returning to the original automation curve.

Using Control Surfaces

Although the mouse is suitable for setting controls, you will quickly discover that it is not the ideal tool for performing common mixing moves (such as dragging sliders and faders). With it you can click only one thing at a time, which is an inefficient way to refine your mix.

To truly benefit from using real-time automation, you need to control the channel with something other than the mouse. A hardware control surface that is designed to integrate with the Logic Mixer will provide the best control for real-time automation, but any MIDI controller will do. In addition to standard MIDI controllers like mod and pitch bend wheels, most modern MIDI keyboards have integrated faders, knobs, and buttons that send out MIDI messages that can be assigned to Logic.

In this set of exercises, you will assign the buttons, knobs, and faders on a MIDI controller to both transport and channel controls in the Mixer, giving you hands-on control over your mixes.

> **NOTE** ▸ Logic supports many leading hardware control surfaces with little or no setup. See the Logic Pro X Control Surfaces Support manual for details on supported devices and individual configuration directions.

Assigning Transport Controls

Most modern MIDI controllers have integrated transport buttons that send out MIDI messages. When assigned to the Logic transport controls, these buttons provide remote control of the project from wherever you are playing.

The easiest way to assign MIDI controllers is through the Key Commands window.

> **NOTE** ▶ This exercise requires a connected MIDI controller, preferably with integrated transport controls. However, you can still try the outlined steps with any MIDI button, pad, or key, as long as they are set to send an on/off MIDI command. Refer to your MIDI controller manufacturer's manual for further information as to what would send an on/off message on your keyboard.

1   Press 1 to open screenset 1, making all tracks visible.

2   Choose Logic Pro > Key Commands > Edit.

The Key Commands window opens. Note the Assignments field below the standard "Learn by Key Label" and "Learn by Key Position" buttons. This field displays MIDI messages that have been assigned to the selection in the command column.

You can assign MIDI messages to selected commands by clicking the Learn New Assignment button.

3   If necessary, clear out any text in the search field by clicking the cancel button.

4   Scroll to the top of the key commands list. Click the Global Commands disclosure triangle to display its commands, if necessary.

All the basic transport controls are listed in the Command column (Record, Play, Stop, Rewind, and Forward).

5   In the Command column, select Play.

6   Click the Learn New Assignment button.

At this point, Logic is "listening" for MIDI messages coming in (as evidenced by the selected Learn New Assignments button) and will assign the next message coming in to the play command.

7   On your MIDI controller, press the play button.

The incoming MIDI message is displayed in the Assignments window followed by "Learned," and the Learn New Assignments button is turned off.

NOTE ▶ Avoid sending double commands by making sure that you press only a single button on your MIDI controller, and that you press it only one time. Also make sure to wait for the Learn New Assignment button to turn off before playing your MIDI controller.

Most likely, you noticed that the project started playback when you assigned the MIDI command. This illustrates that the command assignment worked.

8   Stop playback by clicking the Stop button in the transport bar (the key command will not work while the Key Commands window is open).

Let's continue to assign transport buttons in the same manner.

NOTE ▶ Some MIDI controllers' transport buttons send "toggled" values, which sends one value when first pressed, followed by another when pressed again. To make this behavior work with the Logic transport assignments, you need to send and learn both states. Once they are learned, you will see both values in the Assignments window.

9   In the Command column, select Stop.

10   Click the Learn New Assignment button.

11   Press the stop button on your MIDI controller and wait for the Learn New Assignment button to turn off. The button is now assigned to the Stop command.

12   Using the same technique, assign buttons on your MIDI controller to the Forward, Rewind, Cycle Mode, and Record commands.

> **NOTE ►** When you first assign the Record command, it will put Logic into record mode, possibly prompting you for a save location and even initiating recording onto the currently selected track. After assigning the command, make sure to click Stop and delete any unintentional recordings.

13   Close the Key Commands window.

14   Try out your new key commands by locating around the project, playing selected material.

Assigning Channel Controls

The knobs and faders on most modern MIDI controllers are commonly found in sets of eight or more, perfect for pairing each with a specific channel control in the Mixer (volume, pan, sends, and so on).

When assigning a set of MIDI controls to a set of channel controls, think of them as a consecutive series (fader 1, 2, 3, and so on), or bank, instead of isolated controls. These controls should be linked in a one-to-one relationship: For example, the control surface's fader 1 only controls the Logic volume fader; fader 2 should control only channel 2's volume fader; and so on.

In this exercise, you will assign a series of eight MIDI controller knobs or faders to the volume faders on channels 1 through 8 in the Logic Mixer. You can assign and edit all MIDI controllers in the Controller Assignments window.

> **NOTE ►** The following exercises are designed for MIDI controllers with at least eight knobs or faders. However, you can still complete the lesson by creating a similar setup using a smaller set of knobs or faders.

1 Press 1 to open screenset 1.

2 From the Logic Pro X menu, choose Control Surfaces > Controller Assignments. The Controller Assignments window appears.

3 Click the Expert View button, if necessary.

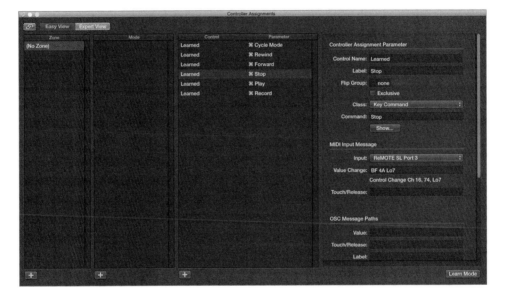

In the Control/Parameter list, you can see all the transport assignments previously made in the Key Commands window.

The right side of the window contains specific information for the selected assignment (the most recently used), including the assigned parameter, MIDI input message, and any value settings.

4   In the Control/Parameter list, select a few assignments and observe their settings in the Controller Assignment Parameter, Input Message, and Value areas. (Scroll down to view the latter.)

> **NOTE** ▸ A MIDI controller sends only 128 different values. To achieve smooth control over parameters that inherently have much finer resolution, Logic scales the MIDI value. This is the default behavior when you make a channel control assignment, and it appears in the Value area in the Mode menu. Also in the Value area, the Min/Max fields let you set a range for the scaled controller, and the Multiply field lets you apply simple math to the input message, thereby changing the speed at which the parameter reacts to the controller's movement.

Now that you've had a look around, let's get started assigning your MIDI controls to the Mixer. To assign each channel independently, first deactivate active groups. Doing so will prevent any unwanted duplicate assignments.

5   Deactivate groups by pressing the Group Clutch key command (Shift-G).

6   In the Mixer, make sure that channels 1 through 8 are not selected (the VCA 1 channel should still be selected from a previous exercise).

7   In the Controller Assignments window, click the Learn Mode button to activate it. Logic is now waiting for MIDI input.

8   Click channel 1's volume fader, which defines the targeted parameter you want to control, as displayed in the Control/Parameter list.

9   Move the first fader or knob of the series of eight on your MIDI controller up and down all the way.

> **NOTE** ▸ When sending continuous controller data, make sure you move the controller from smallest value to largest, so that its entire range is learned.

The assignment is learned, and the MIDI message source and value is displayed in the Input Message area.

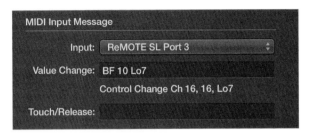

10 With Learn mode still activated, click channel 2's volume fader.

11 Move the second fader or knob of the series of eight on your MIDI controller up and down all the way. The assignment is learned.

12 Repeat the process, clicking the volume fader on channels 3 through 8 and moving the appropriate knob or fader on your MIDI controller one at a time (while Learn mode is still activated).

13 When done, click the Learn Mode button to deactivate it.

You now have a series of assignments that appear in the Control/Parameter list.

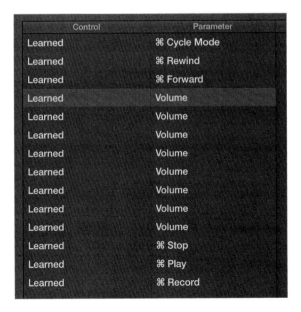

NOTE ► If you make a mistake when assigning a parameter, you can delete the assignment by selecting it in the Control/Parameter list and pressing Delete.

If you look at the Channel Strip settings for the selected assignments, you will see that they are set for Fader Bank. This indicates that each channel will be part of a consecutive series of faders, as specified in the number field to the right.

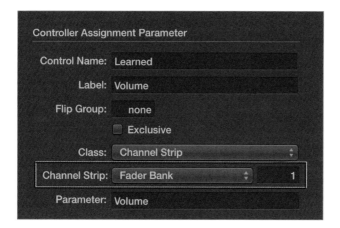

14 Close the Controller Assignments window.

15 Move the knobs or faders you assigned while watching the Logic channel volume faders move.

TIP ► You can also press Command-L (Learn New Controller Assignment key command) to put Logic into Learn mode when the Controller Assignments window is not open. When doing this, you need to hold down the Command key while you are moving the physical control on your MIDI controller, and then release Command when you're done. Essentially, Logic is listening for MIDI input as long as the Command key is pressed.

Mapping the Same Controls to Multiple Parameters

Even if you have only a single set of eight knobs or faders on your MIDI controller, you aren't limited to controlling a single set of channel controls. By creating zones and modes in the Controller Assignments window's Expert view, you can use the same set of physical controllers for volume, pan, sends, and so on, toggling between these mappings via a button from your MIDI controller.

In this exercise, you will create two mapping modes for volume and pan, allowing you to assign the same set of knobs or faders to achieve independent control over both.

1   Choose Logic Pro X > Control Surfaces > Controller Assignments (or press Option-Shift-K) to open the Controller Assignments window.

You're going to assign the same set of knobs or faders to the pan controls on channels 1 through 8. You could assign them one at a time as before, but using the Logic "fill up" feature is much easier. This process requires you to assign only the first and last of the series, and Logic automatically fills in the missing controller assignment information.

NOTE ▸ To use the "fill up" feature, your MIDI controls must be sending consecutive continuous controller (CC) numbers (for example, CC 8 through 16) or MIDI channel numbers (for example, CC 7, Channels 1 through 8) for Logic to extrapolate the missing assignments. You can check which messages are being sent from the MIDI controller by observing the Logic MIDI Activity display (viewed when the LCD in the control bar is set to Custom) while you move controls. If your MIDI controller isn't sending consecutive messages, you can use your MIDI controller's editing software to create these mappings before you try the "fill up" feature. If all else fails, you can assign the controllers one at a time using the technique you learned earlier.

2   Click the Learn Mode button.

3   Click the pan knob for channel 1.

4   Move the first fader or knob of the series of eight on your MIDI controller up and down all the way.

The assignment is learned.

5   With Learn mode still activated, click channel 8's pan knob.

A dialog asks if you'd like to reassign the duplicate controls.

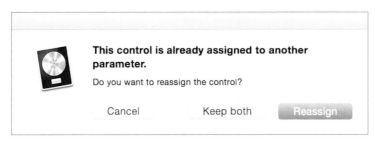

6   Click "Keep both." This step is important, because you want to keep the correct MIDI message assigned to the parameters you specified. Don't worry about doubling the assignment for now.

7   With Learn mode still activated, move the last fader or knob for the series of eight on your MIDI controller up and down all the way.

8   Click the Learn mode button, deactivating it.

A similar dialog asks if you'd like to reassign the duplicate controls.

9   Click "Keep both."

Another dialog asks whether you'd like Logic to automatically fill up in between the two assignments you made.

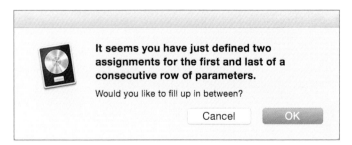

10 Click OK.

Logic creates eight consecutive assignments, mapping the first eight channels' pan controls to the eight consecutive knobs or faders on your MIDI controller.

Creating Zones and Modes

If you move one of the assigned knobs or faders on your MIDI controller, both the volume fader and the pan knob will respond (try this to see). The goal is to have separate modes that can be toggled, allowing you to control volume faders and pan knobs separately. To do so, you first need to create a zone, which represents your MIDI controller. Once created, you can make as many modes as you'd like in the zone.

Currently, the mappings have no zone assignment, indicated by "(No Zone)" in the Zone list.

NOTE ▶ (No Zone) is used to contain assignments that will work irrespective of any active user-created zone.

1   In the Controller Assignments window, click the Add (+) button beneath the Zone list.

A new zone is created in the Zone list, ready to be named.

2   Name the new zone after your MIDI controller. Press Return.

Notice that no assignments are displayed in the Control/Parameter list when this new zone is selected; the assignments still reside in the (No Zone) area. After you create the modes, you can add the assignments you created in the (No Zone) area into their associated modes.

3   Click the Add (+) button beneath the Mode list. A new mode appears in the Mode column.

NOTE ▶ In Logic Pro X, (No Mode) highlights when the first mode is created. This behavior can be a little confusing when you want to name a new mode because this mode cannot be renamed.

4 In the Mode list, double-click New Mode, and then type *Volume*. Press Return.

5 Use the same technique to create another mode named *Pan*.

NOTE ▶ Similar to (No Zone), the default mode, (No Mode), contains assignments that will work irrespective of any active user-created mode.

Now that you have created the modes, you can fill them each by cutting and pasting the volume and pan assignments you made previously in the (No Zone) area.

6 In the Zone list, click (No Zone).

7 Command-click each pan assignment in the Control/Parameter list, and then press Command-X to cut them.

8 In the Zone list, click the zone you created (and named after your MIDI controller).

9 In the Mode list, click the Pan mode, and then press Command-V to paste the assignments. The assignments are added to the Pan mode.

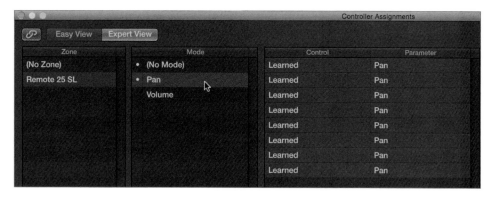

10 Using the same technique, cut and paste the volume assignments from the (No Zone) area to the Volume mode in your new zone.

Now that you've separated the pan and volume assignments into different groups, they will not interfere with each other. The active mode has a small dot next to it in the Mode list. Because you selected the Volume mode last, it will be active.

11 Move one of the assigned knobs or faders on your MIDI controller.

The channel volume faders move, linked to the movement of the physical controller.

12 In the Mode list, select the Pan mode.

A dot appears next to it, indicating that it is the active mode.

13 Move one of the assigned knobs or faders on your MIDI controller.

The channel pan knobs move, linked to the movement of the physical controller.

Assigning a Button to Switch Modes

You can select modes with the mouse, but doing so defeats the purpose of liberating yourself from mouse-based mixing (not to mention keeping the Controller Assignments window open). Instead, you can assign a button on your MIDI controller to change modes and switch between the two modes you created.

Because you want this control to work regardless of the active mode, you need to create this in the (No Mode) area.

> **NOTE** ▶ You need a button that sends a simple on/off MIDI message to make the following exercise work. This can be a dedicated button, pad, or even a key on the MIDI controller, as long as it sends either a note on/note off or a toggled (on/off) continuous controller message. To find out which message the physical control sends, try pressing it while observing the Logic MIDI Activity display.

1   In the Mode list, select (No Mode).

2   Click the Learn Mode button.

3   Press a button on your MIDI controller.

4   Click the Learn Mode button to deactivate it.

You probably noticed in the Controller Assignment Parameter area that Pan is listed in the Parameter field. That's because a pan knob was the last selected channel control. To create a mode switch, you need to assign the MIDI button to a different class in the Class menu.

5   In the Controller Assignment Parameter area, from the Class menu, choose Mode Change.

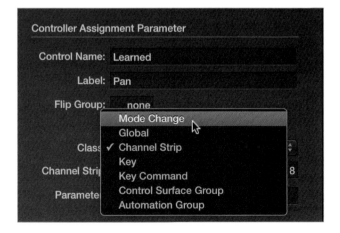

In order for the MIDI button to step through the modes, you need to make one more change in the Value area.

6   In the Value area, from the Mode menu, choose Rotate.

Now you'll test your assignment.

7   Press the button on the MIDI controller you assigned to switch modes. The Volume and Pan modes become active in turn with every button press.

8   Try toggling between the Volume and Pan modes while moving the knobs or faders you assigned previously.

You can now use the same set of knobs or faders to control both volume and pan in the Mixer, changing their function with a button press.

Changing Fader Banks

The assignments you have made so far work great, but only for the first eight channels of the Mixer. You can use the same set of knobs or faders to control all channels of the mix by assigning two bank buttons that shift their targets to the next or previous group of eight channels. Like the mode change switch you created in the preceding exercise, you need to place this control in the (No Mode) area so that it remains functional regardless of the active mode.

1   Activate Learn Mode.

2   On your MIDI controller, press the button you want to assign to move to the next bank of faders.

3   Turn off Learn Mode. A new assignment is created.

Considering that you will be assigning two buttons with nearly identical functions (next and previous bank), naming them is a good idea.

4   In the Controller Assignment Parameter area, click the Control Name field and enter *Bank +*. Press Return.

5   From the Class menu, choose Control Surface Group.

6   From the Parameter menu, choose Fader Bank for Current View.

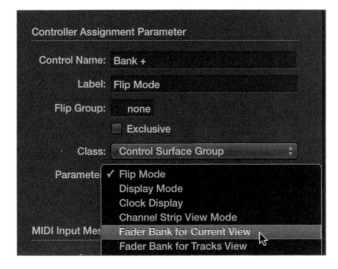

By choosing Fader Bank for Current View, you are specifying that the bank control will work regardless of the view mode in the Mixer.

7 From the Bank Type menu, choose By Bank.

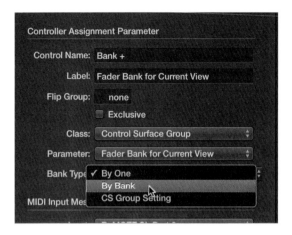

8 In the Value area, from the Mode menu, choose Relative.

This setting is used for buttons that increment/decrement by the amount set in the Multiply field just above it. Logic views banks as 16 channels, so you will need to divide the current value in half to match the set of eight faders/knobs you assigned earlier.

9 In the Value area, change the Multiply field to 0.50.

This completes the setup for the next bank button. The previous bank button assignment is almost identical, except for two small things.

10 Using the same technique, assign another button on your MIDI controller to the same Class, Parameter, and Bank Type settings.

11 In the Control Name field, type *Bank –*.

12 In the Value area, from the Mode menu, choose Relative.

13 In the Value area, change the Multiply field to –0.50.

This step specifies that the button will move by bank decrementally.

Now that you've assigned your bank buttons, you'll test them.

14 Close the Controller Assignments window.

15 Press the button you assigned to Bank + and Bank –, and move one of the previously assigned knobs or faders, observing the channels in the Mixer.

You can now move in the Mixer in banks of eight channels, accessing the volume and pan controls via your MIDI controller.

16 Try your hand at using your new assignments to mix the project live, moving around the project, dynamically setting volume and pan levels, and writing automation.

NOTE ▶ All the assignments you created in the preceding exercises are saved in the com.apple.Logic.pro.cs preference file located in ~/Library/Preferences. All mappings done in the Controller Assignments window are global and apply to all project files. This file is updated whenever you quit Logic.

Lesson Review

1. Where do you enable Snap Automation?
2. How do you scale automation data in real time (live)?
3. How do you apply automation to multiple tracks at once?
4. How can you edit automation on a VCA channel?
5. Where do you assign MIDI controls to the Logic transport?
6. How do you assign MIDI controllers to channel controls?

Answers

1. Snap Automation is enabled in the Tracks area's Snap menu.
2. You can scale automation data using the Trim or Relative automation modes.
3. To apply automation to multiple tracks at once, you must group the channels.
4. You can edit VCA channel automation by first adding the channels to the track list using the Create Tracks for Selected Channel Strips command.
5. MIDI controls are assigned to the Logic transport in the Key Commands window.
6. MIDI controllers are assigned to channel controls in the Controller Assignments window.

Advanced Topics

13

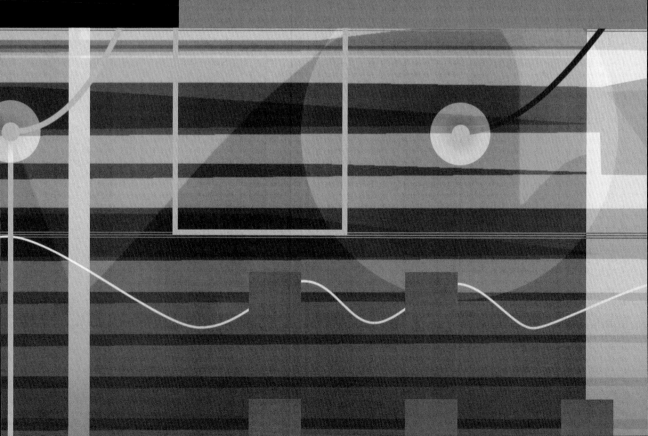

Lesson 13
Working with Surround

The demand for surround sound production has rapidly increased in recent years, due mostly to the proliferation of home theater systems. Not only is surround sound the de facto standard for video (film, DVD-Video, Blu-ray, and so on), but it also has growing influence on interactive media (video games, web-based) and music.

As surround sound becomes more and more prevalent in the audio world, acquiring at least a working knowledge of surround mixing becomes increasingly important. Logic provides sophisticated tools to produce a professional surround sound mix, whether you are creating content for video or interactive media, or producing music-only projects in surround sound.

In this lesson, you will explore the entire workflow of a surround music project, from setup to mixing to encoding.

> **NOTE** ▸ To complete this lesson, you will need an audio interface with at least six outputs wired to a six-channel surround sound playback system. If you do not have such a setup, you can still follow the exercises, but you will hear the results in stereo only.

Configuring Logic for Surround

Working in surround can encompass multiple surround formats, depending on the target playback system (home theater, movie theater, and so on). Logic can accommodate all popular surround configurations from quadraphonic to 7.1, but you will most likely work in the 5.1 (ITU 775) format for your surround productions. This format consists of three speakers across the front (left, center, right) and two speakers in the rear (left surround, right surround). The .1 in the name represents a sixth channel for low-frequency effects (LFE) sent to a subwoofer.

> MORE INFO ▶ The Logic Pro X User Manual provides excellent explanations and diagrams of the various surround formats. See the "Additional surround information" section for details.

In this lesson, you will mix a jazz quintet session in 5.1 surround format and place the listener in the middle of the performers. Let's start by opening the project file used in this lesson.

1   Choose File > Open.

2   Select Music > Advanced Logic X_Files > Lessons > **13_A Blues for Trane_Start.logicx**.

3   Play the project to familiarize yourself with the material you will be mixing.

Assigning Audio Interface Outputs

To enable Logic to play a project through each speaker in your surround sound setup, the amplifier for each speaker must be connected to a separate output in your audio interface. Before you can begin mixing, you need to configure Logic to specify which output is connected to which speaker.

1   Choose Logic Pro > Preferences > Audio. The Audio preferences are displayed.

2   Click the I/O Assignments tab.

The I/O Assignments tab contains options for configuring your surround setup.

3 Click the Output tab, if it's not already selected.

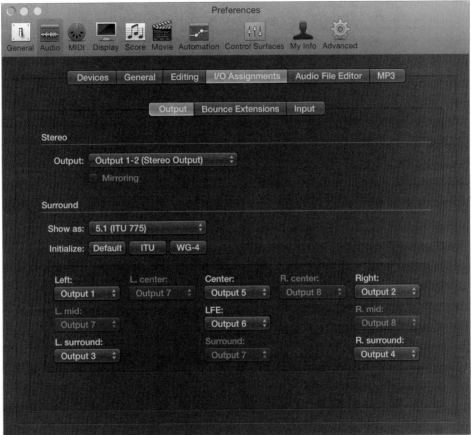

In the Output pane, you can specify which surround channel connects to which output of your audio interface (and, ultimately, to your speakers). Although you can match all conceivable setups, the default configuration is highly recommended, and it represents the established 5.1 (ITU 775) standard.

Notice that several channel assignments are dimmed and cannot be set in the Output Assignment area (L. center, R. center, L. mid, R. mid, Surround). These channels are filtered by the Show As menu, which is set to 5.1 (ITU 775) by default. The surround format chosen in the Show As menu makes available only the appropriate output channels.

4   Click the "Show as" pop-up menu to see the available configurations. When you're done, make sure to leave the setting at its default, 5.1 (ITU 775).

5   Look at each of the channel assignments in the Output Assignments area to verify that your system corresponds to this routing.

6   Close the Preferences window.

Setting the Project Surround Format

The Surround preferences are global (and remain the same from project to project), but each project can be independently configured to any surround format. The surround format is set in the Audio project settings.

1   Choose File > Project Settings > Audio. The Audio settings for the project are displayed.

By default, a project's surround format is set to 5.1 (ITU 775), as shown in the Surround Format menu.

2   Click the Surround Format pop-up menu to see the available configurations, making sure to leave the setting at its default value, 5.1 (ITU 775).

3   Close the Project Settings window.

Mixing in Surround

In the Mixer, look at the output assignments of the channels. The mix includes mono and stereo channels set to output through a single stereo output channel (Output 1-2). In this session, the trumpet, bass, and drum parts are made up of multiple tracks using different mic placements, which were then submixed to Aux channels in summing track stacks, also set to output through the output channel.

To create a surround mix, you need to change the channel outputs from stereo to surround. You can do this in the Output slot by changing the assignment from stereo output to surround. However, before you select all channels, you have something to consider: Don't change the output settings for the channels being routed to submixes because doing so would change the signal flow. Instead, change the output settings for only their respective submix channels (Tpt Sub, Bass Sub, and Drums Sub). Collapsing the subtracks for the track stacks first is a good idea.

1   Click the disclosure triangle at the bottom of the Tpt Sub, Bass Sub, and Drums Sub channels, collapsing the track stacks for the submix channels.

2   Press Command-A to select all the channels in the Mixer.

3   On any of the selected channel strips, click the Output slot, and from the pop-up menu, choose Output > Surround.

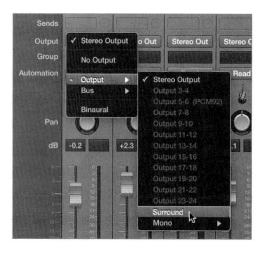

The Pan or Balance control on each selected channel changes to a Surround Panner. To the right of the Mixer, you'll notice that the Stereo Output channel has been eliminated and that the Master channel now has a multisegment level meter.

4   Click the Mixer background to deselect all channels.

Using the Surround Panner

The Surround Panner is used to position signals in the surround field. Each speaker in the output array (except for the LFE) is represented by a small gray dot on the circumference of the circle, and the green dot represents the signal position. You can change a channel's position in the surround field by dragging the green dot in the Surround Panner.

1   In the Tracks area, click the Show/Hide Global Tracks button to display the Marker track.

2   In the Marker track, drag the Head marker up onto the bar ruler to create a cycle area.

3   Solo the Sax M130 channel.

4   Start playback, and listen to the saxophone.

5   In the Surround Panner, drag the green dot to about the 10 o'clock position, slightly in from the edge.

The saxophone emanates from the front left side of the surround field.

As you most definitely discovered, precisely positioning a sound is difficult using the channel's tiny Surround Panner. Fortunately, you can open the Surround Panner in a magnified window.

6   Unsolo the Sax M130 channel.

7   Solo the Tpt Sub channel.

8   Double-click the Tpt Sub channel Surround Panner.

The Surround Panner window opens.

9   Drag the blue dot to the 2 o'clock position, just in from the edge.

10 Stop playback.

In this enlarged view, you can easily and accurately position a signal in the surround field. In addition, the Surround Panner window also provides precise visual feedback as to the angle (±180°) and diversity (distance from the surround field's edge) of the positioning. These values are represented both graphically and numerically.

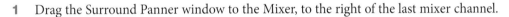 **TIP** ▶ You can mute the signal sent to the speakers by clicking the speaker icons in the Surround Panner.

Adjusting Center and LFE Levels

The Surround Panner window includes sliders to independently adjust the amount of signal sent to the center and LFE channels. By default, the Center Level slider is set to unity (feeding signal to the center channel), while the LFE is muted.

In this exercise, you will adjust the center and LFE levels of various channels. To most easily do this, start off by improving the Mixer's ergonomics.

1 Drag the Surround Panner window to the Mixer, to the right of the last mixer channel.

2   At the top left of the Surround Panner window, click the Link button.

You used this technique earlier (Lesson 8) with plug-in windows. When the Link button is on, you can use a single window to display the Surround Panner of any channel strip, without the clutter of multiple windows.

3   Unlock and lock the screenset to save the layout configuration you just created.

4   Play the project.

5   In the Surround Panner window, drag the Center Level slider all the way to the left, muting the output.

As the amount of signal sent to the center channel is eliminated, the placement of the trumpet becomes more focused on the front right side of the surround field.

6   Unsolo the Tpt Sub channel and solo the Bass Sub channel.

7   On the Bass Sub channel, double-click the Surround Panner.

The Surround Panner window displays the settings for the Bass Sub channel (because linking is turned on).

8   While watching the visual readouts, position the blue dot at an Angle of about 150 (degrees) and a Diversity of about 0.40.

   TIP   Double-clicking the numeric displays at the top of the Surround Panner window and entering a number will precisely set angle and diversity.

9   Drag the Center Level slider all the way to the left, muting the output.

10 Drag the LFE Level to the right, to a value of –15.5 dB.

As you increase the amount of signal sent to the LFE channel, the bass frequencies become more pronounced, reinforced by the subwoofer (LFE channel).

NOTE ▸ The LFE channel and subwoofer speaker are not the same. The LFE is an independent channel used mostly with visual media (film, video, video games) to produce occasional low-frequency effects (supplying rumble at just the right moment.) The subwoofer is a speaker, and in many monitor setups it does double duty, both outputting the LFE channel content, as well as reproducing the lower bass frequencies of the entire system.

11 After you've had a chance to hear the results of your actions, stop playback.

12 Unsolo the Bass Sub channel.

Balancing Stereo to Surround Signals

Depending on the type of input signal (mono, stereo, or surround), Logic uses slightly different types of Surround Panners. So far you've been working with mono source signals. In this exercise, you will use the Surround Panner to accurately position stereo signals in the surround field.

NOTE ▸ A signal's channel input format is indicated by the number of level meters and by the symbol on the button next to the input field. See the section "Set channel strip input formats" in the Logic Pro X User Manual's "Mix a project" chapter for detailed descriptions and illustrations of each input format.

1 Solo the Sax M130, Piano LR, Tpt Sub, and Bass Sub channels.

In this exercise, you will adjust the surround placement of the stereo piano channel in the context of other instruments that are already positioned.

2 On the Piano LR channel, double-click the Surround Panner.

The Surround Panner window displays the Piano LR channel, which is a stereo source.

When using a stereo source, the Surround Panner window contains an additional parameter, Spread, which indicates the width of the stereo signal in the surround field. This is represented graphically by the L and R dots (representing the left and right side of the stereo image), and numerically at the top of the window.

3   Play the project, listening to the piano's position in the surround field.

As you can hear, the piano sounds a bit wide, crowding the saxophone and trumpet on either side of it.

You can adjust the spread of the signal by dragging the L and R dots in the Surround Panner window.

4   Try dragging the L dot to the left and right, increasing and decreasing the spread while listening to the results.

You have to be careful when dragging the L or R dots because you can inadvertently change the angle and diversity. To avoid doing so, Command-drag the L or R dot, which locks down the diversity and angle, allowing you to adjust only the spread.

5   Position the blue dot to an Angle of 0.0 and Diversity of 0.12.

6   Command-drag the L dot toward the center blue dot until the Spread value is +34.

In effect, you narrowed the stereo signal slightly, causing less overlap with the saxophone and trumpet in the surround field.

7   Stop playback.

8   Option-click an active Solo button on any of the soloed channels.

All the Solo buttons are turned off at once.

Let's do the same thing with another stereo source, placing the drums submix in the surround field while listening to the entire mix.

9   In the Drums Sub channel, double-click the Surround Panner to display its settings in the Surround Panner window.

10   Play the project.

11 By moving the dots or changing the numeric values, position the stereo source in the surround field at an Angle of –157.0, Diversity of 0.27, and Spread of +91.

12 Remove any signal fed to the center channel by muting the center level.

The drums now sound behind and to the left side in their own space in the surround mix.

13 Stop playback.

14 Close the Surround Panner window.

> **TIP** Logic offers two ways to smooth dynamic surround panning for live automation. You can lock diversity by Command-dragging the blue dot in the Surround Panner to allow only circular movement. Likewise, the angle is locked when Command-Shift-dragging the blue dot, allowing only linear movement in the Surround Panner.

Using Surround Effects

To preserve imaging, surround mixing often requires the use of specialized surround processors. These are, in essence, effects that independently process the individual channels of the given surround format. Logic has two types of surround processors: multichannel and multi-mono. With multichannel effects, the surround channels are tightly integrated, or coupled, processing the entire surround source at once. Multi-mono effects, on the other hand, are essentially multiple mono plug-ins that are individually applied to each surround channel in the signal path.

In this exercise, you will assign both surround format plug-in types to channels, creating surround send and insert effects to produce a professional-sounding mix.

> **NOTE ▶** The surround plug-ins in Logic work in all surround formats available to the application (Quadraphonic, LCRS, 5.1, 6.1, 7.1, and so on). The surround format chosen for the project determines the surround format of the plug-ins.

Using Multichannel Effects

Immersing the listener in an artificially created ambience is the primary goal of surround production. To aid in this goal, multichannel reverb is used to simulate acoustic environments in the surround field. What differentiates the surround reverb processor from its mono and stereo cousins is its ability to simultaneously receive input from and send output to more than two channels.

For this exercise, you will use a multichannel version of the convolution reverb, Space Designer, as a send effect. This plug-in not only sends and receives over multiple channels, it also utilizes specialized surround recordings of real acoustic spaces for impulse responses.

1   Solo the Sax M130 channel.

2   On the Sax M130 channel, click the first Send slot and choose Bus > Bus 1.

    A new aux channel is created, receiving input from Bus 1.

3 Below the Gain Reduction meter and the EQ display on the Aux 1 channel, click the channel mode button, and from the pop-up menu, choose Surround.

The channel switches from mono to surround, and the level meters now display six segments instead of one or two (mono or stereo, respectively). These represent each of the six channels used in a 5.1 configuration.

4 On the Aux 1 channel, click the first Insert slot and choose Reverb > Space Designer > 5.1. The Space Designer interface opens.

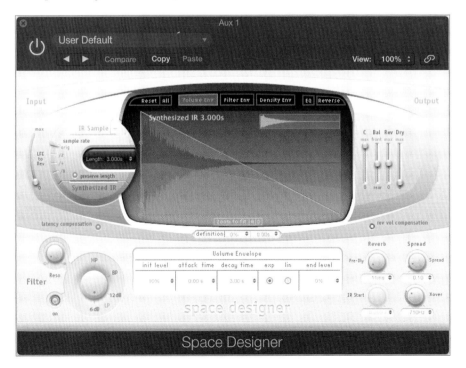

5 From the Settings menu, choose Surround Spaces > Surround Rooms >
02.9 Hansa Studio +.

Space Designer loads the surround impulse response recording and any control
configurations saved to the preset.

NOTE ▶ The Logic surround impulse responses were recorded with a variety of surround recording techniques, such as circle B-format, omni B-format, and discrete
omni. You will even find different format recordings of the same acoustic space.

At first glance, the Space Designer interface looks identical to the stereo version.
However, closer inspection reveals that the wet/dry controls are replaced by four
sliders. Using these you can adjust the amount of wet and dry signal, and you can
control the balance between the front and rear speakers. An additional slider is
provided to adjust the amount of signal sent to the center channel.

6 Drag down the center channel output slider (labeled C) to a value of –4.0 dB.

You've reduced the amount of reverb signal sent to the center channel, thereby creating a more or less equal dispersion of reverb across the surround field.

7 Close the Space Designer window.

As it is now, the Sax M130 channel is set to send to the surround reverb post fader,
but pre Surround Panner. In order to have the surround reverb preserve positional
information when generating reflections, you need to assign the send post pan.

8 On the Sax M130 channel, click-hold the Send slot and choose Post Pan.

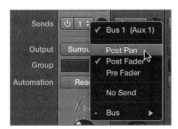

NOTE ▶ Contrary to stereo channels, sends are instantiated as post-fader (and pre-pan) on surround channels by default.

9   Play the project.

10   On the Sax M130 channel, increase the send amount to Bus 1 (Aux 1) to –14.0 dB.

You hear the saxophone localized off to the left front of the surround field along with the processed signal in all five speakers. This creates a convincing ambient effect of the saxophone in a three-dimensional space.

NOTE ▶ The color of the Send level knob ring denotes pre- or post-pan routing. A blue ring denotes pre-pan, a green ring post-pan routing.

11   Unsolo the Sax M130 channel.

12   Assign the sends on the Piano LR, Tpt Sub, Bass Sub, and Drums Sub channels to Bus 1 (Aux 1), and set each to Post Pan.

13   Adjust the send amount of each of the channels in step 12 to the surround reverb, listening to how they sit in the ambient surround field.

14   Stop playback.

NOTE ▶ In addition to its suite of surround effect plug-ins, Logic Pro includes surround versions of the EXS24 mkII, ES2, and Sculpture software instruments.

Using Multi-mono Insert Effects

When used as an insert on a surround channel, any effect not specifically configured for multichannel audio is offered in the multi-mono format (this includes third-party plug-ins). These are applied specifically to surround input signals and can be thought of as multiple instantiations of the same effect, one for each surround channel. What makes these multi-mono effects especially powerful is the ability to independently process the LFE channel, which is often called for when you're creating a surround mix.

The surround professional generally can't predict how a carefully crafted mix will translate to consumer setups because the subwoofer is often the most inaccurately configured component in a typical home theater system.

In addition, the bass-management systems used in consumer receivers vary widely from manufacturer to manufacturer. For this reason, applying a low-pass filter to the output of the LFE channel is recommended while mixing and mastering to catch any stray high frequencies that might otherwise get through. You can accomplish this by inserting a multi-mono version of the Channel EQ on the Master channel, processing the LFE channel differently from the others.

1   On the Master channel, click the first Insert slot and choose EQ > Channel EQ > Multi Mono.

The Channel EQ interface appears.

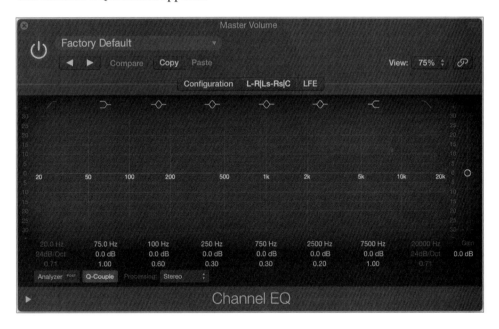

Multi-mono versions of plug-ins display an additional set of buttons in the plug-in header compared with their mono or stereo versions. These buttons provide access to surround routing and configuration options.

2   At the top of the interface, click the Configuration tab.

The plug-in interface changes to display the configuration of the multiple channels.

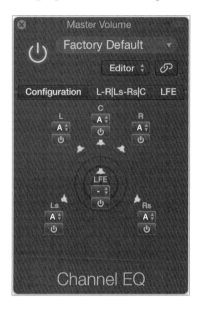

In the Configuration pane, you can bypass the effect on a channel-by-channel basis. The small pop-up menu located under each channel represents a form of grouping, not unlike the channel groups you created in Lesson 9.

Each group represents a separate instantiation of the EQ, as shown in the tabs you viewed at the top of the interface. By default, the Left, Right, Left Surround, Right Surround, and Center channels are assigned to a group (A), with the LFE unassigned. This configuration creates two instantiations of the EQ: one for group A, and the other for the LFE (none).

NOTE ▶ You can also use the Configuration area to simultaneously bypass all the channels in the same group.

3   At the top of the interface, click the LFE tab.

The plug-in interface changes to display the EQ settings for the LFE channel.

4   Click the Low-Pass Filter button (at the far right) to enable the filter band.

5   Double-click the Frequency setting for the Low-Pass Filter band and enter *120.*

6   Drag the Gain/Slope setting for the Low-Pass Filter band up to 48 dB/Oct.

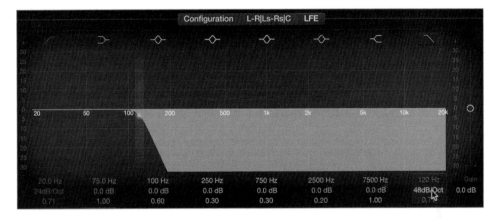

By using a low-pass filter on the LFE channel, you will remove all frequencies that might cause undue muddiness in the subwoofer channel.

NOTE ▸ No hard and fast rule exists for selecting the low-pass filter frequency used on the LFE channel. Usually it is set between 80 Hz and 120 Hz, and it can be different for each monitoring system. To make matters more confusing, some consumer surround systems utilize their own low-pass filters for removing unwanted high frequencies sent to the subwoofer.

In most consumer surround systems, the speakers outputting the Left, Right, Left Surround, Right Surround, and Center channels are often "satellites" incapable of accurately producing extreme low frequencies. For this reason, filtering out the extreme low frequencies for these channels is a good idea, similar to the way you filtered out unwanted frequencies for the LFE channel. You do this by applying a high-pass filter in the L-R|Ls-Rs|C tab.

7   Click the L-R|Ls-Rs|C tab.

The plug-in interface changes to display the EQ settings for the Left, Right, Left Surround, Right Surround, and Center channels.

8   Click the High-Pass Filter button (at the far left) to enable the filter band.

9   Double-click the Frequency setting for the High-Pass Filter band and enter *50*.

10   Drag the Gain/Slope setting for the High-Pass Filter band to 12 dB/Oct.

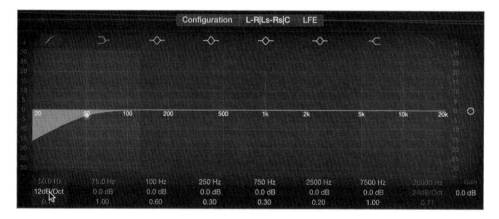

These settings help ensure that your mix translates well to most home playback systems.

11   Close the Channel EQ window.

Checking the Surround Mix

Logic also offers specialized surround plug-ins that enable you to check your mix. These help identify problem spots by isolating individual channels as well as visually displaying the surround field's content.

1 On the Master channel, click the second Insert slot and choose Utility > Multichannel Gain > 5.1. The Multichannel Gain plug-in appears.

The Multichannel Gain plug-in allows you to independently control the gain and polarity inversion of each channel of a surround track or bus. You can also use the plug-in to individually mute each of the surround channels, allowing you to isolate the speaker output.

2 Play the project.

3 Using the Multichannel Gain plug-in, try muting channels individually or in combination to isolate speaker output.

NOTE ▶ The order of channels displayed in the channel level meters is determined by the Channel Order setting in the Display preferences (Logic Pro > Preferences > Display, and then click the Mixer tab). The default Internal setting (L, R, Ls, Rs, C, LFE) can be somewhat confusing when you're using the Multichannel Gain plug-in because the two interfaces display the channels in a different order. However, you can remedy this situation by choosing the Clockwise setting (Ls, L, C, R, Rs, LFE) in Logic preferences, which reflects the Multichannel Gain order.

4 After you have had a chance to experiment, stop the playback.

5 In the Multichannel Gain plug-in, make sure that all channels are unmuted.

6 On the Master channel, click the third Insert slot and choose Metering > MultiMeter > 5.1. The surround MultiMeter plug-in appears.

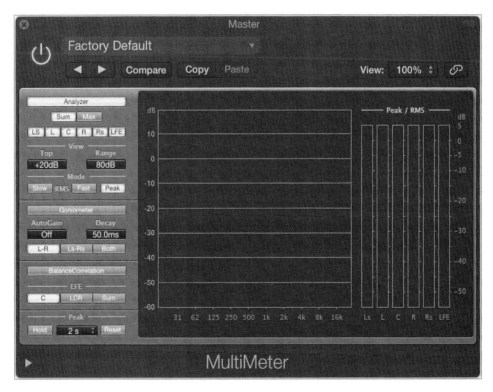

7   Play the project, observing the MultiMeter's frequency analyzer and level meters.

The surround version of the MultiMeter plug-in provides a suite of helpful analysis tools for examining the channels of your surround mix. In addition to a multichannel frequency spectrum analyzer, level meters, and goniometer, the MultiMeter includes an excellent surround balance analyzer.

8   At the lower left of the plug-in interface, click the Balance/Correlation button.

The main window displays sound position in the surround field, which responds dynamically to the signal. You can use this to check the balance of the mix between the Ls, L, C, R, and Rs channels.

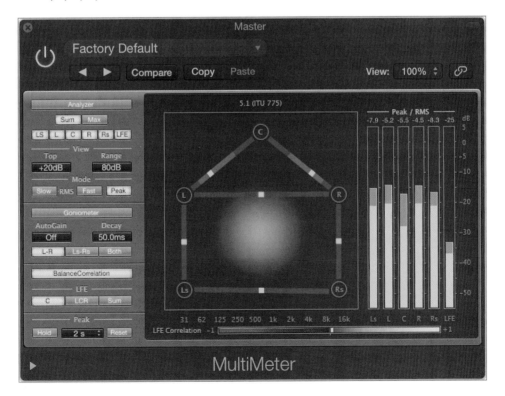

9   Turn off Cycle mode.

10   As the project is playing, listen to your surround mix while watching the balance display.

     Now that you've checked sound placement for your surround mix, you can check the LFE Correlation meter to see if the LFE is causing any phase cancellation. You can display this meter in a variety of ways, comparing the phase of the LFE channel to the center, the front (left, center, and right), or the sum of all channels.

11   In the LFE section just below the Balance/Correlation button, click the Sum button.

12   If necessary, rewind to the beginning of the project and start playback, watching the LFE Correlation meter at the bottom of the MultiMeter interface.

     The LFE Correlation meter moves to the left of the middle point toward –1, indicating that the LFE channel is out of phase with the other channels. You can remedy this situation in the Multichannel Gain plug-in by reversing the phase of the LFE channel.

13   In the Multichannel Gain plug-in window, click the Phase Invert button for the LFE channel.

     The MultiMeter's LFE Correlation meter now moves to the right of the middle, toward +1, indicating that the LFE channel is in phase with the rest of the surround channels.

14   Stop the playback after you've checked your mix.

15   Close the MultiMeter and Multichannel Gain plug-in windows.

Downmixing

The act of reducing a surround mix to a four-channel (quadraphonic, LCRS), two-channel (stereo), or mono version is called *downmixing*. To aid in downmixing, Logic Pro includes a specialized Down Mixer plug-in you can apply to the Master channel, automatically folding down the surround mix to a specified format. Because most consumer DVD-Video players have a built-in downmixing process, this enables you to check your mix's compatibility with these downmixing systems, as well as quickly create new format mixes for delivery.

1 On the Master channel, click the fourth Insert slot and choose Utility > Down Mixer > 5.1 > Stereo.

The Master channel changes to display stereo level meters, and the Down Mixer plug-in window appears.

The downmixing process on most consumer systems folds the Left Surround and Right Surround channels into the Left and Right channels, respectively. Combining signals can cause gain build-up and distortion, so applying gain reduction on those channels is recommended to provide a little headroom. You can create these attenuations in the Down Mixer plug-in using the level sliders.

2 Drag the L-R Level slider down to –6.0 db.

3 Drag the Ls-Rs Level slider down to –6.0 db.

The center channel is sent to both Left and Right channels equally, and therefore must be further reduced when downmixing to create an accurate representation of the mix in stereo.

4   Drag the Center Level slider down to –9.0 db.

The LFE channel is frequently dropped altogether when downmixing to stereo because this channel most often includes only low-frequency effects that are not integral to the mix.

5   Drag the LFE Level slider all the way down to mute.

Now you're set up to hearing the surround mix downmixed to stereo.

6   Play the project, listening to the stereo downmix, which should now be emanating only from the left and right speakers. Stop the playback.

7   In the Master channel, click the Down Mixer plug-in, and from the pop-up menu, choose No Plug-in, thereby removing the Down Mixer plug-in from the channel strip.

Bouncing the Surround Mix

Depending on the delivery format, various techniques exist for encoding a surround project for distribution. To support the work of the mastering engineer or post-production house, you need to create a master multi-channel file of your mix, which they can encode for a variety of media (DVD-Audio disc, Dolby Digital (AC3) format, DTS, and so on.)

You can create a master multi-channel file in the Bounce window.

1   At the bottom of the Master channel, click the Bnce (Bounce) button to open the Bounce window.

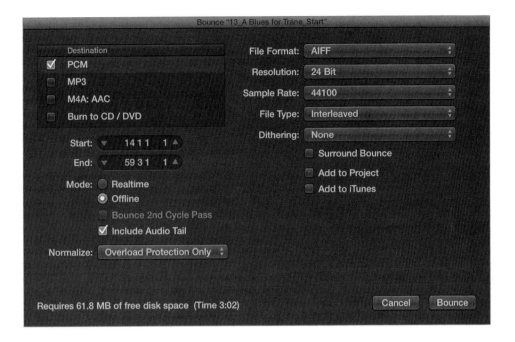

2   If necessary, in the Start field, enter *1 1 1 1* to ensure that the bounce is performed from the beginning of the project.

3   Select the Surround Bounce checkbox.

4   At the lower right of the window, click the Bounce button.

5   In the Save As field, type *Working with Surround*. Press Enter.

> **NOTE** ▶ Logic automatically directs bounces to a Bounces folder created in the project folder.

A bounce is performed, creating an interleaved multi-channel file named **Working with Surround.aif**.

Now that the master multi-channel file is created, it can be encoded as a Dolby Digital (AC3) file in a program such as Compressor.

> **NOTE** ▶ To create encoded Dolby Digital (AC3) surround files, some encoder applications need to import multiple *stems*, or submix files, corresponding to each surround output channel (instead of a single interleaved multi-channel file.) You can create these stems when bouncing by choosing Split from the File Type menu in the Bounce window. Extensions will be added to the names of the resulting files that correspond to their derived channels (L, R, C, Ls, Rs, LFE, and so on.)

Lesson Review

1.   How do you assign the outputs of your audio interface to corresponding surround channels?

2.   Where do you set the surround format for an individual project?

3.   How does the stereo input Surround Panner differ from that of other input formats (mono and surround)?

4.   How does the surround version of the Space Designer plug-in differ from the mono and stereo versions when used as a send effect?

5.   How do multichannel insert plug-ins differ from the mono and stereo versions?

6.   How can you quickly create a four- or two-channel version of your surround mix?

Answers

1. You assign the outputs of your audio interface to corresponding surround channels by choosing Preferences > Audio > I/O Assignments and clicking the Output tab.

2. The surround format for a project is set in the Audio tab of the Project Settings window.

3. The stereo input to the Surround Panner offers an additional Spread control.

4. The surround version of the Space Designer plug-in loads surround format impulse responses, and it has additional controls to adjust the center level as well as the balance between the front and rear speakers.

5. Multichannel insert plug-ins have additional configuration settings that allow you to bypass any surround channel. In addition, the LFE channel can be processed independently from the rest of the surround channels.

6. You can quickly create a four- or two-channel version of your surround mix by applying the Down Mixer plug-in to the Master channel.

14

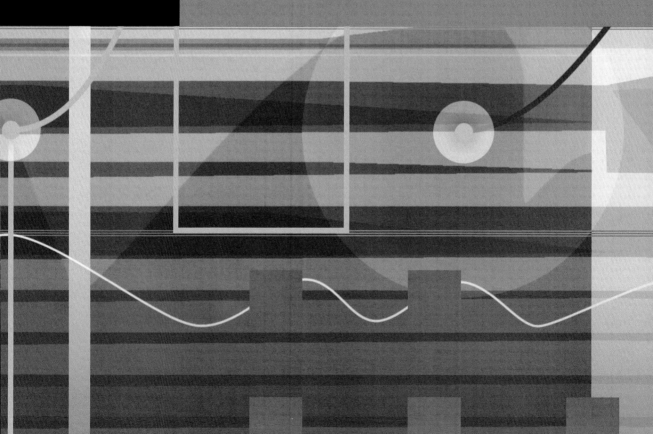

Real-time MIDI Processing

In Lesson 9 you used a variety of editing functions to manipulate recorded MIDI data. Not only can Logic transform pre-existing data in such a manner, but it can also process MIDI data in real-time, even as it is being recorded, changing and modifying the data to produce highly musical and oftentimes surprising results.

In this lesson, you'll explore tools for real-time MIDI processing, starting with the new Logic MIDI plug-ins, and continuing to the deep processing functions offered in the Logic Environment.

Processing MIDI with MIDI Plug-ins

The suite of MIDI plug-ins enables you to process a track's MIDI data via a channel insert, not unlike audio plug-ins. To be truthful, these transform functions are not entirely new, as this functionality has long existed in the Logic Environment (more on that later). However, MIDI plug-ins distinguish themselves because you can insert them directly into a channel's signal flow without having to leave the Mixer.

You were introduced to MIDI plug-ins in the basic book by looking at the Arpeggiator plug-in. You'll start off your exploration of real-time MIDI processing by investigating another one of the MIDI plug-ins, the Modulator.

1   Choose File > Open.

2   Open Music > Advanced Logic X_Files > Lessons > **14_MIDI Processing_Start.logicx**.

The project opens with the Calm FM track selected. On this channel is the EFM1 synthesizer, followed by a Chorus plug-in.

3   In the inspector, double-click the EFM1 in the Calm FM channel to open the plug-in window.

4   Play the project, listening to the Calm FM region. Stop the project after you've auditioned the material.

As you can hear, the synth sounds nice, but besides a subtle pulsing created through the tuning relationship of the oscillators, it doesn't change much. You can create greater interest by modulating some of its parameters via an LFO (low-frequency oscillator) or envelope, creating subtle changes in timbre over the length of the passage. You would usually do this on the synth itself. While the EFM1 does offer an internal LFO (situated at the bottom of the interface), it is extremely limited and lacks the ability to change waveforms and adjust rate in bars/beats (sync to tempo).

Fortunately, the Modulator MIDI plug-in can create the desired effect regardless of the software synthesizer being used, sending MIDI controller data to the EFM1 in the signal chain, thereby circumventing the synth's own limitations.

5   On the Calm FM channel, click the MIDI FX slot and choose Modulator.

The Modulator interface is displayed.

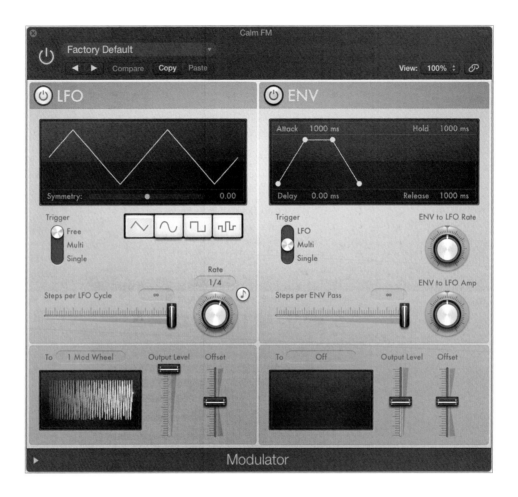

NOTE ▶ The LFO section is turned on by default; to use the Envelope section, you need to click the power button located in the upper-left corner of the section.

The Modulator interface is divided into two sections: The left comprises a fully featured LFO, and the right contains controls for an envelope. Both sections can be set independently or even cross-fed into each other to send MIDI data to the software instruments located down the signal chain (in this case, the EFM1).

You can create the subtle change in timbre by modulating the EFM1's FM (frequency modulation) amount via the Modulator plug-in's LFO. Although the EFM1 does not have the needed modulation source, it does provide an easy way for MIDI signals to control the FM amount via controller assignments located in the hidden controls.

6   Click the disclosure triangle to display the EFM1's extra parameters.

Note that the Ctrl FM parameter is already configured to receive MIDI controller messages via Controller 1 (mod wheel). To avoid interfering with this manual control, set the Ctrl FM parameter to another controller number for sending the LFO control from the Modulator plug-in.

7   From the Ctrl FM menu, choose 3.

Now that you've set the receiving end of the MIDI signal flow, let's configure the LFO to send out the appropriate messages to control the FM amount.

8   In the LFO section of the Modulator plug-in, choose 3 in the To field.

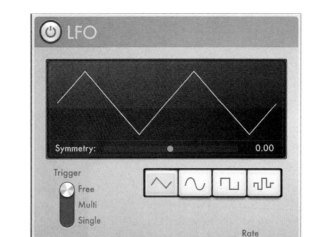

9   Rewind to the beginning of the project and play it, listening to the EFM1.

You hear a regular change in timbre as the LFO sweeps the FM amount of the EFM1 back and forth. The rate of change is set via the Rate knob.

10   Drag the Rate knob to 1/2t.

The rate of change is now set to half-note triplets.

TIP ▶ Clicking the small musical note button to the right of the Rate knob toggles the rate control between musical divisions (bars/beats) and frequency (Hz). The former will sync with project tempo changes, whereas the latter remains constant.

As of now, the wave shape of the LFO is still set to the default triangle. You'll try out the various wave shapes the Modulator plug-in offers.

11 While the project is playing, click the various wave shape buttons and listen to the results. Finish by selecting the Square wave.

You can further modify the wave shape by using the Symmetry and Smoothing controls in the LFO.

12 Drag the Symmetry slider back and forth while observing the results both sonically and visually.

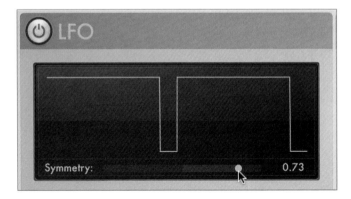

By changing the symmetry, you can vary the pulse width to change the positive/negative relationship of the LFO source.

13 Option-Click the Symmetry control to reset it to 0.

14 Drag the Smoothing slider all the way to the right to a value of 1.00.

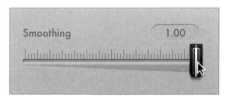

The wave shape changes to a peaked curve, changing the sweeping relationship of the LFO.

15 Stop the project.

16 Close the Modulator and EFM1 windows.

> **TIP** ▶ The Envelope section can modulate the LFO controls via the ENV to LFO Rate and ENV to LFO Amp knobs. Doing so can create some intriguing cross-modulation relationships that help to animate the source sound.

MIDI Processing in the Environment

From the very beginning, its Environment has set Logic apart from other sequencers. The Environment is often thought of as a virtual studio, containing objects that represent your audio channels and MIDI devices. However, the Environment is much, much more. It enables you to process data from MIDI and software instruments in real time by creating complex signal routings and transformations to augment your music.

In this lesson you will explore useful MIDI processors in the Environment by creating signal routings to affect MIDI input a variety of ways.

> **NOTE** ▶ You will need to set the "Display Middle C as" preference (Preferences > Display > General tab) to C3 (Yamaha) to accurately follow the directions in this exercise (and others throughout the book).

Navigating in the Environment

The Environment is tucked neatly away in its own window, which you can access like any other via the main Window menu. As you can with other windows, you can make the Environment window part of a screenset, which helps to keep your screen organized.

1   Press 3 to open screenset 3.

Screenset 3 consists of a Main window (with the inspector displayed) and an Environment window placed on top.

NOTE ▸ Although the window configuration is locked in the screenset, the Environment window is not floating and therefore you may lose it during the lesson after clicking the Main window. Not to worry, just press Command-` (grave accent) to reveal the hidden Environment window below, or open screenset 3 to return to the default configuration.

The Environment is divided into layers, displaying objects of like type or function to help keep things organized. You are currently looking at the All Objects layer, which provides an easy way to look at all objects currently in the project's Environment. Here, you can see the three software instruments (Marimba, 8bit Kit, and Analog Lead) assigned to the track list, as well as other objects being used "behind the scenes" for MIDI input.

NOTE ▸ The top two tracks in the track list are placeholders currently assigned to a special No Output destination. Tracks assigned to No Output will not send any data.

2   Press the Up and Down Arrow keys to scroll one at a time to the Marimba, 8bit Kit, and Analog Lead tracks (tracks 3 through 5), playing your MIDI keyboard to familiarize yourself with the sound of the software instruments.

When you select a track in the track list, MIDI input from your controller is routed to the track's assigned channel. Notice that when you select tracks in the track list, the corresponding Environment object is also selected.

3   Press the Up and Down Arrow keys to select the Marimba track (track 3) in the track list, and select it for MIDI input.

Navigate layers by clicking the Layer menu.

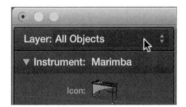

4   From the Layer menu, choose Click & Ports.

The layer switches and displays the contents of the Click & Ports layer. (You may need to scroll up to see all the objects.)

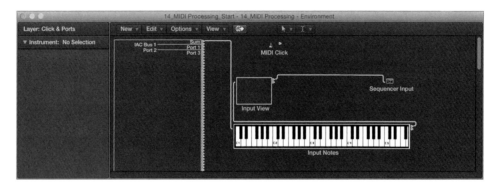

The Click & Ports layer contains objects specific to the routing of MIDI signals from their initial input until they reach the sequencer. The physical input object at the far left represents your MIDI interface or MIDI controller (with direct MIDI-to-USB or

FireWire connection). All available ports from your MIDI input devices are listed in the physical input object (including the Caps Lock Keyboard and virtual ones like the IAC Bus and Network MIDI). Their corresponding cable outputs are depicted by the small triangles running along the right side.

NOTE ▶ The Sum output at the top carries a combination of all MIDI input ports displayed in the physical input object that are not currently cabled. When a cable is connected from one of the remaining MIDI ports, its signal will not be passed through the SUM output.

MIDI signals are passed from object to object in the Environment by cabling them together. The left side of an object represents the input, while the right side represents the output. As you can see in this layer, the physical input is cabled to a keyboard object labeled Input Notes.

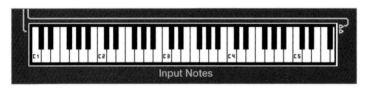

5   Play a few notes on your MIDI controller, observing the keyboard object.

NOTE ▶ If you don't have a MIDI controller, the Musical Typing window will work equally well for the exercises in this lesson.

As you play the MIDI controller keys, the software instrument you selected in the track list (Marimba) is triggered, and the corresponding pitches are displayed in the keyboard object.

6   Click some of the keys on the keyboard object in the Environment window.

The Marimba is triggered each time you click the keyboard object.

When you play a note on your MIDI controller or click the keyboard object, MIDI events are displayed in the Input View object cabled to the keyboard object output. This is a monitor object, which displays all MIDI data passing through it in list form.

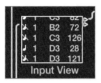

The signal chain finally ends with a sequencer input object. It represents the connection to the Logic sequencer and routes to the selected track in the Arrange track list.

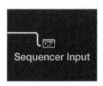

With the physical input cabled to the sequencer input (passing through the keyboard and monitor objects), the MIDI signal flows from the MIDI interface or controller providing input, ultimately arriving at the selected Arrange track via the sequencer input object.

TIP If the connection between the physical input and the sequencer input is severed, MIDI input signals will not be recorded in the Arrange tracks. If you don't see any signal in the Input View object, or you're having problems receiving MIDI input in the Main window, check this connection first.

Creating Environment Objects

Now that you've had a chance to observe signal flow in the Click & Ports layer, you can try creating Environment objects to process incoming MIDI signals. Although you can insert new objects in any layer, in this exercise you'll create an Environment layer to contain the new objects you will be exploring.

1   From the Layer menu, choose Create Layer.

An empty layer is created.

2   In the Layer menu text field, select Rename Layer, and enter *MIDI Process.* Press Return.

You now have a new layer to house your MIDI processing experiments, ready for you to add new objects.

Using Monitor Objects

As you noticed when working with the Click & Ports layer, you use monitor objects to display MIDI signals passing through them. You can create new objects by choosing them from the Environment window's New menu.

1   From the Environment's local menu bar, choose New > Monitor.

A new monitor object appears.

By itself, a monitor object does nothing. In this exercise, you will use it to both monitor MIDI signals passing through it and to connect to the Marimba software instrument channel selected in the Tracks area. To pass the signal, you need to cable the output of the monitor object to the Marimba software instrument channel, which is contained in a different layer (the Mixer layer). Even though these objects exist in different layers, you can still cable them together by Option-clicking the cable output of the monitor object.

TIP Monitor objects are excellent tools for troubleshooting within the Environment, and you can place as many as you want within the MIDI signal flow. By doing so, you can always be aware of the messages an object is outputting.

2 Option-click the cable output (the small triangle in the upper-right corner) of the monitor object.

A menu appears in which you can set the destination for the cable.

3 Choose Mixer > Software Instrument > Marimba.

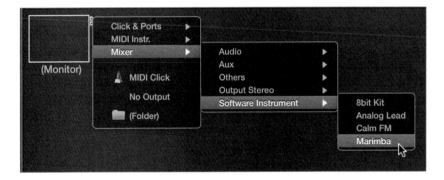

A cable appears, connecting the objects between the Environment layers.

NOTE ▸ When you cable an output from an object to another object, another output triangle automatically appears.

To keep your objects and cabling straight, label objects as you create them.

4   Using the Text tool, click the monitor object to rename it.

5   Enter *To Marimba*. Press Return.

TIP▸ When creating, moving, and naming objects in the Environment, alternate between using the Pointer tool and the Text tool. By default, these are the default (left-click) and alternate (Command-click) tools in the Environment, so you can toggle between them.

Using Arpeggiator Objects

Identical to the Arpeggiator MIDI plug-in, arpeggiator objects receive MIDI note input, outputting each note individually in a variety of selectable patterns, speeds, and lengths. These arpeggiator objects are extremely flexible, and you can configure them to create complex rhythmic patterns out of static chords.

In this exercise you will not only create new Environment objects but also cable them to process MIDI data in ways not possible using MIDI plug-ins.

1   From the Environment's local menu bar, choose New > Arpeggiator to open a new arpeggiator object.

2   Using the Pointer tool, drag the monitor object to the right side of the Environment window to make room for other objects.

To aid in visualizing the signal routing from one object to the next, you can color the objects and their respective cables.

3   From the Environment window's local menus, choose View > Colored Cables.

4   From the Main menus, choose View > Show Colors.

The color palette—in which you can assign colors to selected objects— appears.

5   In the Environment window, select the arpeggiator object; in the color palette, click a shade of green.

The arpeggiator object turns green.

6   Drag the arpeggiator object's cable output to the monitor object.

You now have a connection between the arpeggiator and the Marimba software instrument channel (passing through the monitor).

To route input from your MIDI keyboard to the arpeggiator, you need to bring up the arpeggiator on a track in the Tracks area. Rather than go back to the Tracks area to do this (via Reassign Track or Library), you can use the MIDI Thru tool in the Environment. Any object you click in the Environment using this tool will be configured for the currently selected Arrange track.

7   Press the Up/Down Arrow keys to select the top No Output track (track 1) in the track list.

8   Using the MIDI Thru tool, click the arpeggiator object.

The selected track (track 1) changes to the arpeggiator object.

You can test whether the arpeggiator is receiving input by playing your MIDI controller.

9   Play a few notes on your MIDI controller, observing the monitor in the Environment window.

You hear the Marimba software instrument and see MIDI data displayed in the monitor object.

The arpeggiator object works with tempo-related material, so to have it process the incoming MIDI, the project has to be playing.

10 Play the project.

11 While the project is playing, hold down F, Bb, and C (Fsus4) on your MIDI controller.

You now hear the chord arpeggiated and see the MIDI data displayed in the monitor object.

12 Try adding or subtracting notes to your held chord, observing how they change the arpeggio.

NOTE ▶ The project must remain playing for many of the Environment objects to process incoming MIDI notes. Throughout the lesson, if you reach the end of the project, return to the beginning and restart playback.

In the Object Parameter box, you will find many useful settings for the arpeggiator object. Here, you can select from various patterns and also adjust the velocity, speed, length, and octave of the arpeggiated notes.

NOTE ▶ If you can't reach your MIDI controller with one hand and adjust the Object Parameter box with the other, you can replay the chords after you make the adjustment to hear the result.

13 In the Environment area's Object Parameter box, from the Direction pop-up menu, choose Up/Down.

The pattern direction changes, arpeggiating the notes of the chord up and then down.

14 In the Object Parameter box, from the Direction menu, choose Random.

The pattern changes, randomly arpeggiating selected notes from the chord.

The Velocity parameter allows you to adjust the velocities of the arpeggiated notes of the original chord. You can set a positive or negative offset, or even randomize the velocities.

15 In the Object Parameter box, drag the Velocity parameter (which currently displays Original) to choose Random.

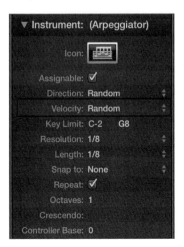

The velocities of the arpeggiated notes are randomized.

The speed of the arpeggio is governed by the Resolution parameter, which is defined by note divisions (half note, quarter note, and so on).

16 From the Resolution menu, choose 1/16.

The arpeggiated notes change to a sixteenth-note resolution, thereby playing twice as fast as before.

To enable synchronization with other MIDI data, you can set the arpeggiator to wait for a specific note division before starting by using the "Snap to" parameter.

17 From the "Snap to" menu, choose 1/8.

The start of arpeggiated playback is quantized to the following eighth note, keeping it in sync with the project's time grid (bars/beats).

NOTE ▸ You can set the length of each arpeggiated note independent of the speed. You can change note lengths by choosing note durations from the Length parameter's menu. However, doing so won't affect the Marimba software instrument because the percussive sound does not sustain very long.

18 Stop playback.

TIP ▶ You can record the output of arpeggiator objects (and others) by inserting them between the physical input and sequencer object in the Click & Ports layer. This ability offers the distinct advantage of allowing you to further manipulate the recorded data within Logic's editors. If you do this, be aware that all input will be arpeggiated until the object is removed from the signal chain.

Using Chord Memorizer Objects

Chord memorizer objects are similar to the Chord Trigger MIDI plug-in in that they can map a single note to a set of up to 12 user-selected notes. This object allows you to trigger complex chords by pressing a single MIDI controller key.

1   Choose New > Chord Memorizer.

A chord memorizer object appears in the Environment window.

NOTE ▶ You might need to move objects around to get them out of the way of one another throughout this lesson. Generally, signal flow in the Environment should flow from left to right, as cable outputs are on the right side of objects.

2   With the chord memorizer object selected, click a shade of dark blue in the color palette.

The chord memorizer object turns blue.

3   Using the Pointer tool, cable the chord memorizer object's output to the monitor object.

4   Double-click the chord memorizer object to open the Chord Memorizer window.

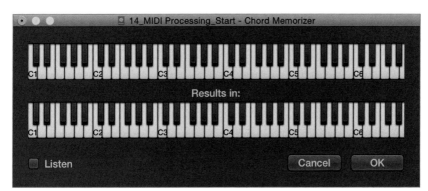

The Chord Memorizer window contains two keyboards. The upper keyboard corresponds to the incoming note, and the lower keyboard corresponds to the notes or chords assigned to the incoming note.

5   On the upper keyboard, click the C4 note.

C4 is automatically selected in the lower keyboard.

6   On the lower keyboard, click C4 to deselect it.

7   On the lower keyboard, click C3, D3, Eb3, F3, D4, and F4 to select them.

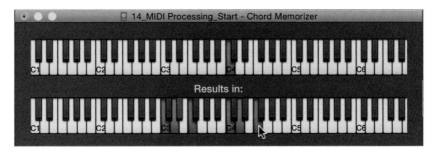

8   Click OK.

For the chord memorizer to process the input from your MIDI controller, you need to open it in the Arrange track list. Instead of doing so using the MIDI Thru tool as you did previously, try changing the track's assignment in the Reassign Track menu.

9 Control-click track 1 and choose Reassign Track > MIDI Process > (Chord Memorizer).

The selected Arrange track (track 1) changes from the arpeggiator object to the chord memorizer object.

10 Press Command-` (grave accent) to reveal the Environment window again.

Because the chord memorizer is not time based, you don't need to play the project to process MIDI input.

11 Press C4 on your MIDI controller.

A full chord sounds, outputting the notes you specified in the lower keyboard of the Chord Memorizer window (C3, D3, Eb3, F3, D4, and F4).

Using Delay Line Objects

Similar to the Note Repeater MIDI plug-in, delay line objects repeat the MIDI events passing through them, achieving a result similar to that of a delay processor creating echoes from audio signals. The most important difference between the two is that instead of sampling and playing bits of audio, the delay line object creates these echoes with additional generated MIDI notes that mirror the incoming MIDI event.

1 Choose New > Delay Line.

A delay line object appears in the Environment window.

2 Select the delay line object, and in the color palette, click a shade of yellow.

The delay line object turns yellow.

3   Cable the delay line object's output to the monitor object.

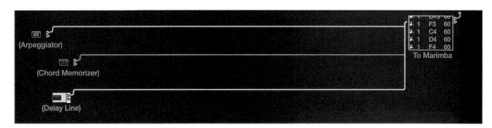

Like with other objects, you need to place the delay line in the Arrange track list so it can process the input from your MIDI controller.

4   Using the MIDI Thru tool, click the Delay Line object.

The selected Arrange track (track 1) changes from the chord memorizer object to the delay line object.

As with the arpeggiator object, the project must be playing to hear the results of the delay line object's processing.

5   Play the project.

6   While the project is playing, play any note on your MIDI controller and listen to the signal through the delay line object. The incoming note is echoed by a single repeat.

You can adjust the number of repeats, timing, velocity, and transposition in the Object Parameter box.

7   In the Object Parameter box, double-click the number next to the Repeats parameter, and enter 4. Press Return.

8   While the project is playing, play any note on your MIDI controller, listening to the signal through the delay line object.

The incoming note is repeated four times. It doesn't sound much like natural echoes, in which the repetitions fall off in volume. You can simulate this effect by adjusting the Velocity parameter to a negative value. By doing so, each successive repeat will lower in velocity by the entered amount.

9   Double-click the number next to the Velocity parameter, and enter *–19*. Press Return.

10 While the project is playing, play any note on your MIDI controller while listening to the signal through the delay line object.

The incoming note is echoed four times, each echo quieter than the previous one.

You can set the speed of the repeats by the Delay parameter. The left value represents divisions; the right value represents ticks. These values allow you to make musical repeats that sync with the tempo of the project.

11 In the Delay parameter fields, double-click the rightmost number, and enter *240*. Press Return.

NOTE ▶ You need to enter tick values when using a computer keyboard to input numbers for the Delay parameter. A sixteenth note equals 240 ticks.

12 While the project is playing, play any note on your MIDI controller, listening to the signal through the delay line object.

The delay time between the repeats is cut in half.

So far you have emulated the results you'd get from a typical audio delay processor. The delay line also allows you to do something unusual: transpose the pitch of each repetition.

13 Double-click the Transpose parameter, and enter –7. Press Return.

14 While the project is playing, play any note on your MIDI controller and listen to the signal through the delay line object.

Each successive repetition drops seven semitones (a perfect fifth).

15 Stop playback.

Creating Signal Chains

So far, you've applied only single processors (arpeggiator, chord memorizer, and delay line) to incoming MIDI signals. The Environment starts to show its potential, however, when you cable processors to each other to enable complex serial and parallel processing.

In this exercise, you will not only learn how to chain processors together in a series but also how to split signals for parallel processing.

1 Drag the topmost cable output from the chord memorizer object to the arpeggiator object (thereby severing the connection to the monitor object).

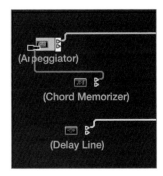

2 Using the MIDI Thru tool, click the chord memorizer object.

The selected track changes to the chord memorizer object.

The incoming MIDI signal now passes from the chord memorizer object to the arpeggiator object, finally ending up at the Marimba software instrument channel (after passing through the monitor object). With these two objects in series, you can trigger complex arpeggiated chords by pressing a single note on your MIDI controller.

3 Start playback.

4   While the project is playing, hold down C4 on your MIDI controller (which you earlier set to play a chord).

The chord generated by the chord memorizer object is arpeggiated.

You'll add to this creation by inserting the delay line object into the signal path.

5   Drag the cable output from the arpeggiator object to the delay line object.

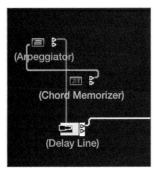

With this arrangement, each note from the arpeggiated chord generated by the chord memorizer and arpeggiator objects will repeat four times, dropping seven semitones each time. This is all triggered by playing a single note on a MIDI controller.

6   While the project is playing, hold down C4 on your MIDI controller.

A whole slew of notes is created with various pitches and rhythmic durations.

7   Stop playback.

Using Transformer Objects

Now that you've investigated chaining MIDI processors in a series, you'll create a parallel processing arrangement in which specified notes are sent down two different signal paths. You can do so using the transformer object.

The transformer object is an extremely powerful processor that can change one type of MIDI data to another. However, that function barely scratches the surface of its capabilities. It also works equally well as a MIDI filter, track automation splitter, Sysex mapper, condition splitter, and much more. For this exercise, you will use the transformer as a condition splitter, sending data down one of two cable outputs depending on criteria you set.

1   Choose New > Transformer.

A transformer object appears in the Environment window.

2   With the transformer object selected, in the color palette, click a shade of red. The transformer object turns red.

3   Double-click the transformer object to open the Transformer window.

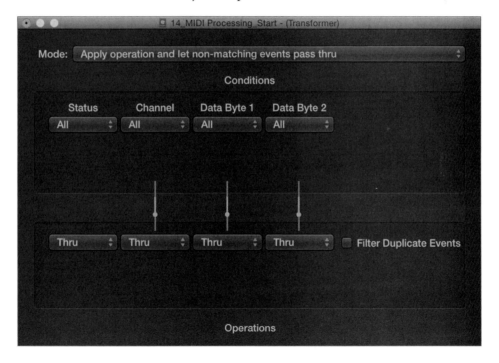

This window is almost identical to the Transform window you explored in Lesson 9 (in the section "Using Transform Functions"). Like the Transform window you used in the MIDI editors to select and edit MIDI data, the Transformer window allows you to specify criteria for selection and transformation. Like the Transform window, the Transformer window also has many available modes.

4 From the Mode menu, choose Condition splitter (true -> top cable).

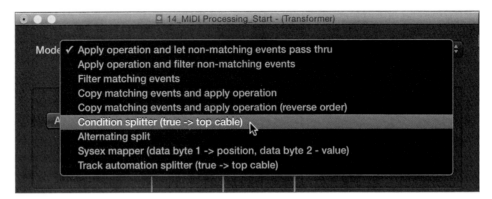

The condition splitter mode sends MIDI data that meets the specified conditions through the uppermost cable output and sends MIDI data that does not fit the criteria to the other output. In this exercise, you will use the condition splitter to deliver specific notes generated by the chord memorizer object to one of the two cable outlets for separate processing chains.

5 From the Status menu, choose = (equal sign).

A pop-up menu displaying Note appears below the Status menu.

6 From the Pitch menu, choose <=.

A value field appears just below the pop-up menu.

7 Double-click the value field and enter *C4*. Press Return.

With this configuration, incoming note values equal to and below C4 will be sent to the upper cable output, and all others will be sent to the lower output.

8   Close the Transformer window.

Next you'll reorder the existing objects to visually reflect the signal flow, which moves from left to right and top to bottom.

9   Move the transformer object to place it to the left of the other Environment window objects.

10 Move the chord memorizer to place it above the transformer object.

The results look like this:

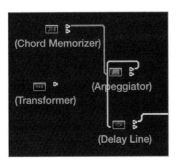

Next you'll cable things up and insert the Transformer into the signal chain.

11 Drag the topmost cable output from the chord memorizer object to the transformer object (thereby disconnecting it from the arpeggiator object).

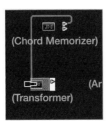

The chord memorizer object will provide the input to the transformer object.

12 Drag the cable output from the transformer object to the arpeggiator object.

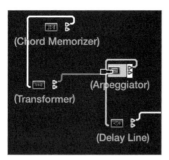

You've now set up one of your signal chains distributed by the transformer object. To complete the arrangement, you need to just set up another signal path to process data that doesn't meet the conditions specified in the transformer object. Begin by creating another monitor object cabled to a different software instrument channel.

13 Choose New > Monitor.

A new monitor object appears.

14 Drag the new monitor object down and to the right, moving it out of the way of the first signal chain.

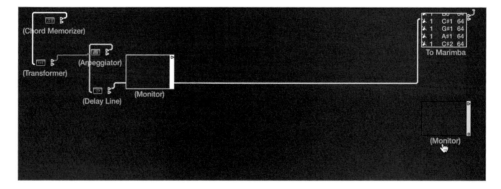

15 Using the Text tool, click the new monitor object, and enter *To 8bit Kit*.

16 Using the Pointer tool, Option-click the cable output on the monitor object and choose Mixer > Software Instrument > 8bit Kit.

A cable appears, connecting the objects between the layers of the Environment.

17 Choose New > Arpeggiator. A new arpeggiator object appears.

18 With the new arpeggiator object selected, click a shade of orange in the color palette. The arpeggiator object turns orange.

19 Drag down the new arpeggiator object, moving it out of the way of the first signal chain.

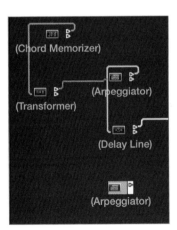

20 In the Object Parameter box, set the Direction and Velocity parameters to Random, and the Resolution and "Snap to" parameters to 1/16.

21 Cable the new arpeggiator object's output to the monitor object labeled To 8bit Kit.

22 Cable the transformer object's lowest cable to the new arpeggiator object.

You've now set up two complete signal chains with separate processing. The source events are generated by the chord memorizer object, with the transformer object splitting the data by note range (those equal to or below C4, and those above C4). Now all that's left is to try it out.

23 Start playback.

24 While the project is playing, hold down C4 on your MIDI controller.

The result is pulsating, surging polyrhythms that never repeat twice, activated by a single key on your MIDI controller.

25 Stop playback after you've listened to your creation.

Using Cable Switcher Objects

Like a transformer object, a cable switcher object can help direct signal flow. Basically, this object is a switch that you can trigger manually to direct the signal flow out of its outputs. The switch can take on different forms, such as a fader button or pop-up menu, which allows you to interact with it in different ways.

In this exercise, you will insert a cable switcher into the signal path, enabling you to switch between two routes at any given time.

1 Choose New > Fader > Specials > Cable Switcher.

A cable switcher object appears.

2 With the cable switcher object selected, click a shade of light blue in the color palette.

3 Close the Color window. (You won't need it for the rest of the lesson.)

4 Click the cable switcher's name, and drag the cable switcher to the right of the upper-most arpeggiator object (the green object connected to the Marimba software instrument channel).

5 Drag the uppermost cable output of the green arpeggiator to the cable switcher.

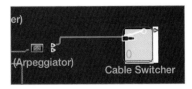

6   Drag the cable switcher object's cable output to the monitor object labeled To Marimba.

Doing so forms one signal path that feeds directly into the Marimba software instrument channel.

7   Drag the lower cable output of the cable switcher object to the delay line object.

To make the signal flow easier to view, you'll move the delay line object to the right of the cable switcher object.

8   Drag the delay line object to the right, placing it below and to the right of the cable switcher object.

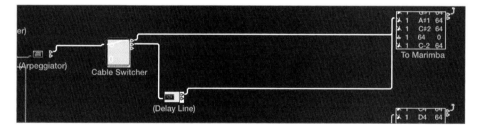

This setup forms the other signal path, passing through the delay line object and eventually reaching the Marimba software instrument channel.

9   Try clicking the cable switcher object a few times.

The cable switcher changes configuration, routing the input to a different cable output each time you click.

Notice that you have three output destinations from which to select, and only two are cabled to signal paths. Like any other Environment object, the cable switcher adds an additional cable output (up to 128) when you connect a new output cable.

To route the cable switcher only to the used outputs, you need to alter its range in the Object Parameter box. The Range parameter is expressed by two numbers that form the upper (left number) and lower (right number) values of a specified range.

10 Click the cable switcher's name to display its parameters. In the Object Parameter box, drag down the rightmost Range parameter (127) until it reaches a value of 1.

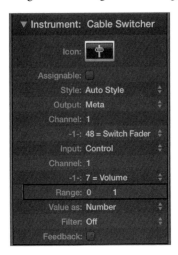

Doing so sets the Range from 0 to 1 (two outputs) and allows the cable switcher object to toggle between the two signal paths connected to its cable outputs.

As mentioned earlier, you can change the cable switcher object's interface to reflect different types of switches. You can do so by choosing an option from the Style menu in the Object Parameter box.

11 From the Style menu, choose As Text.

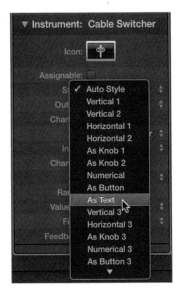

The cable switcher object changes to display text. By default, the displayed text corresponds to the numbered cable output (0 or 1); you can toggle the number by clicking the cable switcher itself. This is not a particularly elegant solution for labeling and accessing the signal paths cabled to the cable switcher's outputs. However, you can enter your own text instead of the default range numbers to create clearer labels in the signal paths.

12 Double-click the cable switcher object to open the Cable Switcher window.

13 Double-click the uppermost field of the Value Names of Text 'Fader' column and enter *Bypass*. Press Return.

14 In the second field, enter *Delay*. Press Return.

NOTE ▸ The Cable Switcher window has 128 fields that can contain text. When using cable switcher objects with large ranges displayed as text, select the "Behave as Menu" checkbox at the top of the Cable Switcher window. Doing so lets you access the entire range via a pop-up menu, instead of clicking the cable switcher.

15 Close the Cable Switcher window.

The cable switcher object now displays the text you entered in the Cable Switcher window.

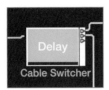

TIP ▸ You can resize any Environment object by dragging its lower-right corner, similar to the way you adjust window size. Resizing enables the cable switcher object to display longer text.

Now you'll try out the cable switcher object while the project is playing. To have your hands free to interact with the cable switcher object, you can create a MIDI region with a C4 note held to trigger the rhythmic patterns played on the Marimba and 8bit Kit software instrument channels.

16 In the Tracks area, use the Pencil tool to create a one-measure MIDI region in the Chord Memorizer track (track 1), starting at 1 1 1 1.

17 Double-click the region you just created to open the Piano Roll Editor.

18 In the Piano Roll Editor, use the Pencil tool to create a C4 note with a velocity of 80 that lasts the entire length of measure 1.

19 Close the Piano Roll Editor.

20 In the Arrange window's Region Parameter box, select the checkbox next to Loop.

The region is now looped and will continually play a C4 to drive the rhythmic patterns played by the Marimba and 8bit Kit software instruments.

21 Press Command-` (grave accent) to reopen the Environment window.

22 Play the project.

23 While the project is playing, click the cable switcher object to switch between the signal paths (with the delay line object and without).

24 Stop playback.

Using Touch Tracks Objects

Touch tracks objects allow you to trigger MIDI regions or folders by playing single notes. This technique works especially well in a live performance setting because you can trigger anything from short passages or phrases to entire songs by pressing a single key on your MIDI controller.

When triggered in a touch tracks object, MIDI regions or folders play through the instruments assigned to their tracks, sharing the same track-channel relationship they have in the Arrange window. As a result, you can play a single touch tracks object that includes MIDI regions from multiple tracks, each through its respective channel (and sound source).

In this exercise, you will use a touch tracks object to play the MIDI regions present in the Arrange tracks. Notice that these regions are muted and have not been sounding when the project is played. However, muted regions will sound when triggered via a touch tracks object. This behavior allows you to create MIDI recordings via normal methods in the Arrange window for import to a touch tracks object and then mute the regions so they don't sound when the project is played.

1   Choose New > Touch Tracks.

A touch tracks object appears in the Environment, and its corresponding Touch Tracks window opens.

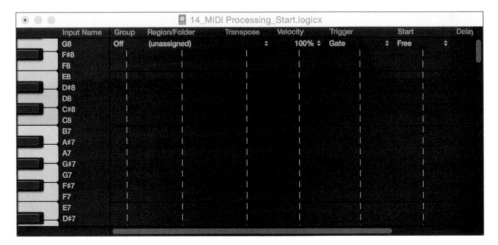

In this window you can assign different MIDI regions (or folders) to each key represented to the left of the window. Dragging a region or folder from the Tracks area to
the target row in the Region/Folder column will assign that region or folder to a key.

2   Scroll down in the Touch Tracks window until you can see a range of roughly C2 to E3.

3   Drag the first region (Lead 1) on the Analog Lead track to the Touch Tracks window
and drop it on the C3 row in the Region/Folder column (the pointer will change to
the Pencil tool).

NOTE ▶ You might need to reposition the Touch Tracks window to see both it and
the Arrange tracks window.

NOTE ▶ If you mistakenly drop the region in the wrong place, you can delete it by
double-clicking its name (Lead 1) and choosing Delete from the dialog.

The region's name now appears in the Region/Folder column for C3.

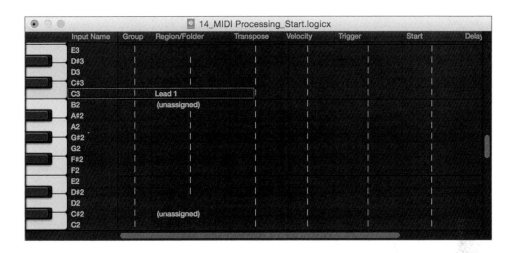

4   Drag the second region (Lead 2) on the Analog Lead track to the Touch Tracks window and drop it on the D3 row in the Region/Folder column.

The region's name now appears in the Region/Folder column for D3.

5   Drag the third region (Lead 3) on the Analog Lead track to the Touch Tracks window and drop it on the E3 row in the Region/Folder column.

The region's name now appears in the Region/Folder column for E3.

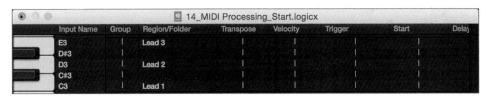

Now that you've specified the regions to be played and assigned them to MIDI notes, you need to place the touch tracks object on a track to enable it to receive MIDI input.

6   Press the Down Arrow key to select the No Output track (track 2).

7   Using the MIDI Thru tool, click the Touch Tracks object to assign the selected track.

> **NOTE ▶** The touch tracks object must receive MIDI note input in order to work. However, it will not pass MIDI events through to its output, so generally it's a good idea to place it at the end of a chain of objects.

To allow the touch tracks object to play the MIDI regions, the project has to be playing.

8   Play the project.

9   With the project playing, try playing the C3, D3, and E3 keys one at a time on your MIDI controller, holding them down for various lengths of time.

Whenever you press a key, the triggered Lead 1, Lead 2, and Lead 3 regions play for as long as you hold that key or until the regions end. This playback behavior is referred to as the *gate* trigger mode, which is the default mode for any region imported into the Touch Tracks window.

In the Touch Tracks window, you can change the triggering behavior for any region by changing the setting in the Trigger column.

10 In the Touch Tracks window, click the Gate setting in the Trigger column for the C3 note (Lead 1) and choose GateLoop.

This setting acts similarly to Gate, except that it will continue to repeat the region for as long as you press the key.

11   Change the Trigger setting for D3 (Lead 2) and E3 (Lead 3) to GateLoop.

12   With the project playing, try playing the C3, D3, and E3 keys one at a time on your MIDI controller, holding them down for various lengths of time.

The region playback loops for as long as you hold down a key.

13   Stop playback.

Using Apple Loops with Touch Tracks

Any type of MIDI region is fair game for use with touch tracks. So, you can use imported MIDI regions as you would use Standard MIDI files and software instrument Apple Loops (green Apple Loops). In particular, software instrument Apple Loops consist of MIDI regions paired with a sound source (software instrument and effects settings are instantiated when you drag them to your project), and you can drop them into the Touch Tracks window for triggering. In effect, you can use touch tracks to trigger these loops much as a sampler would trigger audio files by mapping individual loops to the keyboard.

In this exercise, you will import a few software instrument Apple Loops for use in the touch tracks object you created earlier.

1   Click the Apple Loops button to open the Loop Browser.

2   In the search field, enter *disco pickbass*, and press Return.

The Loop Browser displays a variety of software instrument Apple Loops with the words "disco pickbass" in their names.

3   In the Loop Browser, click the Disco Pickbass 02 loop, and play it to familiarize yourself with the material.

4   Drag the Disco Pickbass 02 loop to the blank area below the existing tracks.

A new track is created with the Disco Pickbass channel strip, and the Apple Loops region (Disco Pickbass 03) appears on the track.

5   In the Loop Browser, click the Disco Pickbass 06 loop (you will need to scroll down the list), and play it to familiarize yourself with the material.

6   Drag the Disco Pickbass 06 loop to 6 1 1 1 on the Disco Pickbass track (track 7).

The Apple Loops region (Disco Pickbass 06) appears on the track.

7   Mute both Disco Pickbass regions.

8   Drag the Disco Pickbass 02 region to the Touch Tracks window and drop it in the Region/Folder column for C2.

NOTE ▶ You might need to scroll down in the Touch Tracks window. The window will automatically scroll when you drag regions to its upper and lower edges.

9   Drag the Disco Pickbass 06 region to the Touch Tracks window and drop it in the Region/Folder column for D2.

Previously, you set up the Lead regions to trigger when you pressed a key and to repeat until you released the key (GateLoop). This time, you will set up the triggering a little differently by allowing the region to continue looping even after you release the key, and not stopping until you press a subsequent key. You can do so using another Trigger setting, ToggleLoop.

10 In the Touch Tracks window, click the Gate setting in the Trigger column for both the C2 and D2 notes (Disco Pickbass 02 and Disco Pickbass 06) and choose ToggleLoop.

In the current setup, you could trigger the regions at any part of the measure, on or off the beat. This configuration is fine for the rubato Lead regions, but the Disco Pickbass regions could play out of sync with the rhythmic patterns being generated by the arpeggiator and delay line objects.

For just this sort of situation, the Touch Tracks window provides a way to quantize the playback start by changing settings in the Start column.

11 Expand the Touch Tracks window to view the Start column, if necessary.

12 In the Start column, click the vertical white line for the C2 note (Disco Pickbass 02), and choose Next 1/1.

The 1/1 setting quantizes playback to the next whole note, starting the region playback at the beginning of the bar.

13 In the Start column, click the vertical white line for the D2 note (Disco Pickbass 06), and choose Next 1/1.

The Touch Tracks window allows you to transpose individual regions by entering an offset in the Transpose column.

14 In the Transpose column for the D2 note (Disco Pickbass 06), drag upward to a value of +5.

This setting will transpose the Disco Pickbass 06 region up five semitones (a perfect fourth) upon playback.

NOTE ▶ This transposition is different from the typical transposition behavior of samplers because the length and speed of the region will not be altered and will remain in perfect time with the project.

15 Play the project.

16 While the project is playing, press the C2 and D2 keys one at a time on your MIDI controller.

NOTE ▶ Remember, because Trigger is set to ToggleLoop for both keys, you don't need to hold down a key. It will continue sounding until you press the key again.

The Disco Pickbass regions play in time with the project, and they toggle on or off when you press subsequent keys. In addition, the Disco Pickbass 06 region plays a perfect fourth higher, changing the harmonic underpinning of the composition.

17 While one of the Disco Pickbass regions is still playing, try triggering one of the Lead regions (C3, D3, and E3) on top.

You probably noticed that the Disco Pickbass regions stopped playing when you triggered one of the Lead regions, and vice versa. This is because when regions are initially assigned in the Touch Tracks window, they have the same group assignment. When you trigger a region, any other region in the same group will stop playing (similar to the behavior of a monophonic synthesizer).

This relationship makes sense for regions of a similar kind, but not if you want to trigger regions independently of each other without stopping their playback (similar to a polyphonic synthesizer).

18 In the Touch Tracks window, double-click the Group setting for all the Lead regions (C3, D3, and E3), and enter *1*. Press Return.

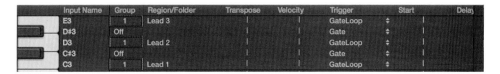

	Input Name	Group	Region/Folder	Transpose	Velocity	Trigger	Start	Delay
	E3	1	Lead 3			GateLoop	↕	
	D#3	Off				Gate	↕	
	D3	1	Lead 2			GateLoop	↕	
	C#3	Off				Gate	↕	
	C3	1	Lead 1			GateLoop	↕	

19 In the Touch Tracks window, double-click the Group setting for both of the Disco Pickbass regions (C2 and D2), and enter *2*. Press Return.

Now you are ready to test your creation.

20 While the project is playing, try triggering one of the Disco Pickbass regions (C2 and D2), and let it loop while triggering the Lead regions (C3, D3, and E3) on top.

21 Stop the project and close the Touch Tracks window.

22 Choose File > Save As.

23 Name the project *14_MIDI Processing_Finished* and save it to Music > Advanced Logic X_Files > Lessons > Completed.

> **TIP** ▶ If you have created a useful tool or widget in the Environment, you can import Environment layers from one project to another by choosing Options > Import Environment > Layer.

Lesson Review

1. What distinguishes MIDI plug-ins from other real-time MIDI processors in Logic (like the Environment)?
2. How are layers used in the Environment?
3. What does the physical input object represent?
4. What does the keyboard object do?
5. What does a monitor object do?
6. What does the sequencer input object represent?
7. How do you cable an object from one layer to another?
8. What does an arpeggiator object do?
9. What does a chord memorizer object do?
10. What does a delay line object do?
11. What does a transformer object do?
12. What does a cable switcher object do?
13. What does a touch tracks object do?

Answers

1. MIDI plug-ins can be inserted directly into a channel's signal flow without having to leave the Mixer.
2. Layers are used to organize objects of similar type or function in the Environment.
3. The physical input object represents the ports of your MIDI interface or MIDI controller (with direct MIDI-to-USB connection).
4. The keyboard object displays incoming MIDI notes as well as generating new notes from its output.
5. A monitor object displays MIDI events passing from its input to its output in a list form.
6. The sequencer input object represents the connection to the Logic sequencer.
7. You can cable across layers by Option-clicking the output of the object and selecting the input object from the menu.

8. An arpeggiator object arpeggiates harmonic input (chords) by outputting each note individually in a selectable pattern.

9. A chord memorizer object maps a single note to a set of up to 12 user-selected notes.

10. A delay line object repeats MIDI events passing through it, achieving a result similar to that of a delay processor creating echoes from audio signals.

11. A transformer object primarily changes one type of MIDI data to another. It can also act as a MIDI filter, track automation splitter, SysEx mapper, and condition splitter.

12. A cable switcher object manually directs the signal flow out of multiple outputs.

13. A touch tracks object allows you to trigger MIDI regions or folders by playing single notes.

15

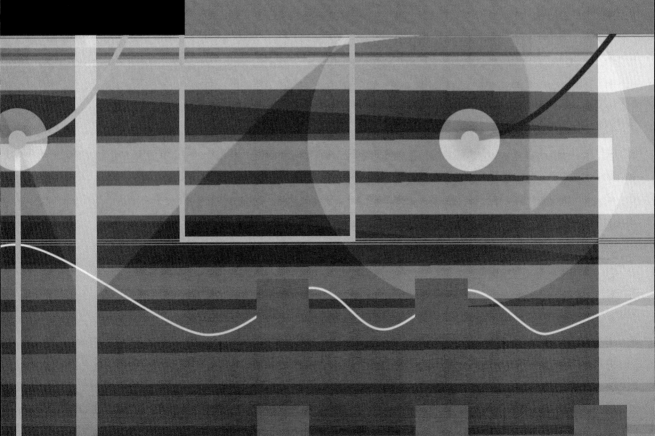

Working with Notation

Logic was built from the ground up with musical notation as a central part of MIDI sequencing. (In fact, Logic evolved from a 1980s notation application called Notator.) As a result, Logic includes comprehensive notation capabilities for creating and printing parts and scores. You can enter notes directly into the Score Editor or automatically transcribe an existing MIDI recording.

This marriage of notation and MIDI data is integral to Logic. Every note in the score represents a MIDI note event. Logic is often called a *notating sequencer* because you can access all the powerful arranging and composing functionality of its sequencer in the notation environment of the Score Editor.

In this lesson you will explore the Logic Score Editor, inputting notation and transcribing audio and MIDI regions for the composition "Sintra," a Latin guitar piece with drums, percussion, and bass.

Creating Notation

You can employ a variety of methods when inputting notation, including graphic input, step input, and real-time transcription. In this exercise you will focus on the first two techniques, entering notes directly into the Score Editor.

Let's start by opening the project file you will be using for this lesson and notating the rhythm guitar part, transcribing the audio file into notation.

> **NOTE ▶** You will need to set the "Display Middle C as" preference to C3 (Yamaha) to accurately follow the directions in this exercise and others throughout the book. This is set by default, but it is best to verify this setting before you continue. You'll find this option in Logic Pro X > Preferences > Display > General.

1   Choose File > Open.

2   Go to Music > Advanced Logic X_Files > Lessons and open **15_Sintra_Start.logic**.

3   Play the song to familiarize yourself with the material.

    As you can see in the Tracks area, the song mainly consists of software instrument tracks outputting to the EXS24 mkII software sampler, mixed with audio recordings of nylon string guitar. Because the Score Editor interprets MIDI data to create nota-tion, you will be working with a transcription of the main nylon string guitar part (track 3), inputting and adjusting notes where needed.

    > **NOTE ▶** Guitar notation sounds an octave lower than written. In order to have the Score Editor display the notation correctly and maintain an accurate playback for this project, all regions in the Guitar Score track have a Transposition value of +12 in the Region Parameter box.

4   If the first region (Guitar Score_Intro) in the Guitar Score track (track 3) is not already selected, click to select it.

5   Press the number 3 to recall screenset 3.

    This screenset places the Score Editor in the top half of the screen, Piano Roll Editor in the bottom half, and Transport bar in the middle. Both editors display the selected Guitar Score track's contents.

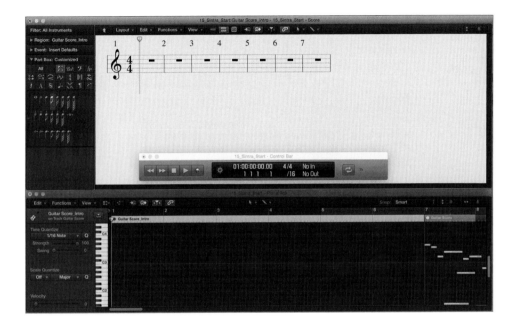

You are viewing a blank region that was created as a place for you to input notational data. Notice that rests are automatically displayed.

NOTE ▶ Like most of the other editors in Logic, the Score Editor can be displayed both in the Main window and in an independent window. To open the Score Editor in a separate window, choose Window > Score Editor in the main menu bar, or drag the Score tab from the bottom of the Tracks area.

Entering Notes Using Graphic Input

You can graphically input notes and other notational elements in the Score Editor by selecting them from the Part box, a palette of notational symbols in the inspector (at the far left of the Score Editor).

Each group button acts as a filter, allowing you to view only specific notational symbols at any given time.

1   In the Part box group menu (the upper section), click each object group button.

The objects associated with each group are added to the panel just below the group menu. The most recently selected object group appears at the top of the panel.

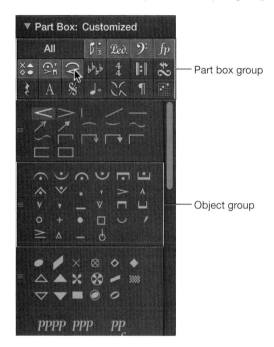

Part box group

Object group

When a group filter button is inactive, the notational symbols are hidden in the palette. To help keep the palette organized, you can select Part box sets that combine groups for common tasks.

2   In the Part box pop-up menu, choose Notes & Rests.

Only notes, pedal markings, key signature, and rests groups appear in the palette.

3   Choose the Pencil tool.

4   Since the song is in the key of D major, click D in the key signature object group. (You might need to scroll downward.)

5   Click the staff between the treble clef and the time signature.

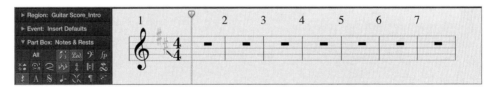

A D major key signature is inserted.

6   In the Part box, scroll upward to view the note object groups.

Various rhythmic lengths are displayed.

7 In the object group, select the eighth-note duration.

8 Using the Pencil tool in the Score Editor, hold down the B line in the middle of measure 5, using the help tag to position an eighth note at 5 2 3 1. Then release the mouse button.

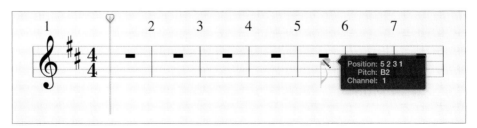

NOTE ▶ When the MIDI Out button is enabled (at the top of the Score Editor), you'll get aural as well as visual feedback as you drag a note around the staff. The note is played by the EXS24 mkII plug-in (using a nylon string guitar sampler instrument) on the current track.

An eighth note is inserted on the B line at 5 2 3 1.

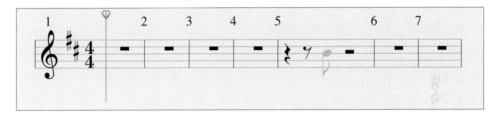

NOTE ▶ The note also appears in the Piano Roll Editor, and it provides a good reference, especially for length.

9 Use the same technique to insert a note on the D line above the first note you created.

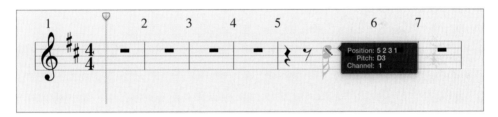

You might have difficulty landing on the correct pitch when graphically inserting a note. If your composition falls into a consistent key, you can make input easier by turning on the Diatonic Insert feature. With this feature activated, you are limited to entering only those notes in the current key signature.

10 Choose Edit > Diatonic Insert.

11 Still using the Pencil tool, click anywhere above the D eighth note you created, and then drag up and down while looking at the help tag.

The pitch choices are limited to diatonic pitches (so in D major, your pitch choices will not include C natural or F natural).

12 Release the mouse button to place an eighth note at E above the D eighth note you previously created.

   NOTE ▶ The note heads automatically change position, correctly notating adjacent pitches.

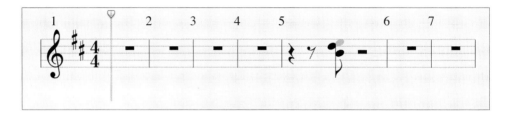

Just as in any of the other MIDI editors in Logic, you can copy and paste note data.

13 Choose the Pointer tool.

14 In the Score Editor, drag a selection rectangle around the chord you just created.

15 Option-drag the chord to 5 3 1 1.

A copy of the chord is created at the new position.

   NOTE ▶ When you move and transport notes, they automatically snap to the division value set in the Transport bar.

Dragging Notes into the Score

Another way to input notes is to drag them directly from the Part box.

1   Drag a quarter note from the notes object group to the B line at 5 3 3 1.

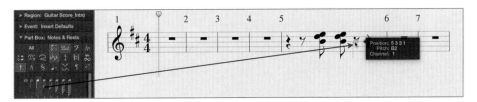

A quarter note is created where you dropped the note.

Although this can be a good method for inputting notes with a variety of durations, journeying back and forth across the screen can get tedious. Fortunately, you can tear off the Part box as a floating palette and position it anywhere on the screen.

2   Drag the Part box title bar near the measure you are working on.

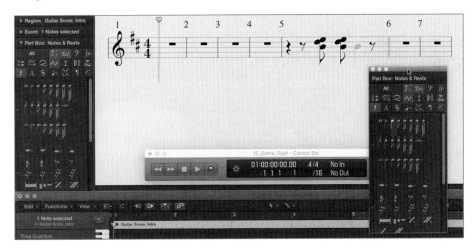

3   To create a chord, drag two more quarter notes from the floating palette, dropping them on the D and A above the B you just input.

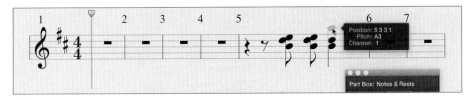

4   Create another chord at 5 4 3 1 by dragging half notes to B (on the same line as the previous B), and to D and F#, above the previous B.

A chord lasting two beats is created, tied across the bar line between measures 5 and 6.

NOTE ▶ In Logic you cannot insert ties graphically when using standard notation. Logic creates and displays them automatically according to the length of the MIDI note.

Adjusting Note Length

Musical notation depicts note length using a specific set of symbols (sixteenth notes, eighth notes, and so on). As you can see in the Piano Roll Editor, length is depicted proportionally: The longer the duration, the more horizontal space a note takes up. You can adjust note length in the Score Editor by inputting in the Event inspector, but you can also lengthen a note by dragging it directly on the staff.

1   Drag a selection rectangle around the final chord, and then Option-drag it to 6 2 3 1.

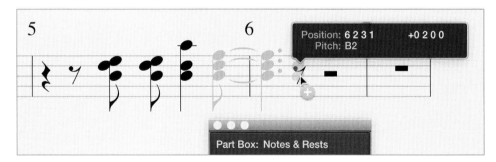

2   On the left side of the Score Editor window, click the disclosure triangle for the selected chord to display the Event inspector.

The Event inspector displays the parameters for the selected chord, as indicated in the header by "3 Notes selected."

Notice that Logic also supplies a chord analysis of the selected notes (identifying these notes as a B minor chord).

NOTE ▸ When notes are graphically input into the Score Editor, they are given lengths that are slightly less than the full value (hence the high tick numbers) to avoid overlaps in note length.

3   In the Event inspector, double-click the numbers next to the Length parameter and enter *0 0 2 0* (with spaces), signifying an eighth note, in the text field. Press Return.

TIP ▸ When entering numbers into the Event inspector, you can also use periods, instead of spaces, to separate the digits.

The lengths of the selected notes change from half notes to eighth notes.

NOTE ▶ The division value setting for a project impacts how you interpret the Length parameter. In the project file you are using for this lesson, the division value is set for sixteenth notes (/16), so 0 0 2 0 represents an eighth-note value (two sixteenth notes).

4 Option-drag the chord to 6 3 3 1.

A copy of the chord is placed and selected at the new position, ready for editing.

5 Choose View > Duration Bars > Selected Notes.

The chord you copied now displays duration bars around each selected note.

6 Drag one of the selected duration bars to the right (while watching the help tag) to reach a duration of 0 1 2 0 (a dotted quarter note).

The note lengths of the chord change to dotted quarter notes.

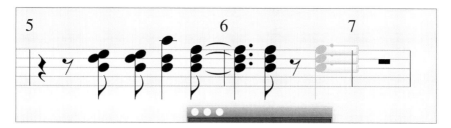

7 Close the floating notes group palette.

Entering Notes Using Step Input

Although graphic input allows you to enter notes precisely, it can be slow. A faster technique is step input, which allows you to insert notes at the current playhead position while Logic automatically moves the playhead forward based on the selected rhythmic length. You can set a note's pitch and length by clicking an onscreen piano keyboard, pressing a key on your computer keyboard, or using a MIDI input device.

To begin step input, you need to place the playhead at the position where you want to begin.

1   Option-click the staff at 5 1 1 1 (use the help tag) to place the playhead at the beginning of measure 5.

> **TIP** ▶ Option-clicking in the staff (not on notes or other symbols) is a quick way to locate the playhead in the Score Editor for playback or editing.

2   In the main menu bar, choose Window > Show Step Input Keyboard.

The Step Input keyboard opens. You can use the buttons in this window to set the pitch, length, and dynamics (velocities) of a note.

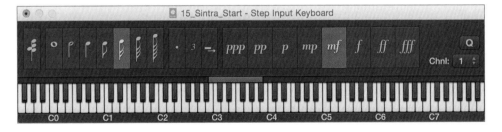

> **TIP** ▶ You can use the Step Input keyboard in any Logic editor; it is especially effective when you control it with an extensive set of key commands (including commands for specific note pitches). This feature allows you to quickly input notes entirely from your computer keyboard for non-real-time purposes such as creating notation.

3   If necessary, reposition the Step Input keyboard so it does not cover up the score.

4   At the left side of the window, click the whole-note button.

5   On the Step Input keyboard, click the D2 key.

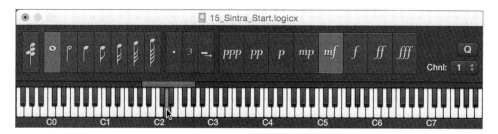

A D note is inserted just below the staff, and the playhead jumps to the end of the inserted whole-note value.

NOTE ▸ Don't panic! The note you just input is displayed as a dotted quarter note for the reason explained in the "Creating a Polyphonic Staff Style" section later in this lesson.

Instead of clicking the note on the Step Input keyboard, you can also use a MIDI controller to insert notes by clicking the MIDI In button in any editor so that Logic can receive MIDI incoming data. When MIDI In is enabled, Logic "listens" for MIDI note input.

6   While looking at the MIDI Activity display in the Transport bar, find the D2 and A1 keys on your MIDI controller.

7   In the Score Editor, click the MIDI In button to turn it on.

8   On the Step Input keyboard, click the half-note button.

9   On your MIDI controller, press the D2 key, then the A1 key.

A D note is created at 6 1 1 1 and an A note at 6 3 1 1 (spaced by a half-note interval).

As long as the MIDI In button is on, Logic assumes that you are using step input, and it will create notes based on MIDI input. For this reason, you need to turn off MIDI input when you are finished using MIDI for note input.

10 Click the MIDI In button to turn MIDI input off.

11 Close the Step Input keyboard.

Working with Guitar Notation

Just as text can be formatted depending on its context (such as paragraphs for standard text, stanzas in poetry, and outlines), musical notation can be represented in a variety of formats, depending on the instrument, transposition, number of voices, and so on.

Logic allows you to format notes using staff styles, which incorporate multiple attributes of the notes in a MIDI region such as clef, staff size, instrument transposition, and various voice-display parameters. A staff style acts like a notation-display filter, and you can change it at any time.

To enable Logic to accurately display the guitar part you input previously, you must first choose an appropriate score style. You will explore the two distinct types of guitar notation—tablature and standard—in the following exercises.

1 Above the Event inspector, click the disclosure triangle to show the Region inspector (Guitar Score_Intro).

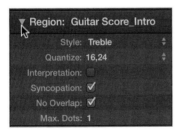

The Region inspector contains parameters that affect the display of the selected MIDI region. The Style parameter designates the staff style assigned to the region.

2   Click and hold the Style pop-up menu.

The staff style options appear.

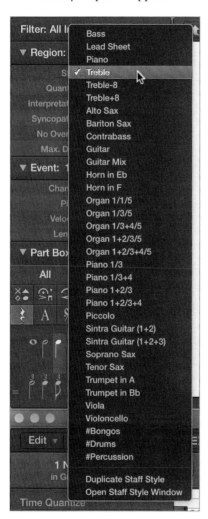

Logic includes many staff styles that each contain several attributes, such as clef assignment and display transposition.

NOTE ► Logic saves staff styles in a project file, which you can import into other songs by choosing File > Project Settings > Import Project Settings.

3   From the Style menu, choose Guitar.

The notation in the Score Editor changes to display guitar tablature.

NOTE ► Logic has extensive options for creating the tablature of all types of string instruments (guitar, bass, banjo, and so on). You can set the string tunings, type of note head, and other appearance options in Project Settings > Score by selecting the Tablature tab. In addition, you can insert tablature-specific symbols such as hammer-ons, pull-offs, and palm mutes into your score by selecting the Chord Grid group in the Part box.

As you can see, staff styles are extremely versatile in their displays of note data.

4   From the Style menu, choose Treble, returning the notation to its default setting.

NOTE ► Logic automatically assigns a default staff style (Treble, Bass, or Piano) to a MIDI region based on its octave and range.

Creating a Polyphonic Staff Style

You probably noticed that the three bass notes you created by step input are displayed incorrectly in the Score Editor. The notes do not appear to sustain for the full amount of time and are cut off by the notes that follow. However, if you look at the notes in the Piano Roll Editor (in the bottom half of the screen), you'll notice that the lengths of those notes are displayed correctly.

Our guitar part was input as a single voice, and therefore the note lengths are cut off because there is no voice independence. To solve this problem, you need to create a polyphonic staff style that can display multiple independent voices at once.

1   Shift-click to select the three notes you just created via step input (D2, D2, and A1).

The corresponding notes are highlighted in the Piano Roll Editor.

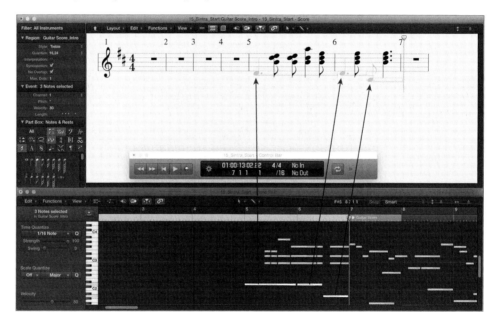

Notice the difference in the notes' representation in the Piano Roll and Score Editors. The first note is sustained for the entire measure, and it should be notated as a whole note instead of a dotted quarter note. The reason for this discrepancy lies in the established system for the notation of a polyphonic instrument. A polyphonic instrument, such as a guitar, notated on a single staff needs to display rhythmically different melodic lines in the same staff. These voices, in turn, must be able to display length, stem direction, and rests independent of each other.

2   In the Score Editor's local menu bar, choose Layout > Show Staff Styles.

The Staff Style window opens, displaying the contents of the default Treble staff style.

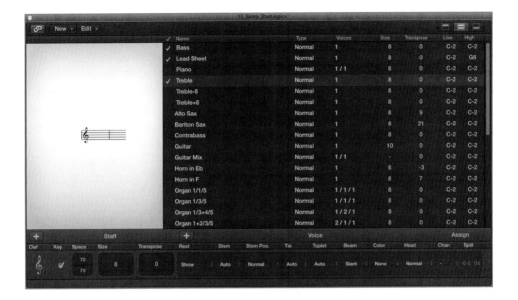

The top of the Staff Styles window contains staff overviews that display information for each of the available staff styles. (Staff styles that are currently used in the project have a check mark next to their names.) The lower area of the Staff Styles window contains the Staff, Voice, and Assign parameters for the selected staff style.

The data currently displayed in the parameter area is for the selected Treble staff style, a single-voice staff with various display attributes.

3   From the New menu, choose Duplicate Staff Style.

A new staff style is created with the attributes of the Treble staff style (temporarily named "Treble*copied"). Let's rename it.

4   In the name field, double-click the staff style name, enter *Guitar 1+2*, and then
    press Return.

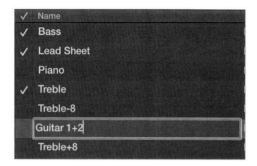

Notice that the new staff style contains a single staff and voice. A staff style can have
multiple staves with independent settings, each containing as many voices as you need.

In guitar notation, multiple voices are displayed on a single treble staff. Each voice is
differentiated by the direction of the stems, ties, and tuplets. Let's continue customizing
the staff style to reflect these display parameters by first inserting an additional voice.

5   Click the Add (+) button to the left of the Voice column.

A new voice is added to the staff style and represented by an additional row of menus
in the Voice parameter area.

NOTE ▸ You can delete voices by selecting any parameter in the respective row, and
pressing Delete.

In guitar notation, when more than one voice is displayed at the same time, the stems,
ties, and tuplets of the top voice always point upward. You can reflect this in the staff
style by modifying the Voice attributes for the top voice.

6   In the top voice, from the Stem parameter menu, choose Up.

7   Do the same for the Tie and Tuplet parameter menus.

8   In the bottom voice, click the Stem, Tie, and Tuplet menus one at a time and choose Down.

By default, each voice in a staff style can display rests. This can create multiple rests in a staff, which are appropriate for divided (divisi) parts but not for a solo part.

9   From the Rest parameter menu for the bottom voice, choose Hide.

The rests for the bottom voice are hidden.

TIP ▶ You can insert rests manually by dragging them into the score from the Part box. These are graphic indicators only and have no effect on the playback of the MIDI region.

The last thing to consider is how to assign individual notes in the region to each voice. By default, a staff style will use a split note to do this. Pitches that fall above the split note are assigned to voice one, and pitches that fall below the split note are assigned to voice two. You can change this split note in the Assign parameters in the Staff Style window.

However, this technique usually won't work for guitar notation because voices are assigned primarily to represent melody (or bass lines) and the accompaniment, and they can consist of any range of pitches. Instead, you can assign voices in a staff style using the individual notes' MIDI channel numbers.

NOTE ▸ Each note can have its own MIDI channel in Logic. The MIDI Out channel setting of the MIDI controller applies the channel setting on input, or you can apply it after the fact using Logic editors.

10 In the Assign columns (far right), from the Chan(nel) menu for the top voice, choose 1.

11 From the Chan(nel) menu for the bottom voice, choose 2.

With these settings, all notes using MIDI channel 1 are assigned to the top voice, and all notes using MIDI channel 2 are assigned to the bottom voice.

Now that you have created the polyphonic Guitar staff style, you'll apply it to the displayed region.

12 Close the Staff Style window.

13 In the Region inspector, from the Style menu, choose Guitar 1+2.

The notation changes slightly, displaying the notes with all stems pointing up. When you insert notes manually, the same default MIDI channel is assigned to all notes (in this case, channel 1). When you applied the staff style, all the notes in the region were assigned to the top voice.

You don't have to individually change the MIDI channel for each note you want to assign to the bottom voice. Instead, you can quickly assign notes to adjacent voices by using the Voice Separation tool. This tool allows you to draw a line between voices you want to separate. Notes below the line are bumped to the adjacent voice below their current assignments, and notes above the line are bumped up a voice.

14 Choose View > Duration Bars > Off. Choose the Voice Separation tool.

15 Using the Voice Separation tool, draw between the bass notes and the chords in one continuous line.

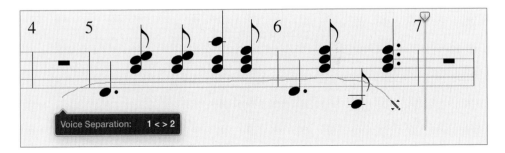

The bass notes are assigned to the bottom voice and displayed correctly.

NOTE ▶ You can continually adjust voice assignments with the Voice Separation tool by drawing lines above and below individual notes or entire passages.

Working with Text

Text appears in various ways in a score, supplying everything from lyrics to performance indications. Although you can only select specialized text objects (lyrics, chords, song titles, and so on) for insertion from the text group in the Part box, you can also add standard text by simply using the Text tool.

To illustrate this, let's create a basic performance indication for the guitar part.

1   Choose the Text tool.

2   Click in the first measure.

A text insertion point is created.

3   Type *Latin* and press Return.

4   Using the Pointer tool, drag the newly created text above the staff in the first measure.

NOTE ▶ Logic automatically justifies newly created text depending upon where you click the page. To ensure that the new text is tied to the staff, click in the staff first, and then drag the text to the appropriate position.

You can format inserted text in any font or size in the Fonts window.

5   From the Score Editor's local menu bar, choose Functions > Text Attributes > Fonts.

The Fonts window opens.

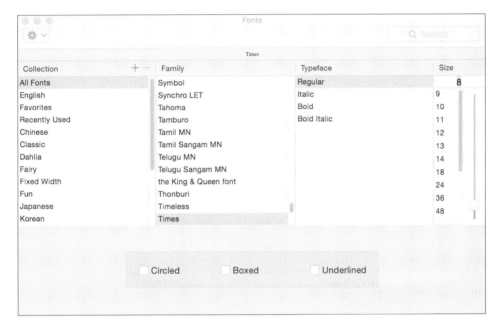

6   In the Size column, click 12.

The selected text increases in size.

7   Close the Fonts window.

Using Text Styles

Just as you can format notes using staff styles, you can also create text styles to format text elements in the Score Editor. Each text style contains attributes, such as font and size, you can apply to specific types of text objects as a group. In this exercise, you will create a new text style you can assign to any inserted text in the current score.

1   In the Score Editor's local menu bar, choose Layout > Text Styles.

The Text Styles window opens. (You may need to resize the window to view its entire contents.)

2   In the text style window, click the Add (+) button.

A new text style is created at the bottom of the list.

3   Double-click the new text style in the Name column, and then enter *Performance Indications*. Press Return.

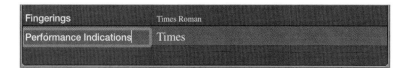

4   In the Example column for the Performance Indications text style, click the selected font (Times).

The Fonts window opens.

5   In the Family column of the Fonts window, select Arial.

6   Select the checkbox next to Boxed.

7   In the Size column, select 10.

8   Close the Fonts window.

9   Close the Text Styles window.

Text styles are assigned to a text element in the Event inspector.

10   If necessary, select the performance indication you input earlier in the exercise (Latin).

11   In the Event inspector, from the Style menu, choose Performance Indications.

The text you inserted earlier adapts to the specifications you defined for the assigned text style.

TIP ▶ Text styles are useful for creating specialized text formats commonly used in musical notation, such as rehearsal markings. The Fonts window also includes check-boxes for circling or boxing the text (useful for rehearsal markings).

Creating Chord Charts

Let's create some chord symbols in the Guitar score to indicate the accompaniment chords for the guitar solo. Instead of using the Score Editor/Piano Roll Editor screenset, you'll work with the Score Editor in the Tracks area. So far you've been accessing the editors in the Main window by clicking the tabs at the bottom of the window. You can speed up workflow considerably by using the various toggle key commands, which allow you to open and close an editor in the Tracks area with a single keystroke.

1   Press the number 1 to open Screenset 1.

2   In the Guitar Score track, select the last region (Guitar Score_Chords).

3   Press N (Toggle Score Editor) to open the Score Editor in the Tracks area.

The Guitar Score_Chords region is displayed in the Score Editor.

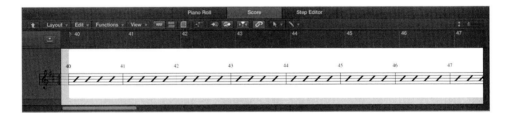

NOTE ▶ The Guitar Score_Chords region doesn't contain any MIDI events or added notational symbols. The chord slashes displayed are actually part of the Lead Sheet staff style, which is set for the region. You can display chord slashes for any staff style instead of rests by choosing them from the Staff Style window's Rest parameter menu.

4   In the Part box group menu, click the Chord Grid group button to view its contents.

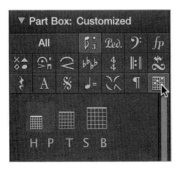

5 Drag the smallest chord grid object to just above the staff at 40 1 1 1.

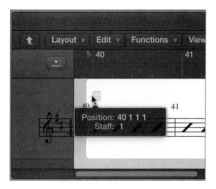

NOTE ▶ You can make chord grids in three sizes, each represented by objects in the Part box. You can always change the size after insertion by Control-clicking the object and choosing one of the scale options (reduced, normal, and enlarged) from the shortcut menu.

The Chord Grid Library window opens.

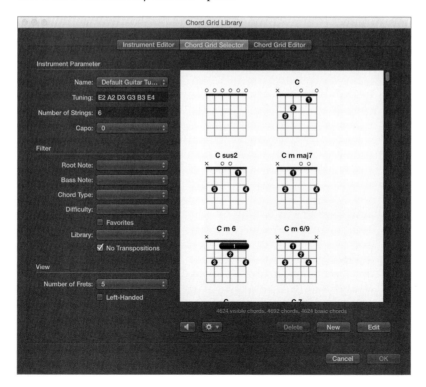

The Chord Grid Library contains a database of more than 4,000 chord grids you can use in your compositions. Chords are listed by position (fret).

6   Scroll through the chord choices in the Chord Grid Library.

Given the overwhelming number of chords displayed, you need to filter the view to center in on the chord you want. A good place to start is by specifying the root and chord type in the Filter area.

7   In the Filter section, from the Root Note menu, choose D.

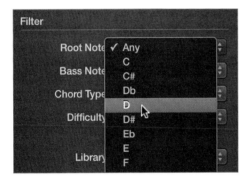

Only chords with D in the root are displayed in the Chord Grid Library.

8   From the Chord Type menu, choose major.

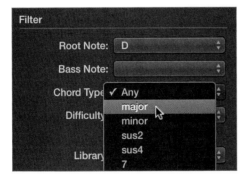

Only major chords with D in the root are displayed in the Chord Grid Library.

9   In the upper-left corner of the Chord Grid Library, click the root position D major chord and click OK.

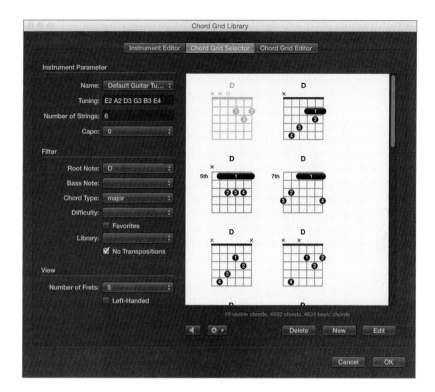

The D major chord grid is added to the score at 40 1 1 1.

TIP ▶ If you need to adjust the position of any inserted score object (including text), you can drag it from one location to another using the Pointer tool. However, when exact positions are required (as they often are), use the Event inspector. When an object is selected, you will find parameters in the Event inspector you can use to adjust both the vertical and horizontal positions by single pixels, and align the object in relation to the page borders.

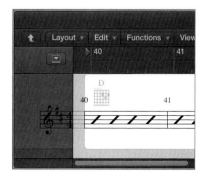

Creating Chord Grids

You can easily create your own chord grids in the Chord Grid Library. Once you create these chord grids, you can access them in any project.

1   Drag the smallest chord grid object to just above the staff at 44 1 1 1.

2   In the lower-right corner of the Chord Grid Library, click the New button. The Chord Library displays an Undefined chord, ready for editing.

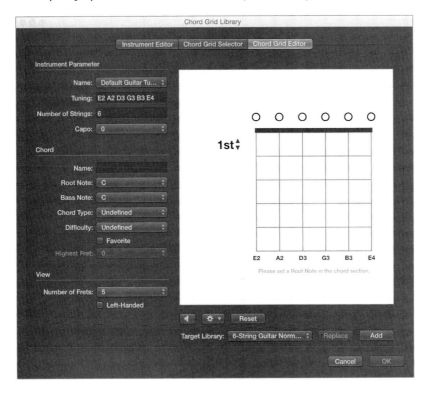

When creating your own chord grids, a good place to start is by specifying the root note, bass note, and chord type.

3   From the Root Note menu, choose C.

4   From the Bass Note menu, choose D.

5   From the Chord Type menu, choose add9.

Now you're ready to specify the chord's notes by clicking the desired fret and string.

6 Click at the first fret, second string (C4).

A fingering dot is added to the chord grid.

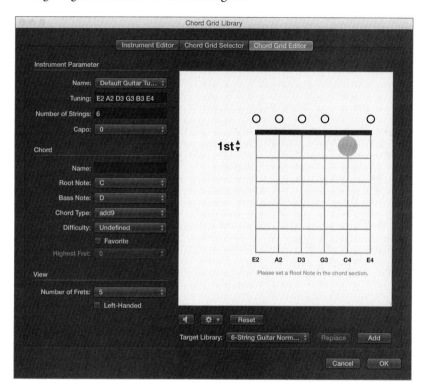

You can specify a finger number for each fingering dot by Control-clicking it.

7 Control-click the fingering dot you just created, and from the shortcut menu, choose 1.

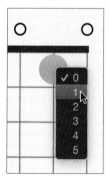

You can indicate whether open strings are played by clicking the area above those strings.

8   Click the area above the low E string (E2) and the area above the A string (A2) to specify that those strings will not be played.

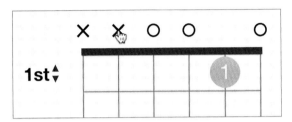

The chord name updates to indicate the harmony (Cadd9/D). Now that you have finished creating your chord, you can add it to the Chord Grid Library for future use.

9   Click Add to add the chord grid to the library.

The Chord Grid Library window provides a convenient way to audition selected chords, enabling you to hear the result before you add them to your score.

10   Click the Playback button to turn on playback.

The chord plays.

11   Click the Playback button to turn off playback.

12   Click OK.

The chord grid is inserted at 44 1 1 1.

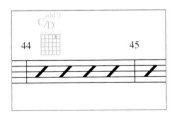

You will probably need to adjust the chord grid's position after you insert it into the score. You can make that job easier by using guides, which allow you to visually align an object's position in relation to the time grid (bars, beats, divisions, and so on).

13 From the View menu, choose View > Guides > All Objects.

A dotted line extends from the chord grids to the staff below, showing its position in relation to the time grid.

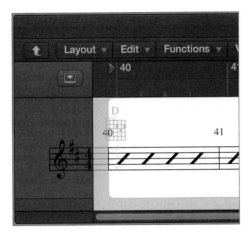

14 Using the guide, Option-drag the D chord grid from 40 1 1 1 to 46 1 1 1 to copy it.

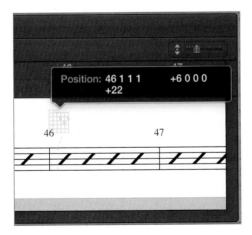

You needn't worry if your inserted chords are not aligned. You can easily align them using the Align Object Positions Vertically command.

15 Drag a selection rectangle around the three chord grids you inserted.

16 Control-click any of the chord grids, and from the shortcut menu, choose Align Object Positions Vertically.

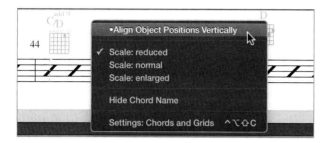

The chord grid objects align vertically.

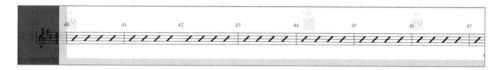

TIP ▶ If you need to create chord charts without the guitar-oriented chord grids, you can use the Chord object in the text group in the Part box.

Transcribing a Performance

The Logic notation engine is designed to preserve the subtleties of an actual performance while representing that performance data as cleanly notated scores. With a little finessing, you can create accurate parts and scores based on existing MIDI tracks without sacrificing any of the original "feel" of the sequenced material.

Logic accomplishes this demanding task by using a separate notation display system that allows you to adjust the look of the notation without changing the original MIDI data.

In this exercise, you'll prepare MIDI regions in the Tracks area to aid in the transcription process, and adjust parameters in the Score Editor to correctly notate the parts without modifying the performance data.

Preparing MIDI Regions for Notation

During sequencing, you may end up with tracks made up of noncontiguous regions (that is, regions with spaces between them). However, the Score Editor displays notation in regions only, and it displays nothing (not even a staff!) where no region is present.

For the purpose of notation, therefore, fill in noncontiguous MIDI tracks with regions by inserting blank regions, or by merging multiple regions into a single composite region. Doing so has no effect on the performance data of a part but does enable the Score Editor to create staves filled with rests.

1 In the Tracks area, scroll down and select the Bongos track (track 6).

The Bongos track consists of two separate regions.

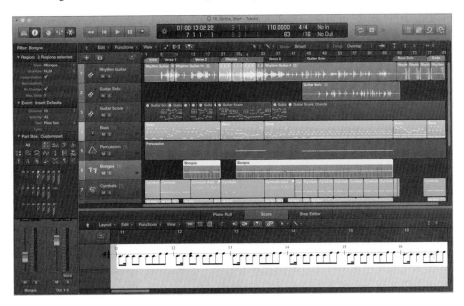

As you can see in the Score Editor, the display starts at measure 11, which corresponds to the start of the first region in the track.

2 In the Tracks area, choose the Pencil tool, and click the beginning of the Bongos track (at 1 1 1 1) to create a blank region.

3 Create another blank region at 81 1 1 1 in the Bongos track.

4   In the track list, click the Bongos track to select all of its regions, including the new ones.

5   Choose Edit > Join > Regions.

One contiguous region is formed for the Bongos track.

6   Scroll through the Score Editor to view the part. Rests are now displayed for areas with no activity.

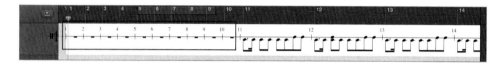

TIP ▶ The Score Editor is currently displaying the track's data in Linear view, which allows you to scroll to the left and right to view the contents. You can also choose to display the data in Wrapped view, which is similar to a lead sheet and enables you to view data by scrolling vertically. The last view mode, Page view, also organizes the data vertically, but is mainly used when laying out a score for printing. The Score Editor view buttons, which you can use to turn the views on and off, are located next to the View menu.

Viewing the Data Accurately

The settings in the Region inspector (with the exception of Style) form the basis for the rhythmic interpretation and display of MIDI data. These settings apply only to the score display and do not change the playback data of the MIDI regions in any way.

Let's look at how these parameters affect the notation of a selected region.

1   In the Bongos track, click the Solo button to solo the track.

2   Press the "Go to Position" key command (/) to locate the playhead to 11 1 1 1.

3   Play the song, listening to the bongo part while watching the notation.

4   When you're familiar with the material, stop playback.

5   Make sure that the Score Editor has key focus by clicking the upper part of the score area, or by pressing the Tab key.

6   In the upper-left corner, open the Region inspector (if it's not already open) by clicking the disclosure triangle next to Bongos.

You can use the Quantize setting to apply visual quantization to the notes, dictating the shortest value displayed in the selected MIDI region.

7   From the Quantize menu, choose 8.

The notation changes to display eighth notes as the shortest value.

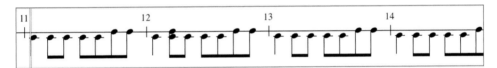

8   Play the song again, and listen to the bongo part while watching the notation.

Notice that what you are hearing is not rhythmically the same as the notation. This illustrates the independence of display quantization from the actual MIDI performance data.

9   Use the "Go to Position" key command (/) to locate to 11 1 1 1.

10 From the Quantize menu, choose 16,24.

This default setting works well for the part. It permits sixteenth notes and sixteenth-note triplets (indicated by 24) to appear as the shortest note lengths in the Score Editor.

Let's move on to the Interpretation parameter, which is specifically used to create an easy-to-read score from real-time MIDI recordings. Performed notes generally aren't held for the full length of a given note; rather, they are shortened depending on the articulation and the time needed to move to another note on the instrument. With Interpretation turned on, Logic fills in those performance gaps between notes and makes a guess as to the appropriate notation for each note.

11 In the Region inspector, deselect the Interpretation checkbox.

The notes are now displayed as isolated sixteenth notes with rests.

This notation might be more technically accurate because it displays the actual length of the notes as they are played, but it is much harder to read! Considering that the part is a percussive one, it makes sense to have Interpretation turned on (the default setting).

12 Select the Interpretation checkbox to turn on Interpretation.

TIP ▶ Turn off Interpretation when you're using graphic or step input, because you want the full value of the selected notes to be displayed.

Each note in Logic can have unique display attributes, independent of the region settings in the Region inspector. These attributes are set in the Note Attributes dialog.

13 Double-click the first note of measure 11 to open the Note Attributes dialog.

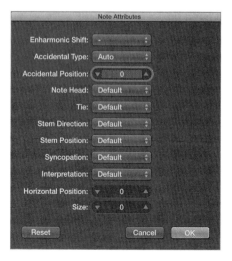

Here you can adjust individual notes using various menus, including one for Interpretation.

14 Click Cancel to close the Note Attributes dialog.

15 Press N to close the Score Editor.

16 In the Bongos track, click the Solo button to turn off soloing.

Working with Drum Notation

Logic has a unique and powerful way of notating drum parts using mapped instruments. Traditionally, mapped instruments are created in Logic to represent a drum machine or drum channel in a multi-timbral synthesizer, but they also enable you to assign specific notes to voice groups in the Staff Style window and thereby create drum notation.

In this exercise you will create a mapped instrument to generate a score from the drum tracks used in the song.

Consolidating the Tracks

To create a single drum staff, you first need to consolidate the multiple drum part tracks into a single contiguous region.

1 Press Option-Shift-D to deselect all regions.

2 Shift-click tracks 7 through 11 (Cymbals, Hi Hat, Toms, Rim Shot, and Bass Drum) to select the regions in each track.

3 Choose Edit > Convert > Loops to Regions.

4 Choose Edit > Join > Regions.

The drum tracks combine into a single region on track 7.

5   Press Option-Shift-D to deselect all regions.

6   In the track list, delete the tracks left empty by the merge (tracks 8 through 11).

7   If necessary, select track 7, which now displays Cymbals as its name.

Creating a Mapped Instrument

Now that everything is consolidated into a single region, you can create the mapped instrument object in the Environment.

1   Choose Window > Open MIDI Environment.

The Environment window opens, displaying the Instruments layer, which has nothing in it yet.

2   From the Environment window's local menu bar, choose New > Mapped Instrument.

A mapped instrument object is created in the Instruments layer, and the Mapped Instrument window appears.

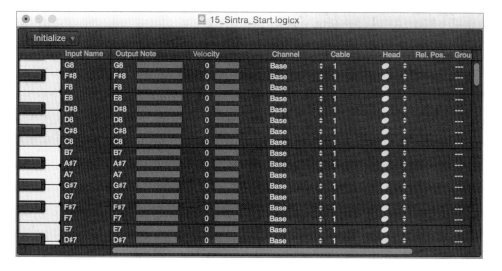

You can use the Mapped Instrument window to edit individual notes in a mapped instrument. It automatically opens when creating a new mapped instrument object.

NOTE ▶ You can also open a Mapped Instrument window by double-clicking a mapped instrument object.

3 In the Mapped Instrument window, scroll down until you can see the drum names displayed in the Input Name column (and so that Kick 2 is at the bottom of the list).

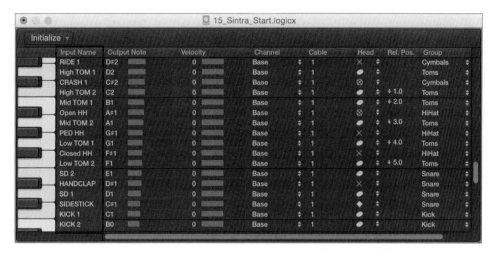

4 Look at the three columns to the right: Head, Rel. Pos. (for Relative Position), and Group.

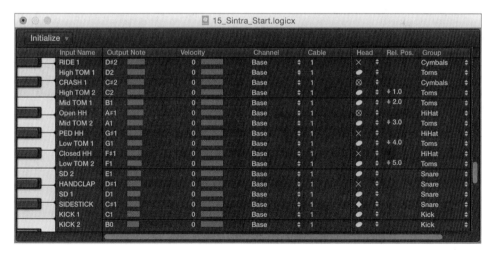

Altering the information in these columns has a direct impact on the drum notation. You can assign note heads and adjust the relative position of the clef for each note. In addition, you can assign each note to drum groups, which carry common attributes that the Score Editor's staff style interprets.

NOTE ▶ The default settings in the Mapped Instrument window correspond to the standardized General MIDI (GM) Drum Kit note assignments, which enables you to easily create drum notation from an EXS24 mkII sampler instrument that also reflects the GM note assignments. If you aren't using a GM-mapped drum sampler instrument to output the part, you can adjust note mapping in the Output Note column to trigger the appropriate sounds.

5   Close the Mapped Instrument window.

6   In the Object Parameter box (for Mapped Instr.), click the object's name, enter *Drums*, and press Return.

The mapped instrument object's name changes to Drums.

To enable the track in the Tracks area to display the drum notation, you need to assign it to the mapped instrument you created. To ensure that it still outputs to the EXS24 mkII plug-in inserted on the software instrument channel, you need to cable the objects together in the Environment.

7   Option-click the cable output from the Drums object, and from the shortcut menu, choose Audio > Software Instrument > Inst 1 (the software instrument with the EXS24 mkII sampled drum kit).

NOTE ▶ Option-clicking a cable output allows you to connect objects in different layers of the Environment.

An alert message appears, asking if you want to remove the port setting for the object.

8   Click Remove.

NOTE ▶ By removing the port and channel settings for the object, you are setting the Drums object to output only to the software instrument object.

A cable appears, connecting the objects between the layers of the Environment.

You're now ready to assign the newly mapped instrument to the consolidated drums track (Cymbals) in the Tracks area. Instead of Control-clicking the track in the track list and choosing an object from the shortcut menu, you can quickly assign the selected track to any object in the Environment using the MIDI Thru tool.

9   Choose the MIDI Thru tool.

10 Move the Environment window to the right, so you can see the Tracks area's inspector and track list.

11 In the Environment window, click the Drums object while observing the inspector in the Tracks area (Cymbals).

12 Close the Environment window.

In the Tracks area, the selected drums track (track 7) is now assigned to the Drums mapped instrument. (You can verify the assignment by looking at the Arrange channel strip, which now displays a MIDI fader.)

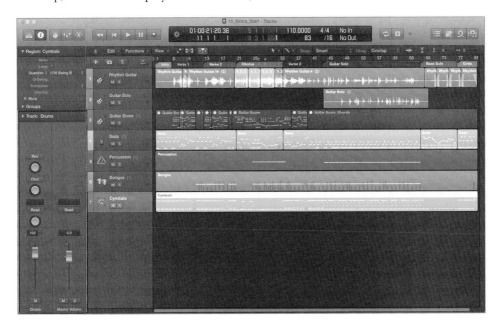

Now all that's left for you to do is assign the staff style in the Score Editor.

13 Press N to open the Score Editor.

The Score Editor displays the contents of the drums track but uses the default Bass staff style. To enable the settings in the Mapped Instrument window to be translated into notation, you must assign a mapped staff style to the region. Mapped staff styles are designated in the staff style list by a # symbol preceding the name.

14 In the Region inspector, from the Style menu, choose #Drums.

The region now displays in correct notation.

Display the #Drums staff style to see how it affects the settings.

15 From the Score Editor's local menu bar, choose Layout > Show Staff Styles.

The #Drums staff style is displayed in the Staff Style window.

As you can see, this is a polyphonic staff style of sorts, consisting of multiple voices assigned to drum groups instead of a split point or MIDI channel. These drum groups correspond to the Group column entries in the Mapped Instrument window.

NOTE ▶ You might need to resize the Staff Style window to see its entire contents.

16 Close the Staff Style window.

Creating Scores and Parts

The Score Editor allows you to use score sets to control which instruments are displayed (and printed) in a score. In a score set, you can include as many (or as few) of the existing track instruments as you want, and you can arrange instruments independently of their order in the Tracks area. In a score set you can also assign instrument names and determine if the group shares bar lines, brackets, or braces.

Creating a Score Set

You can create multiple score sets to display everything from a full score to individual parts. In this exercise, you will use score sets to lay out the full score and to quickly generate individual instrument parts.

1   Click Stop to return the project to 1 1 1 1.

2   Open Screenset 4.

The screenset contains a full-screen Score Editor in page view. Don't worry if the lines appear crowded at this point. You will address this later in the lesson.

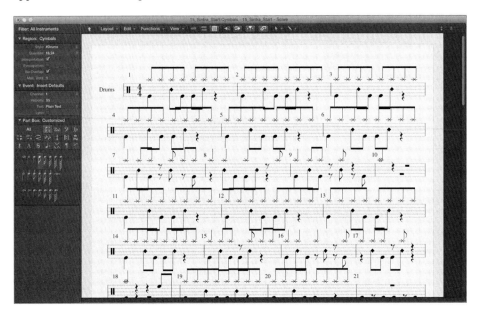

NOTE ▶ You can use Page view in any Score Editor window. From the Score Editor's local menu bar, choose View > Page View, or click the turquoise Page View button next to the menu bar.

Prior to the creation of any score sets, Logic displays selected instruments using a default score set named All Instruments that appears at the top of the inspector in the Score Set menu.

However, you aren't seeing all the instruments at the moment because you recently selected the Drums region. To display all the instruments, you need to move up a few levels (reflecting the Tracks area).

3   In the upper-left corner of the window, click the Display Level button twice.

All Tracks area instruments appear in the Score Editor.

Although the default All Instruments score set works as a basic display of the instruments, you can refine the score display by creating your own score set.

4   In the Score Editor's local menu bar, choose Layout > Show Score Sets.

The Score Set window opens. (You might need to resize the Score Set window to see its entire contents.)

5   In the Score Set window's local menu bar, choose New > New Complete Set.

A new score set, made up of all the instruments used in the Tracks area, is created.

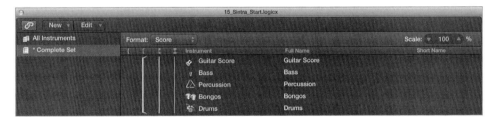

6   Double-click the score set name, and enter *Ensemble* in the text field. Press Return.

NOTE ▶ The instrument names that appear in the score relate directly to the contents of the Full Name column. By default, these contents include the names of the objects in the Environment that are assigned to the tracks (channels, mapped instruments, and so on). You can, however, enter whatever you like in the Full Name and Short Name columns.

A score set also allows you to scale the size of the displayed staves, enabling you to fit more systems onto a page. This function is especially useful when creating full conductor scores.

7 Double-click the number next to the Scale parameter (below the score set name) and enter *65*. Press Return.

To apply the score set you created, you need to assign it in the inspector.

8 At the very top of the inspector area, click and hold the Score Set menu and choose Ensemble.

The score displays at a smaller scale.

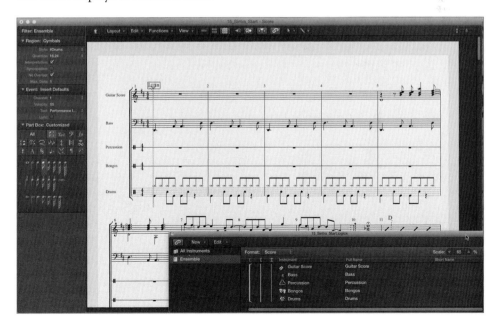

Creating Parts for Printing

Creating individual score sets for each instrumental part in the score gives you the most control over naming and other display attributes and also allows you to print parts by choosing from the Score Set menu.

In this exercise, you will create an individual, printer-ready score set for the guitar part by creating a new empty score set and then adding the Guitar Score instrument to the set.

1   In the Score Set window, choose New > New Empty Set.

An empty score set is created.

2   Double-click the score set name, and in the data field, enter *Guitar*. Press Return.

3   Choose New > Add Instrument Entry.

A single instrument entry is added to the score set. By default, the first instrument in the track list is added, which in this case is the Guitar Score instrument.

To complete the part, you'll rename the default instrument in the Score Set window.

4   Double-click the Full Name field and enter *Guitar*. Press Return.

Instrumental parts can reflect different layout preferences. To designate a score set as a part, you need to change the Format parameter.

5   From the Format pop-up menu, choose Parts.

6   Close the Score Set window.

7   In the inspector, click the Score Set menu and choose Guitar.

The Score Editor displays the guitar part.

Now that you've designated the Guitar score set as a part, you can change its layout settings without affecting the Ensemble score set you created previously. The layout settings for both scores and parts are located in the Global Score project settings.

8   In the Score Editor's local menu bar, choose Layout > Global Format.

The Project Settings window opens, displaying the Global tab.

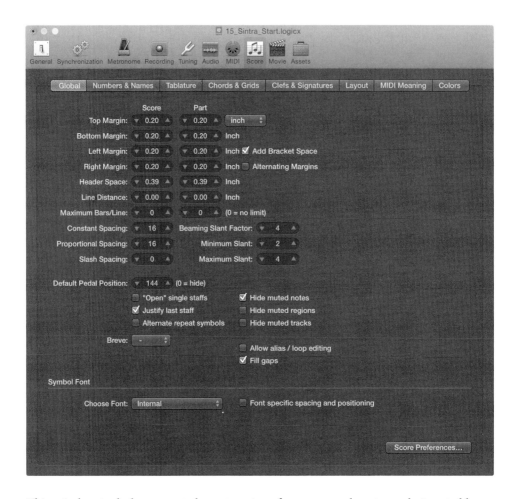

This window includes separate layout settings for scores and parts, as designated by the two columns titled (appropriately enough) Score and Part.

The notation in both the guitar part (and the ensemble score from earlier in this lesson) is a bit crowded. You can create more space between the systems by adjusting the Line Distance setting in both the Part and Score column.

9   In the Score column, click the Line Distance field and enter *0.10*. Press Return.

10 In the Part column, click the Line Distance field and enter *0.25*. Press Return.

11 Close the Project Settings window.

The staves for the guitar part are now more spread out, making them easier to read.

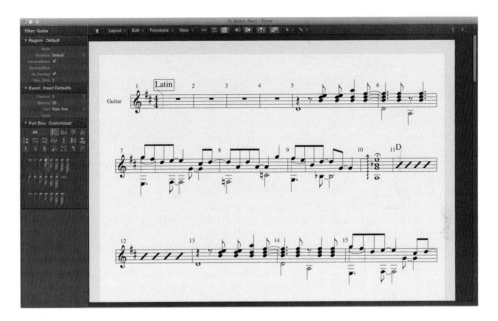

Let's finish by comparing the two score sets you have created. You can see the differences most easily if you view the pages in their entirety. By zooming out in the Score Editor, you can see entire pages side by side.

12 Press Command-Up Arrow repeatedly to vertically zoom out until you see two pages.

13 From the Score Set menu, choose Ensemble.

The Score Editor displays the full score.

The two score sets display independent scale and line distance settings.

14 Try printing the scores of both the Guitar and Ensemble score sets by selecting them in the inspector and choosing File > Print.

NOTE ▶ If you don't have a printer connected, you can save the score as a PDF file by choosing File > Print and then verifying the settings and clicking OK in the Page Setup window. Then, in the Print window, click the PDF button, and choose "Save as PDF."

Lesson Review

1. In what ways can you enter notation in the Score Editor?
2. Where do you edit note length?
3. What do you use to assign display attributes to notation?
4. How do you assign voices in a score style?
5. What do you use to assign voices in a part in the Score Editor?
6. What do text styles do?
7. Does the Quantize parameter in the Score Editor change both notation and playback?
8. How do you create drum notation?
9. What do you use to display and print only selected parts?
10. Can you retain independent formatting for both parts and scores?

Answers

1. Notation can be entered in the Score Editor using graphic input, step input, and real-time transcription.
2. Note length is edited in the Event inspector or by adjusting the note's duration bar.
3. Staff styles are used to assign display attributes to notation.
4. Voices are assigned using a MIDI split note or an individual MIDI channel.
5. The Voice Separation tool can be used to quickly assign voices in a polyphonic staff style using MIDI channel assignment.
6. Text styles assign display attributes to text elements in the Score Editor.
7. No. Quantize in the Score Editor changes the notation display but does not affect the performance data.
8. Drum parts can be notated by assigning a mapped instrument and a mapped staff style to a track.
9. Score sets are used to display and print individual parts up to full scores.
10. Yes. You can assign separate format settings for parts and scores in the Global Score project settings.

16

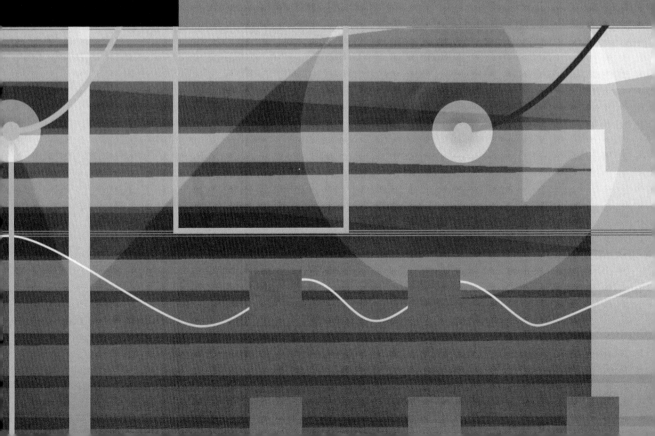

Working with Picture

Creating and editing music and audio for picture is a collaborative effort integrating a variety of media that is often produced by more than one person or facility. As a result, a key skill is the ability to import and work with many media elements in several formats while maintaining the same timing references—especially when the audio needs to synchronize with critical moments in the film or video footage. Computer-based production has greatly facilitated the creation of music and audio for all visual media. Computers powerful enough to stream digital video and audio in the same application have simplified the methods for ensuring synchronization between music and picture.

In this lesson you will work with a short video scene, walking through the workflow from setting up the project to delivering the soundtrack.

Creating Post-Production Audio

Creating and editing audio for post-production has its own unique workflow compared to music production. To streamline the process, creating a template is useful, especially for working with video. In this exercise you will start off by creating a basic template that will suit the majority of post-production needs from sound effects editing to musical scoring.

1   Choose File > New.

2   In the New Tracks dialog, create a single Software Instrument track, and open the library.

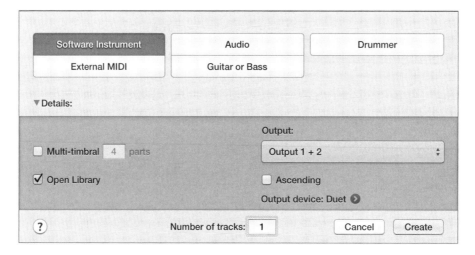

Although not necessary, a basic piano track is a useful addition to your template because it can provide an easily accessed instrument for sketching out musical ideas in the early stages of scoring.

3   In the Library, select Piano > Yamaha Grand Piano.

4   Close the Library area.

5 In the upper left of the Track parameter area, click the disclosure arrow to collapse the window.

One of the most important elements when working with visual media is the presence of timecode you can reference when recording and editing audio. A new project defaults to displaying only bars and beats in the ruler, and while these are important for musical composition, you will be primarily working with SMPTE timecode when placing effects. Fortunately, Logic lets you display both timing references in your project.

6 From the Main window's local menus, choose View > Secondary Ruler.

SMPTE time now appears at the top of the ruler in addition to bars and beats.

7 Press Command-Left Arrow (the Zoom Horizontal Out key command) to zoom out enough to see about two minutes of SMPTE time (01:02:00:00).

Having a giant SMPTE display floating in the Tracks area is also a good idea. This display and the ruler provide you with clear visual references of valuable timing information you will use when working with picture.

8 Click the LCD's Display Mode button and choose Open Giant Time Display.

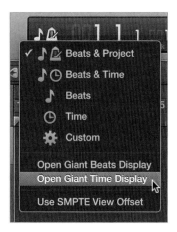

A large floating SMPTE display appears, which you can reposition anywhere on the screen for your convenience.

9 Drag the floating SMPTE display to the lower third of the Tracks area.

Let's finish your template by displaying a few global tracks that lend themselves to working with video.

10 Click the Global Tracks button.

11 Control-click any of the global tracks headers, and from the shortcut menu, choose Configure Global Tracks.

12 In the Global Tracks Configuration dialog, select the Marker, Movie, Signature, and Tempo checkboxes. Click anywhere outside the dialog to close it.

Your screenset now looks like the following figure.

13 Lock the screenset.

14 In the File menu, choose Save As Template.

15 Enter *Working with Picture* for the name. Press Return.

For more about creating templates, refer to Lesson 1, "Speeding Up Your Workflow."

Opening the Movie

Using digital video clips simplifies video-to-music synchronization, enabling you to instantly locate to any point in the project and the video. What's more, you can save the digital video (along with all the synchronization settings) in the project folder for easy archiving and retrieval.

Logic leverages the Apple QuickTime engine for video playback, and can therefore open a digital video clip (commonly referred to by the term *movie*) in any format supported by the QuickTime standard.

In this exercise, you will open a digital video clip in a new Logic project and adjust the synchronization settings to allow for time-locked playback and reference of audio and video.

1   In the Movie global track, click the Movie pop-up menu and choose Open Movie.

The Open window appears.

NOTE ▶ You can also open a movie by choosing File > Movie > Open Movie.

2   Navigate to Music > Advanced Logic X_Files > Media > 2nd Impressions > Movie
     Files, and open 2nd Impressions.mov.

     In the Drop Movie dialog, you can see that the video also contains an audio track. This
     video contains an embedded production audio track you will use for reference.

3   Make sure that the "Open the movie" and "Extract the audio track" options are
     selected. Click OK.

     An alert appears, asking whether not you want the project to match the sample rate of
     the video's audio track.

4   Click Use 48000 Hz.

NOTE ► Nearly all contemporary post-production audio is created at a sample rate of 48 kHz.

One more alert box appears to ask if you want the project to match the frame rate of the digital video clip.

5   Click Use 23.976.

NOTE ► The original footage used in this lesson was shot on film at 24 fps and then transferred to video via telecine at 23.976 fps.

The video opens in a floating window, and a thumbnail in the Movie track displays images from the movie at regular intervals. What's more, an audio track containing the embedded production audio is added to the track list.

Logic performs some useful tasks when it opens a digital video clip, including reading the audio sample rate and video frame rate from the file. This automatic feature is convenient, but knowing where you can manually set synchronization is a good idea.

6   From the File menu, choose Project Settings > Audio.

Here you can see the Sample Rate pop-up menu in which you can set the project's sample rate.

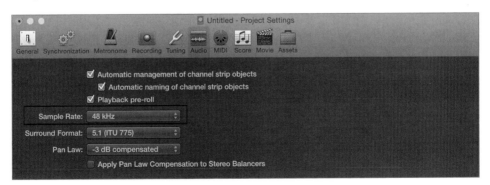

7 Click the Synchronization button.

8 In the Synchronization project settings, click the General tab.

To ensure that the timecode display is accurate, you want the project set to the movie's frame rate in the Frame Rate pop-up menu.

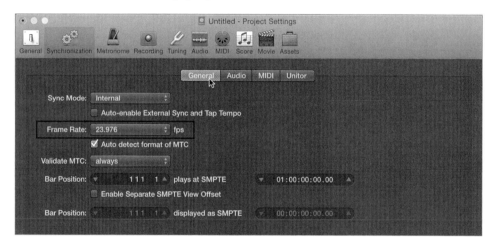

Working with SMPTE Timecode

You can establish synchronization between your video and Logic merely by opening a QuickTime movie in a project, but you should manually adjust a few settings so that the Logic timecode will match the burn-in timecode from the video.

The Bar Position and "Plays at SMPTE" settings align the musical timing of the project to the SMPTE start time of the video. Using these two settings, you tell Logic where the first bar of the project occurs in relation to absolute SMPTE time.

1 Find the starting SMPTE timecode by moving the playhead to the beginning of the video and looking at the displayed burn-in timecode.

As you can see in the Movie window, the beginning timecode displays 01:02:50:13.

2   In the "Plays at SMPTE" field, click the number, and enter *01:02:50:13*. Press Return.

TIP ▸ By default, the Logic SMPTE readout displays subframes, or bits, as its last digit (after frames). You can choose from various options for the SMPTE display in the Display Preferences under the Display SMPTE menu.

You might have noticed that the video display changed and is not currently seen in the Movie global track. This is because the Movie Start time is now not in sync with the burned-in time code. (It defaults to 01:00:00:00.00.) When you set the Movie Start time, the movie will start when the project starts (01:02:50:13.00), thereby aligning the burn-in timecode with the Logic SMPTE readout. This information is entered in the Movie project settings.

3   At the top of the Project Settings window, click the Movie button to display the Movie settings.

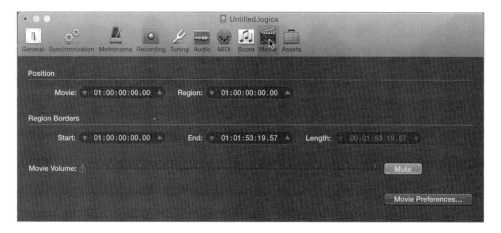

4   In the Movie field, click the number and enter *01:02:50:13.00*. Press Return.

The video will now start at the beginning of the project.

5   Close the Project Settings window.

6   Play the project from the beginning, observing the SMPTE display in relation to the burn-in timecode of the video.

7   Stop playback after listening for 10 or 15 seconds.

Navigating with Video

Movie playback, as manipulated by the Transport bar controls, maintains sync with the project.

1   Resume playback and click anywhere in the Bar ruler to locate to another position.

The movie relocates in sync with the project.

2   In QuickTime Player, drag the playhead to the right.

The project relocates to remain in sync with the movie.

3   Stop playback.

You can resize the QuickTime Player window by dragging its lower-right corner, or by Control-clicking the video, and from the shortcut menu, choosing one of the size options.

4   Control-click the QuickTime player window, and from the shortcut menu, choose 0.5 Size.

The QuickTime window shrinks to half of its original size.

Using Markers to Spot the Movie

When you're identifying (spotting) where music will enhance your project, you can use Logic during or after your spotting session with the director to mark these specific time-code locations where you've agreed to place music cues. Placing markers also enables you to insert text notes at specific SMPTE positions you can later use as timing references.

For the scene in this exercise, the director has specified that music should open the scene to smooth the transition out of the previous scene. The music coincides with the beginning of the video clip, but note that when the music stops it will not cover the dialogue and ambient sound effects that occur later in the clip.

1   Locate the QuickTime playhead to around three seconds into the clip (01:02:53:00.00).

2   From the main menu bar, choose Navigate > Other > Create Without Rounding, or press Control-Option-' (apostrophe), to create a new marker (Marker 1) at the current playhead position.

> **NOTE ▸** The Create Without Rounding command creates a marker at the playhead's precise position on the SMPTE ruler, instead of at the beginning of the nearest bar.

3   Control-click the new marker (Marker 1), and from the shortcut menu, choose Rename Marker. Enter *Music out* for the marker name, and press Return.

4   Click the List Editors button.

5   In the List Editors area, click the Marker tab.

The new marker appears in the list, and its position is expressed in bars and beats. Although this display may be musically useful, in this video-based workflow, displaying this list in SMPTE time is more relevant.

6   From the Marker List View menu, choose "Show Event Position and Length as Time."

The list is displayed with SMPTE timings. To make sure that the new marker won't be affected when changing tempo, you need to lock its SMPTE position. Doing so guarantees that the marker will not move if the project's tempo is changed. You will explore this concept a bit later in this lesson.

7   From the Marker List Options menu, choose Lock SMPTE Position.

A small lock appears by the marker name.

TIP ▶ Use markers as the basis for beat mapping, functioning similarly to the way you used the Beat Mapping track to align both MIDI and audio events to bars and beats in Lesson 2. You can use this same technique to align the downbeat of a measure to an exact moment in the movie as represented by the marker. When the marker is selected, its starting point is displayed in the Beat Mapping track, so you can drag nearby bar and beat lines to align them with the marker.

Adding Scene Cuts

Often a director will want musical cues or sound effects to begin near scene cuts to accentuate a transition from one scene to the next. You can identify relevant visual cues in a video using a function called Adding Scene Cuts. When you enable this function, Logic analyzes the video information and creates a special marker, which is called a *scene marker*, at locations where the image changes drastically (such as at scene cuts).

> **TIP** ▶ You can use the Adding Scene Cuts feature on isolated areas (identified by marquee, cycle, or region selections) or for the entire video.

1   In the global Movie track, choose Add Scene Cuts to Marker Set.

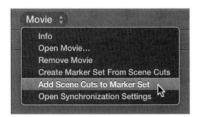

A status bar displays the progress of cut detection.

After the analysis is completed, scene markers (designated by the movie frame symbol) appear in the Marker track, as well as in the Marker List alongside the marker you manually created.

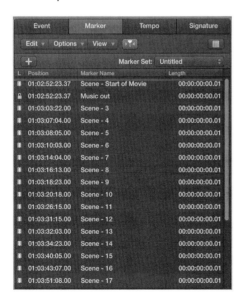

NOTE ▶ Scene markers are automatically locked to SMPTE positions.

2   In the Marker List, hold down the Option key to choose the Finger tool, and then click the markers in the list.

The movie locates to scene cuts and other points where the video image changes drastically.

TIP ▶ The Marker track can contain multiple alternative tracks, similar to those you looked at in the Tempo track in Lesson 2. By choosing New Set from the Marker Set pop-up menu, you can create separate markers for marking musical sections and for spotting sound effects or musical cues.

3   Click the "Go to Beginning" button to return to the beginning of the project.

4   Close the List Editors area.

TIP ▶ Copy and paste marker lists into word-processor documents to create cue sheets and Edit Decision Lists (EDL).

5   Close the QuickTime window in preparation for the next exercise.

The movie now appears above the Region inspector.

To better see the audio assets in the Tracks area, you want to get the video out of the way (but keep it easily accessible). When you close the QuickTime window, the movie does not disappear, but is tucked away in the inspector, where you can still view a small version of it.

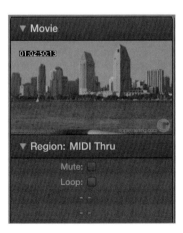

TIP ▶ Open the QuickTime window again as a floating window by double-clicking the movie in the inspector.

Importing Media

Integration between the editing suites used by video editors, sound designers, engineers, and composers has traditionally been a hurdle when these groups collaborate on media projects. However, integration has improved with the development of formats that allow you to exchange media with colleagues while maintaining the SMPTE data relevant to the project.

In the following exercises, you will import media in multiple formats into your project while retaining their timecode information.

Importing XML from Final Cut Pro

Logic supports Extensible Markup Language (XML) files as a data interchange format. XML is used by other Apple applications, such as Final Cut Pro, to store relevant project information. By exchanging XML files between apps, this information can be retained as a project moves from one user (and app) to another. For example, XML exchange allows you to import audio files that a film editor used in a Final Cut Pro project, and retain their timing and automation information in the Logic Tracks area.

For this exercise, you'll use an XML file created for a Final Cut Pro project. This file contains information about the file locations and timing for a few tracks of sound effects that the project's video editor placed in a Final Cut Pro sequence.

1   Choose File > Import > Final Cut Pro XML.

2   Navigate to Music > Advanced Logic X_Files > Media > 2nd Impressions > XML Export and import **2nd Impressions_Ambience.fcpxml**.

3   Click Import.

   A prompt appears, asking you to relink the XML file's associated audio files by choosing the correct file path.

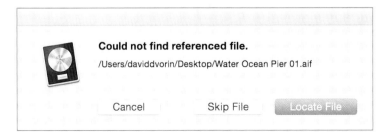

4   Click Locate File. Iin the file selector dialog, open Music > Advanced Logic X_Files > Media > 2nd Impressions > FX from FCP > **Water Ocean Pier 01.caf**.

The audio files associated with the XML file are imported into four new tracks in the Tracks area.

5   Play the project, listening to the imported sound effects in relation to the video. Stop playback.

Importing Broadcast WAVE Files

Broadcast WAVE files are similar to files in other PCM audio file formats (such as AIFF), but they also contain timecode information saved in the header of each file when the file is recorded. You can use that information to import and export these audio files between applications while retaining their absolute positions in time.

Let's test this by importing a sound effect into the Broadcast WAVE format.

1   Open the Browser area, and click the All Files tab.

2   Click the Home button.

3   Navigate to Music > Advanced Logic X_Files > Media > 2nd Impressions > FX.

4   Drag the Cell phone.wav file to a new track in the Tracks area at position 1 1 1 1.

A new track named "Cell phone" is created that contains the audio file you dragged.

5   With the region highlighted, from the Tracks area's local menu bar, choose Edit > Move > to Record Position.

The "Cell phone" region locates to the timecode position contained in the audio file (01:03:15:03.33).

6   Play the project while observing how the "Cell phone" audio works with the movie.

NOTE ▶ You can save newly recorded audio files in the Broadcast WAVE format by choosing Logic Pro X > Preferences > Audio > General, and then choosing WAVE (BWF) from the Recording File Type menu. When you use this feature, all saved audio files will include the region's original record position.

Positioning Events on the Timeline

A common task when working with picture is syncing audio events to specific SMPTE positions. These audio events could be sound effects referenced from an Edit Decision List (EDL), or musical hits in the arrangement that punctuate visual cues. Being able to quickly and accurately place events on the timeline is essential when you're arranging material in a session that has been locked to a SMPTE position.

In this the following exercises, you will learn various techniques for efficiently placing events on the SMPTE timeline.

1   In the Browser area, select the Alarm clock.aif audio file, and click the Prelisten button to audition it.

2   If necessary, reposition the SMPTE display so it doesn't block the Tracks area.

3   Drag the Alarm clock.aif file from the Browser area onto a new track in the Tracks area at position 1 1 1 1.

A new track named "Alarm clock" is created that contains the audio file you dragged.

The simplest technique for positioning an event on the timeline is to manually spot the video as you drag the event in the arrangement.

4   Drag the Alarm clock region to the right, holding down the mouse button and dragging the file back and forth along the timeline while watching the movie.

Notice how the movie syncs with the position of the dragged audio file. You can use this visual reference to place cues at specific locations.

You might have noticed that the region snapped to barlines. Obviously, spotting effects to musical divisions based on bars and beats does not make sense in a video workflow. You can override this setting using the Control key.

5   Click the Alarm clock region, then hold down the Control key while dragging the file back and forth along the timeline and watching the movie.

The region moves in much smaller increments. This technique suffices for placing an effect at an approximate timing, but it is common practice to more precisely place the region by defeating the grid entirely. Hold down Control-Shift to position the region by ticks (a much smaller increment of time than a frame of video).

6   Control-Shift-drag the **Alarm clock** region back and forth along the timeline, while watching the giant SMPTE window.

The region moves in very small increments.

7   Close the Browser area.

> **TIP** ▶ When you drag a timecode-related asset in the Tracks area, the asset's movement is dictated by the Snap menu settings and your zoom level.

Placing Events by Playhead Position

Let's continue working with the Alarm clock region, this time aligning the event precisely to the playhead's SMPTE position using the "Place Region/Event to Playhead Position (Pickup Clock)" command.

1   Use the "Go to Previous Marker and Set Locators" key command—Option-, (comma)— and the "Go to Next Marker and Set Locators" key command—Option-. (period)— to locate the playhead to the scene marker located at 01:04:30:13.

2   With the Alarm clock region still selected, press ; (semicolon), which is the key command for Place Region/Event to Playhead Position (Pickup Clock).

The selected region snaps to the playhead position.

3   Play the project to view the newly positioned region in relation to the movie image.

4   Stop playback.

Creating the Score

One of the most important elements of a musical score is the timing between it and the image it accompanies. In addition to supplying emotional and aesthetic cues to the viewer, a score also establishes and/or reinforces a scene's pace. For this reason, the initial tempo you choose when composing for picture is of utmost importance, and it will dictate choices made from that point forward.

The Logic metronome is an excellent tool for auditioning tempi, but changing the tempo can be problematic when your project also has non-musical audio assets (FX, ADR, foley, and so on) that are synced to picture.

By time-locking nonmusical audio clips to their respective SMPTE positions, you can later adjust the music tempo freely without changing those audio assets' positions in relationship to the movie. Doing so will also give you the added benefit of making them impossible to move by mistake.

1   Choose Edit > Select All.

2   From the Tracks area local menu bar, choose Functions > Lock SMPTE Position.

All regions now display a lock icon in front of their names to indicate that they cannot be moved.

Now that the regions are locked, you'll take a look at how to change tempos without altering those locked regions' SMPTE positions.

3   Click the background of the Tracks area to deselect all regions.

4   Click the "Cell phone" region and hold down the mouse button to observe the SMPTE and bar position displayed in the help tag (and in the giant SMPTE window).

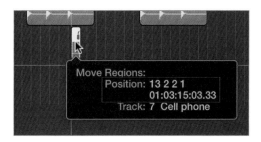

Note that the SMPTE position of the "Cell phone" region is 01:03:15:03.33, which corresponds to the bars and beats position of 13 2 2 1.

5   In the LCD, double-click the Tempo display and enter 66 to change the project tempo to 66 bpm. Press Return.

6   Click the "Cell phone" region and hold down the mouse button, again observing the SMPTE and bar positions displayed in the help tag.

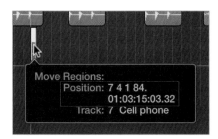

The region's SMPTE position remains the same as previously, but the corresponding bars and beats position is now 7 4 1 84.

When an event is SMPTE locked, it maintains its timecode position, regardless of the project tempo.

NOTE ▶ Audio clips imported from movies are automatically locked to SMPTE position to maintain sync.

7   In the inspector, double-click the movie to open it in a floating window.

8   Select the Click button to turn on the metronome.

9   Play the project.

10   In the LCD, try entering a few different tempi, listening to the metronome click in relation to the visuals. Stop the project when you find a tempo that complements the visual pace of the scene.

11   Now that you've established a tempo for your score, try using the available piano track to sketch out some musical ideas in relation to both the musical tempo and the visual pace.

12   Turn off the Click.

Exporting Audio to Movie

While you are working on a project, you may want to supply the client or director with a new video that includes your soundtrack. You could export high-quality audio to the video, but you'll more likely send a compressed version of your mix, which significantly reduces the file size for faster sharing via the Internet.

In this exercise, you will export your soundtrack to the project's video, and compress it with one of the codecs available in Logic

1   Click the background of the Tracks area to deselect all regions.

2   Choose File > Movie > Export Audio to Movie.

3   From the Audio Format menu, choose AAC.

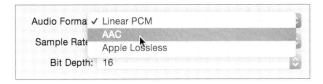

4 From the Bit Depth menu, choose 320 kbps.

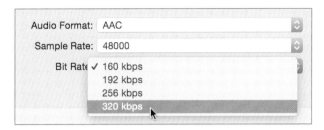

5 In the Save As dialog, name the file *2nd Impressions Mix*, and save it to your desktop.

Another dialog appears asking you to choose which audio tracks from the project's video file to include in the new movie. In this case, you want to include the dialogue track that is part of the video.

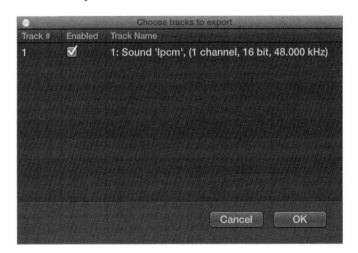

The dialogue track was already imported into the project's Tracks area, so leaving this selected would have the undesirable result of doubling the dialogue track in the exported movie.

6 In the dialog, click the background to deselect the original audio track, and then click OK.

Logic bounces the project's mix to the referenced video file, and converts the audio to the compressed format you chose.

7   Locate the new video on your desktop.

8   Double-click the movie file to play it in QuickTime.

▶ **Creating Stems for Dubbing**

To simplify the daunting task of the final dubbing or mixing stage, tracks of similar function or type are often submixed to reduce the amount of active channels needed in the final mix. Called *stems*, these submixes are highly useful because they allow the audio engineer to make last minute adjustments when creating the final mix while keeping the track count to a manageable amount. You can create these stems in Logic by assigning channels of similar material to specific busses for submixing, and then creating new audio tracks with the inputs set to receive the outputs of the individual stem busses. Using this technique, you can record the outputs of the submixes onto new tracks in the Tracks area. Then you need only copy them from the Audio Bin or Finder for delivery.

Lesson Review

1.   What settings govern how a digital video clip is synchronized in Logic?

2.   Where can SMPTE timecode be displayed in Logic?

3.   What type of Final Cut Pro exported file format can be imported into Logic?

4.   What audio file format contains timing information and can be imported into Logic?

5.   What kinds of markers are created with the Detect Cuts function?

6.   In what ways can regions be positioned on the timeline?

7.   How can you change the project tempo without changing a region's position?

8.   Which command is used to create a new video with your project's soundtrack?

Answers

1. Digital video clips in a Logic project can be synchronized by setting the SMPTE start times, frame rates, and movie start times.

2. Logic can display SMPTE timecode in the SMPTE ruler, Control bar, and giant SMPTE display.

3. Final Cut Pro XML files, including automation information, can be imported directly into a Logic timeline.

4. Broadcast WAVE files can be imported directly to a Logic timeline and retain their original recorded positions.

5. Detect Cuts creates scene markers that can flag scene cuts and other major visual changes.

6. Regions can be positioned on the timeline by placing them manually, by using the Pickup Clock command to align them with the current playhead position.

7. SMPTE positions of regions and events can be locked, enabling you to change tempos without changing the SMPTE timing.

8. Logic's "Export Audio to Movie" command is used to create a new video, marrying the project's mix with the referenced video.

Index

Differentiate yourself. Get Apple certified.

Stand out from the crowd. Get recognized for your expertise by earning Apple Certified Pro status.

Why become an Apple Certified Pro?

Raise your earning potential. Studies show that certified professionals can earn more than their non-certified peers.

Distinguish yourself from others in your industry. Proven mastery of an application helps you stand out in a crowd.

Display your Apple Certification logo. With each certification you get a logo to display on business cards, resumés, and websites.

Publicize your certifications. Publish your certifications on the Apple Certified Professionals Registry (training.apple.com/certification/records) to connect with clients, schools, and employers.

Learning that matches your style.

Learn on your own with Apple Pro Training Series books from Peachpit Press.

Learn in a classroom at an Apple Authorized Training Center (AATC) from Apple Certified Trainers providing guidance.

Visit **training.apple.com** to find Apple training and certifications for:

OS X	Pages
OS X Server	Numbers
Final Cut Pro X	Keynote
Logic Pro X	

"The Apple Certification is a cornerstone of my consulting business. It guarantees to our clients the highest level of dedication and professionalism. And above all, the trusting smile of a client when you mention the Apple Certification can't be replaced."

– Andres Le Roux, Technology Consulting, alrx.net, inc.

 Training and Certification

Apple Pro Training Series

OS X Support
Essentials 10.10
Supporting and Troubleshooting OS X Yosemite

Kevin M. White and Gordon Davisson

Lesson and media files available for download

Pages, Numbers,
and Keynote

Mark Wood

Lesson and media files available for download

Final Cut Pro X 10.1
Professional Post-Production

Brendan Boykin

Lesson and media files available for download

The Apple Pro Training Series

Apple offers comprehensive certification programs for creative and IT professionals. The Apple Pro Training Series is both a self-paced learning tool and the official curriculum of the Apple Training and Certification program, used by Apple Authorized Training Centers around the world.

To see a complete range of Apple Pro Training Series books, videos and apps visit: **www.peachpit.com/appleprotraining**

Apple
Certified